THE EFFECTIVENESS OF INNOVATIVE APPROACHES IN THE TREATMENT OF DRUG ABUSE

Recent Titles in Contributions in Criminology and Penology

Bad Guys and Good Guys: Moral Polarization and Crime
Daniel S. Claster

Innovative Approaches in the Treatment of Drug Abuse: Program Models and Strategies
James A. Inciardi, Frank M. Tims, and Bennett W. Fletcher, editors

Coca and Cocaine: An Andean Perspective
Felipe E. Mac Gregor, editor

Police Under Pressure: Resolving Disputes
Robert Coulson

Punishing Criminals: Developing Community-Based Intermediate Sanctions
Malcolm Davies

Crack and the Evolution of Anti-Drug Policy
Steven R. Belenko

In Defense of Prisons
Richard A. Wright

Police in Contradiction: The Evolution of the Police Function in Society
Cyril D. Robinson, Richard Scaglion, with J. Michael Olivero

Drug Abuse Treatment: The Implementation of Innovative Approaches
Bennett W. Fletcher, James A. Inciardi, and Arthur M. Horton

State Police in the United States: A Socio-Historical Analysis
H. Kenneth Bechtel

Academic Politics and the History of Criminal Justice Education
Frank Morn

Crime History and Histories of Crime: Studies in the Historiography of Crime and Criminal Justice in Modern History
Clive Emsley and Louis A. Knafla, editors

THE EFFECTIVENESS OF INNOVATIVE APPROACHES IN THE TREATMENT OF DRUG ABUSE

Edited by
Frank M. Tims
James A. Inciardi
Bennett W. Fletcher
Arthur MacNeill Horton, Jr.

Contributions in Criminology & Penology, Number 49

GREENWOOD PRESS
Westport, Connecticut • London

Library of Congress Cataloging-in-Publication Data

The effectiveness of innovative approaches in the treatment of drug abuse / edited by Frank M. Tims . . . [et al.].
p. cm. — (Contributions in criminology and penology, ISSN 0732–4464 ; no. 49)
Includes bibliographical references and index.
ISBN 0–313–30065–8 (alk. paper)
1. Drug abuse—Treatment—United States. I. Tims, Frank M. II. Series.
RC564.65.E36 1997
616.86'06—dc20 96–18222

British Library Cataloguing in Publication Data is available.

Library of Congress Catalog Card Number: 96–18222
ISBN: 0–313–30065–8
ISSN: 0732–4464

First published in 1997

Greenwood Press, 88 Post Road West, Westport, CT 06881
An imprint of Greenwood Publishing Group, Inc.

Printed in the United States of America

The paper used in this book complies with the Permanent Paper Standard issued by the National Information Standards Organization (Z39.48–1984).

10 9 8 7 6 5 4 3 2 1

Contents

Introduction: An Overview of the Applied Evaluation Research Portfolio

Frank M. Tims, Bennett W. Fletcher, James A. Inciardi, and Arthur McNeill Horton, Jr.

Community-based drug abuse treatment in its present form dates back only to the mid-1960s. With the exception of newer forms of drug treatment, such as private hospital-based inpatient treatment of about four weeks' duration, which has become widely adapted for treating illicit drug use only in the past 10 years, substantial evidence has been amassed on the effectiveness of drug abuse treatment. This research indicates that problem behaviors, including illicit drug use, heavy alcohol use, drug-related criminal activity, and poor social functioning, tend to improve during the course of treatment and remain at more favorable levels after treatment (for example, Ball & Ross, 1991; De Leon, 1984; Hubbard et al., 1989; McGlothlin, Anglin, & Wilson, 1977; Simpson & Sells, 1990).

However, it is also widely acknowledged that, while drug abuse treatment is effective at the aggregate level, there is wide variability in outcomes among individuals being treated. No single program element or patient characteristic determines outcomes. Favorable outcomes are predicted by such factors as continuing in treatment, adherence to treatment regimens, and engagement in therapeutic processes (Simpson, 1981; Woody et al., 1983). These factors, in turn, are related in complex ways to the capability of the treatment provider and availability of resources; to patient factors, such as motivation, suitability for treatment, and medical and psychological problems (De Leon & Jainchill, 1986; McLellan, Arndt, Metzger, Woody, & O'Brien, 1993); and to external environmental events and influences (Childress, McLellan, Ehrman, & O'Brien, 1986; Siegal, 1986).

THE APPLIED EVALUATION RESEARCH PORTFOLIO

The work reported in this volume, which comprises the Applied Evaluation Research (AER) portfolio, represents an effort to systematically integrate science and practice to improve drug abuse treatment. Strategies to increase access to treatment, to improve the ability of programs to attract and retain clients in treatment, to match interventions to the wide range of problems presented by drug abuse patients, to engage them in a process of change, and to improve outcomes were implemented in these projects.

The AER projects had their genesis in initiatives by the National Institute on Drug Abuse (NIDA) to develop a program of research demonstration projects to improve drug abuse treatment effectiveness and to expand treatment capacity nationwide. These initiatives were driven in part by the urgent need to reduce the spread of HIV infection among drug abusers. HIV, the cause of AIDS, is transmitted by sharing of contaminated drug injection equipment and through unprotected sexual activity. Drug abuse treatment reduces illicit drug use and needle sharing (Ball, Lange, Myers, & Friedman, 1988; Miller, Turner, & Moses, 1990). It was recognized that the spread of HIV could be reduced through expansion of existing treatment, by improving its effectiveness, and through well-conceived harm-reduction strategies.

A large number of projects were funded under the NIDA initiatives, including psychosocial therapy and medication development work which is reported elsewhere in the literature, and the 15 projects in this volume. The AER projects in this volume each focus on applied community-based drug abuse treatment research questions. The AER portfolio makes substantial contributions to our knowledge of drug abuse treatment process and outcomes, as well as forming a basis for continued research to build and integrate this knowledge into a coherent set of principles upon which to base successful treatment.

Those seeking treatment for drug abuse and dependence have diverse problems and needs; these problem areas must usually be addressed during the course of treatment to sustain treatment gains. Because different treatment populations present different needs and constraints, the AER projects vary in their focus. For example, some dealt with methadone maintenance patients, some with criminal justice populations, and others with mentally ill chemical abuse clients. Some of the projects investigated modifications to existing treatment modalities, while others created new configurations of treatment organization and delivery.

This book devotes a chapter to each project included in NIDA's AER portfolio. This introduction does not present a comprehensive summary of each project, but instead highlights one or two of the most interesting or promising findings from what is in each case a substantial body of work. Many of these research projects have multiple foci. For example,

Simpson's project (Chapter 12) breaks important ground in the areas of counselor training, techniques for improving counselor-patient communication, use of relapse prevention techniques in methadone maintenance programs, and use of contingency management.

The reader is referred to Inciardi, Tims, and Fletcher (1993) for detailed descriptions of the research designs of these projects, and to Fletcher, Inciardi, and Horton (1994) for descriptions of how the projects were implemented.

INNOVATIVE APPROACHES TO TREATMENT

The interventions attempted to build on a wide range of theoretical and clinical work to improve understanding of treatment process and outcomes. These foci included outreach and enrolling high-risk populations in treatment; providing comprehensive treatment, including medical and psychiatric care, to those who need it, including the homeless, dually diagnosed, and HIV seropositive; providing comprehensive AIDS education and behavioral change counseling; providing social skills training, including assertiveness training for women and vocational training; providing relapse prevention training; developing and testing improved counseling strategies; testing strategies to increase retention; implementing and testing case management approaches; integrating treatment models, such as methadone and therapeutic community, and day treatment and therapeutic community; varying planned length of treatment; and providing continuity of care and transitional services in a criminal justice population.

IMPROVED ACCESS TO TREATMENT

Methadone maintenance has been shown to be an effective treatment for heroin addicts (Ball & Ross, 1991; Simpson & Sells, 1990), and an effective means of reducing the spread of HIV (Ball, Lange, Myers, & Friedman, 1988; Metzger et al., 1993). Brady, Besteman, and Greenfield (Chapter 3) report findings from a project in which a mobile methadone and health care van provided a means to dispense basic health care to underserved populations. Retention of clients receiving mobile methadone services was significantly greater than retention of clients in established methadone treatment clinics in the same urban area. The mobile van approach overcame community resistance to fixed-site treatment programs, helped integrate drug treatment services with other health services, and helped provide access to areas of highest need for both drug treatment and health services.

IMPROVEMENT OF RETENTION IN METHADONE MAINTENANCE PROGRAMS

Like other medical treatments, methadone maintenance must be given an opportunity to treat its patients if it is to be successful. For a number of reasons, some of which were discussed above, patients tend to leave treatment before its work is done. Barriers to treatment retention were examined by Maddux (Chapter 2) in four randomized clinical trials. In all studies, it was found that both experimental and standard methadone treatment reduced AIDS-related needle risk behaviors.

Study 1: In comparing no-fee treatment with treatment for a nominal ($2.50/day) fee, it was found that significantly more patients were retained in no-fee treatment.

Study 2: Mandatory counseling was inversely related to retention. Patients were more likely to remain in treatment if counseling was optional.

Study 3: Self-regulation of methadone dosage did not increase retention over program-regulated dosing.

Study 4: Preliminary analyses indicate that patients admitted to treatment within 24 hours of applying for it were much more likely to enter treatment than patients following standard (within 14 days) admission practice.

ADDITION OF SERVICES TO METHADONE MAINTENANCE PROGRAMS

Improving Counseling Approaches

Simpson, Dansereau, and Joe (Chapter 12) developed a project (Drug Abuse Treatment for AIDS–Risk Reduction — DATAR) to enhance methadone treatment by using new approaches to counseling that rely on graphic representations (cognitive mapping) and associated materials and training for counselors, contingency management strategies, life skills and ancillary training, and relapse prevention training. The cognitive mapping approach was intended to improve communication with clients and to encourage solution-oriented thinking and action planning. The enhancement was found to be effective in terms of increasing retention in treatment and in significantly reducing illicit drug use and criminality during treatment. A one-year follow-up to assess outcomes is currently in progress.

Vocational Enhancement of Methadone Maintenance

Kleinman and colleagues (Chapter 14) report findings on adding a vocational services component to a methadone maintenance clinic in New

York City. The role of employment in the rehabilitation of addicts has been the subject of much discussion (Platt, Husband, Hermalin, Cater, & Metzger, 1993), but the relative scarcity of vocational services in drug abuse programs and labor market conditions have frustrated attempts to properly assess the impact of such services. In the clinic where the program was introduced, it was found that 75 percent of the 289 subjects who indicated interest in vocational services attended at least one vocational counseling session. Fully 43 percent of clients in the study returned to attend 11 sessions or more. Participation in vocational services was significantly associated with greater abstinence from cocaine, as measured by urinalysis. However, such participation did not predict posttreatment employment at follow-up. Moreover, there were no differences in retention between the clinic with vocational services and a comparison clinic without such services.

Enhanced Methadone Maintenance to Reduce the Spread of AIDS

In the study reported by Grella, Anglin, Wugalter, and Annon (Chapter 1), a combination of harm reduction and an enhanced methadone maintenance (EMM) program were directed at heroin addicts at high risk for HIV infection or transmission in Los Angeles County, where the seroprevalence rate has remained low (3 percent for addicts in treatment versus 6 percent for those out of treatment). Those addicts at high risk of infection or transmission were defined as HIV-seropositives, gay or bisexual males, sex workers (prostitutes), and sex partners of any individuals in these three categories. Outreach was conducted with these target groups to enroll them in treatment, and subjects were randomly assigned to either standard or EMM. The EMM condition included an array of additional services, including HIV risk-reduction interventions. The EMM clients were retained in treatment longer, but did no better than standard methadone clients in terms of drug use and HIV risk behaviors. While results are preliminary (the second follow-up is now in the field) and must be viewed with caution, they point up the difficulty of intervening with clients with multiple problems and risk behaviors. Of particular concern was cocaine use by clients, which tended to be seen in individuals at higher risk for HIV.

ADAPTATION OF TREATMENT MODELS

Intensive Day Treatment Using a Therapeutic Community Model

Guydish, Chan, Werdegar, Tajima, and Acampora (Chapter 13) conducted a randomized trial of residential therapeutic community (TC) treatment versus an intensive seven-day-a-week day treatment program using TC methods. The day treatment program had a somewhat higher dropout rate in the first two weeks of treatment, but data on those staying more than two weeks indicate that the day treatment regimen is both feasible and accepted by clients and staff. While 60 percent of clients initially preferred residential treatment, those who were assigned to the modality of their choice were much more likely to remain in treatment. Retention in the day treatment program was improved by giving more attention to orientation, counselor assignment, and client involvement in structured activities, so that, over time, retention in the two programs became more similar. Outcome data for the two programs are not yet available, but the feasibility and acceptance of the day treatment modality have been demonstrated.

Passages: Therapeutic Community Methods in Methadone Maintenance

In the Passages project (Chapter 10), De Leon and colleagues sought to improve treatment by developing an intensive day treatment methadone maintenance program incorporating TC methods (Passages), which was then compared with typical methadone maintenance. Clients in the study were high in social deficits, had high levels of psychological dysfunction, and reported high levels of crack or cocaine use. Compared to the typical methadone programs, clients in Passages attended treatment sessions more regularly and had greater reductions in drug use and HIV risk behaviors while in treatment. Participation in Passages was associated with reductions in the percentage of clients using needles, the percentage having multiple sex partners, heroin and cocaine use, and illegal activities.

Residential Treatment for Homeless, Mentally Ill, Chemical Abusing Clients

In Chapter 6, Rahav and colleagues report development of a treatment modality adapted for a population that has received little research attention: the homeless, mentally ill, chemical abuser. As Rahav points out, this population is one of the most difficult to treat successfully. Homeless shelters, psychiatric facilities, and drug abuse treatment programs are not designed to deal with the wide-ranging and complex problems of this population; nevertheless, it consumes valuable resources while receiving insufficiently comprehensive care. Rahav's chapter, which is a comparison of a modified TC and a community residence model adapted for the homeless, mentally ill, substance abuser, shows that TC treatment methods can result in significant improvements over other approaches for this population.

Project IMPACT: Residential Treatment Models and Varying Planned Time in Treatment

McCusker, Garfield, Lewis, and Frost (Chapter 4) report on a study that involves two large residential programs in which program structure and length of time in treatment were varied. The structure was varied by having one program retain its TC regimen and having the other incorporate relapse prevention and health education. In each of the programs, clients were randomly assigned to short versus long duration of treatment (three months versus six months in relapse prevention and six months versus one year in TC). Follow-up was scheduled at 3 months post-discharge and at 18 months post-admission. Data from the first follow-up suggest that client outcomes for the four program models (structure and duration) have remarkably similar outcomes. Further interpretation must await the completion of the 18-month follow-up interviews.

Intensive Day Treatment for Cocaine Users

Kirby, Festinger, Lamb, and Pratt report in Chapter 11 on a study in which a comprehensive behavioral model for cocaine addiction was implemented in a day treatment program. The behaviorally oriented treatment elements of this model included contingency management, couples therapy, job skills training, interpersonal problem solving and social skills development, and relapse prevention strategies to maintain abstinence. Patients were taught to schedule their time outside treatment to minimize opportunities for drug use. Those able to structure their time to avoid high-risk situations, and to recognize high-risk situations and employ strategies to cope with or avoid them, achieved greater reductions in cocaine use.

A Therapeutic Community Work-release Facility

Lockwood, Inciardi, and Surratt (Chapter 5) report research on the effectiveness of a work-release program based on TC principles (the CREST program) for drug abusers paroled from state prison, compared to a standard work-release program without drug treatment. Some CREST clients had participated in a prison-based TC (the KEY program), offering a four-way comparison. At six-month follow-up, all graduates of the CREST work-release program were drug abstinent and arrest free. Those who had participated in the prison-based KEY program had a higher completion rate in CREST than those who entered CREST without previous KEY experience (56 percent compared with 47 percent). While both in-prison and TC work-release programs were effective in improving abstinence and reducing recidivism after incarceration, combining in-prison drug abuse treatment with a treatment/work-release program appears to increase overall treatment effectiveness. HIV seropositivity rates were 9 percent among males and 16 percent among females, and were significantly related to history of injection drug use. Based on the research findings, the State of Delaware has assumed funding of the KEY and CREST treatment programs.

APPLICATIONS OF CASE MANAGEMENT TO IMPROVE TREATMENT

Case Management for Injection Drug Users

Mejta, Bokos, Maslar, Mickenberg, and Senay report a study in Chapter 7 in which a case management model for injection drug users was developed and evaluated. This model consisted of assessment of needs and problems, specification of client goals and development of a case management plan to meet them, linkage of the client with treatment and service providers selected to address client needs, monitoring of treatment process and progress, and advocacy on behalf of the client. This model of case management was found to improve treatment access, entry, and retention for injection drug users, resulting in reduced opiate and cocaine use over time.

Assertive Community Treatment for Parolees

Martin, Inciardi, Scarpitti, and Nielsen (Chapter 8) report a study of an assertive case management model, Assertive Community Treatment (ACT), with a sample of parolees. ACT provided intensive outpatient treatment combined with assertive case management to provide drug abuse treatment and needed services to drug-dependent parolees. The use of a case management model as a primary treatment for parolees was not successful. It was concluded that the ACT model was not intensive enough, there were no constraints on the parolee to attend treatment, and that the parolee population was a difficult one, being "system-wise" and mistrustful of the system. The random assignment protocol resulted in the assignment of clients to treatment who would ordinarily have been excluded as not ready or motivated for treatment. Voluntary participation in the study meant that the program had no external leverage to keep subjects in treatment until they became internally motivated to change.

Intensive Induction and Strengths-based Case Management

Siegal, Rapp, Fisher, Cole, and Wagner (Chapter 9) implemented a project in which a standard (outpatient) drug abuse treatment program was enhanced by strengths-based case management, an intensive two-day induction program to orient patients to treatment, or both. Preliminary data at six months post-admission suggest that, compared with the treatment-only control group, the induction program was a positive experience, facilitating treatment. A substantial reduction in cocaine use for those engaged in case management was reported, as well as fewer family, social, and mental health problems. Furthermore, there appeared to be a synergistic effect, so that patients who received the pretreatment induction program and case management had better outcomes than those just receiving one or the other.

OTHER INTERVENTIONS

Outpatient Treatment and Aftercare to Reduce AIDS Risk

In Chapter 15, Cottler, Cunningham, and Compton examined the effectiveness of an intervention to recruit drug abusers into treatment and reduce AIDS risk behaviors. The data reported is from African-American clients who entered a drug-free outpatient program based on a 12-step model, with aftercare services provided. Comparison of drug use and HIV risk behaviors was made between the clients who entered treatment and a group that declined treatment at the referral point. This study found improvement in both the treatment and comparison groups on both drug use and HIV risk behaviors, and that no significant differences in drug use were found between the two groups over the 18-month follow-up period. Greater improvement in HIV sex risk was found in the treatment group, suggesting that AIDS prevention efforts can be effective in reducing risky sexual behaviors.

WHAT WAS LEARNED?

The AER studies have proved valuable in improving our understanding of drug abuse treatment processes and outcomes, in testing interventions developed in the laboratory to see how they perform in the field, in developing and implementing new and innovative models of drug abuse treatment, and in determining the cost-effectiveness and cost-benefits of alternative versions of treatment. As might be expected in a diverse portfolio in which a variety of approaches were tested on a variety of client populations, some interventions were successful, and some studies are as yet inconclusive or have found no differential improvement over standard treatment. Although the research projects have not completed analyses of data, in many cases new interventions or modifications to existing treatment appeared to improve treatment effectiveness or efficiency. Only a few of the large number of insights and findings resulting from this body of research are mentioned below.

An important finding is that it is possible to improve our ability to engage difficult-to-treat populations in treatment by innovations to reduce barriers to treatment delivery. Clients who did not seek treatment at clinics were enticed to enter and remain engaged in a mobile treatment program.

Cocaine use is prevalent among those entering treatment, even for primary opiate users. Use of cocaine prior to admission to treatment was found to be associated with higher HIV risk behavior, psychological and social maladjustment, and treatment engagement problems.

A consistent finding across several studies was that the speed with which individuals are enrolled in treatment affects whether they enter treatment. This is particularly true of those with serious psychological impairment, but was found for others as well. It appears that only a narrow window of opportunity exists to engage those who need treatment in a treatment program. Even a delay of one day in admitting patients to treatment results in substantial attrition among those seeking treatment. Delaying intake to "test the motivation" of those seeking admission may be inappropriate, given the finding that rapid intake processing results in equivalent or better retention, once patients are engaged in treatment. The outcomes for patients admitted under rapid intake and those admitted with usual delays (up to 14 days) were comparable.

Improvement in treatment services can result in improved outcomes, and matching treatment services to individual needs can also improve outcomes by improving retention and motivation. Innovative approaches include new counseling tools to facilitate client-counselor communication, therapeutic alliance, and improve counselor functioning. The work by Simpson, Dansereau, and Joe has been incorporated into NIDA's technology transfer program.

A finding common to virtually all of these projects is that both the intervention and the standard drug abuse treatment were effective in reducing illicit drug use and in improving other behavioral and social outcomes. This replicates previous findings on drug treatment effectiveness, but it is also vexing in view of the research designs of most of these studies. Virtually all of the projects in this portfolio compared experimental research interventions to standard treatment. Thus, the test of these research interventions was to compare their marginal benefit over typical treatment. It is far more difficult to detect statistically significant improvements in an enhanced research intervention in comparison with an effective intervention than in comparison with a no-treatment or placebo condition.

In instances in which no difference was found between the enhanced intervention and the standard intervention, the question is raised whether this is due to a lack of statistical power, an inadvertent enhancement of the standard intervention (as might happen when standard treatment is manualized so it can be measured), or a true failure of the enhanced intervention to improve outcomes.

Use of a no-treatment control group must usually be considered unethical in subjects who seek treatment and when an efficacious treatment is known to exist. When the demand for treatment is greater than its availability, it may be possible to compare treated individuals with those who are waiting for access to treatment. This is a situation that is becoming rarer, which is fortunate from a humanist perspective but which also makes it more difficult to carry out rigorous research.

Finally, although it was not the purpose of these projects to develop methodological or theoretical research models, it is clear that the treatment research field has yet to reconcile different philosophical views of self-selection within a coherent research framework. Randomized clinical trials treat self-selection as a source of bias and seek to eliminate its influence through random assignment of subjects to treatment conditions. Others, particularly those carrying out field research, view self-selection as inextricably tied to motivation, and as a result look askance at random assignment insofar as it isolates motivation from treatment efficacy. The field needs to elaborate the two distinct models that are implicit in these two research views. The first is that treatment is efficacious (or not) regardless of the individual characteristics of the subject, and that random assignment allows the main effects of treatment to be isolated from the interaction effects of the treatment and the individual patient (at least insofar as these individual effects contaminate selection of treatment). The second view is that self-selection is a part of the treatment process itself, and that treatment effectiveness rests more upon the interaction of the individual and the intervention than upon treatment alone. A reconciliation of these divergent views is needed insofar as it regards determination of appropriate research design and methodology for drug abuse treatment research.

REFERENCES

Ball, J. C., Lange, W. R., Myers, C. P., & Friedman, S. R. (1988). Reducing the risk of AIDS through methadone maintenance treatment. *Journal of Health and Social Behavior, 29*, 214–226.

Ball, J. C., & Ross, A. (1991). *The effectiveness of methadone maintenance treatment*. New York: Springer Verlag.

Childress, A. R., McLellan, A. T., Ehrman, R., & O'Brien, C. P. (1986). Classically conditioned responses in opioid and cocaine dependence: A role in relapse? In B. A. Ray (Ed.), *Learning factors in substance abuse* (National Institute on Drug Abuse Research Monograph 84, DHHS Publication No. ADM 90-1576). Washington, DC: U.S. Government Printing Office.

De Leon, G. (1984). *The therapeutic community: Study of effectiveness* (Treatment Research Monograph Series, DHHS Publication No. ADM 85-1286). Washington, DC: U.S. Government Printing Office.

De Leon, G., & Jainchill, N. (1986). Circumstances, motivation, readiness, and suitability (CMRS) as correlates of treatment tenure. *Journal of Psychoactive Drugs, 8*, :203–208.

Fletcher, B. W., Inciardi, J. A., & Horton, A. M. (Eds.). (1994). *Drug abuse treatment*. Vol. 2: *The implementation of innovative approaches*. Westport, CT: Greenwood Press.

Hubbard, R. L., Marsden, M. E., Rachal, J. V., Harwood, H. J., Cavanaugh, E. R., & Ginzburg, H. M. (1989). *Drug abuse treatment: A national study of effectiveness*. Chapel Hill: University of North Carolina Press.

Inciardi, J. A., Tims, F. M., & Fletcher, B. W. (Eds.). (1993). *Innovative approaches in the treatment of drug abuse*. Vol. 1: *Program models and strategies*. Westport, CT: Greenwood Press.

McGlothlin, W. H., Anglin, M. D., & Wilson, B. D. (1977). *An evaluation of the California civil addict program* (National Institute on Drug Abuse Services Research Monograph Series, DHEW Publication No. ADM 78-558). Washington, DC: U.S. Government Printing Office.

McLellan, A. T., Arndt, I. O., Metzger, D. S., Woody, G. E., & O'Brien, C. P. (1993). The effects of psychosocial services in substance abuse treatment. *Journal of the American Medical Association, 269*(15), 1953–1959.

Metzger, D., Woody, G., McLellan, A. T., O'Brien, C., Druley, P., Navaline, H., DePhilippis, D., Stolley, P., & Abrutyn, E. (1993). Human immunodeficiency virus seroconversion among intravenous drug users in- and out-of-treatment: An 18-month prospective follow-up. *Journal of Acquired Immune Deficiency Syndromes, 6*, 1049–1056.

Miller, H. G., Turner, C. F., & Moses, L. E. (1990). *AIDS: The second decade* (pp. 89ff). Washington, DC: National Academy Press.

Platt, J. J., Husband, S. D., Hermalin, J., Cater, J., & Metzger, D. S. (1993). Cognitive problem-solving employment readiness intervention for methadone clients. *Journal of Cognitive Psychotherapy, 7*, 21–33.

Siegal, S. (1986). Drug anticipation and the treatment of dependence. In B. A. Ray (Ed.), *Learning factors in substance abuse* (National Institute on Drug Abuse Research Monograph 84, DHHS Publication No. ADM 90-1576). Washington, DC: U.S. Government Printing Office.

Simpson, D. D. (1981). Treatment for drug abuse: Follow-up outcomes and length of time spent. *Archives of General Psychiatry, 38*, 875–880.

Simpson, D. D., & Sells, S. B. (1990). *Opioid addiction and treatment: A 12-year follow-up*. Malabar, FL: Robert E. Krieger Publishing Co.

Woody, G. E., Luborsky, L., McLellan, A. T., O'Brien, C. P., Beck, A. T., Blaine, J., Herman, I., & Hole, A. (1983). Psychotherapy for opiate addicts. *Archives of General Psychiatry, 40*, 639–645.

I

METHADONE PROGRAMS

1

The Effectiveness of the Los Angeles Enhanced Methadone Maintenance Project: Reducing HIV Risk among Injection Drug Users

Christine E. Grella, M. Douglas Anglin,
Stuart E. Wugalter, and Jeffrey J. Annon

The Los Angeles Enhanced Methadone Maintenance (EMM) Project sought to implement an enhanced methadone maintenance treatment program and evaluate its effectiveness as a vehicle for human immunodeficiency virus (HIV) risk reduction. The goal of the project was to engage in treatment heroin addicts who were at highest risk of HIV infection and transmission within Los Angeles County, an area where the seroprevalence rate among injection drug users (IDUs) remains fortuitously low (approximately 3 percent for in-treatment addicts and 6 percent for those not in treatment) (Longshore & Anglin, 1993). The project focused on retaining these addicts in treatment and reducing their high-risk behaviors for HIV infection and transmission, including both injection drug use and high-risk sex behaviors.

Clients were recruited from four target groups at high risk of HIV infection and transmission determined on the basis of local seroprevalence studies of IDUs (Anglin, Miller, Mantius, & Grella, 1993). The target groups were: HIV-positive individuals, gay or bisexual males, sex workers (prostitutes), and sex partners of individuals in any of the above three categories. This subject pool provides a laboratory for examining the efficacy of treatment protocols for the subgroup of heroin addicts who are at highest risk of HIV infection and transmission. This subgroup is particularly important because it is most likely to be the vector of HIV transmission with other IDUs and with non-IDUs through sexual contact and prenatal transmission of infected mothers.

The project goals of recruitment and retention are consistent with a harm-reduction approach to drug treatment (Ward, Darke, Hall, & Mattick, 1992). The harm-reduction approach focuses on reducing the negative consequences that stem from injection drug use, with the goal of progressively limiting these consequences, in contrast with the rehabilitation approach that favors abstinence as the only goal of drug treatment (Jones, 1990; Ward, Mattick, & Hall, 1992). While many addicts may never achieve total abstinence, they may improve their physical health, mental health, and social functioning while in treatment, as well as reduce the costs to society from criminal involvement and HIV infection. Adherents of a harm-reduction approach advocate the use of outreach, prevention, and health education to change HIV risk behaviors, both within and without drug treatment programs (Brettle, 1991; Des Jarlais, Friedman, Choopanya, & Vanichseni, 1992; Springer, 1991). Methadone maintenance treatment can play an especially important role within a harm-reduction approach because it is the largest drug treatment modality for heroin addiction and has proven effective in reducing injection drug use (Ball, Lange, Myers, & Friedman, 1988).

METHOD

Procedure

Subjects were recruited through outreach to local service providers (for example, AIDS service organizations, social welfare programs, health clinics), distribution of fliers, and word of mouth. Prospective clients were evaluated for their eligibility for methadone maintenance treatment according to federal and State of California[1] regulations and for the study, which required membership in at least one of the high-risk target groups. Eligible subjects were admitted into the project after providing informed consent and then randomly assigned to one of two treatment conditions, either the control group, which received standard methadone maintenance, or the EMM treatment group. Individuals in the enhanced treatment group received an array of additional services: transportation assistance in the first 90 days after admission; case management services, including a reduced ratio of clients to case managers; participation in special groups, including an HIV education group, a cocaine abusers' group, and a women's group; on-site psychiatric treatment and medication; and contingency-based reinforcers to improve quality of life and promote drug-free activities, such as free food coupons, movie passes, and restaurant coupons. (See Anglin, Miller, Mantius, and Grella [1993] for a full description of enhanced treatment.)

All research subjects received free methadone maintenance treatment through the duration of the study and were asked to participate in at least two interviews: one at treatment entry, which assessed behavior in the 12 months prior to admission, and a follow-up interview, which assessed behavior subsequent to treatment entry and was conducted 18 months after admission. Because of time constraints, only the first 300 subjects received a second follow-up interview at 36 months after admission.

Over the five-year implementation period, treatment was delivered through two different treatment providers. (See Grella and Anglin [1994] for a full description of project implementation.) Midway through the project, we established a new research clinic, operated by the Matrix Institute on Addictions, where treatment was provided to all research subjects. The clinic was located in mid-city Los Angeles and shared in the hardships that plagued Los Angeles during the early 1990s. Local businesses and homeowners were hard hit by the sustained recession in California, which resulted in severe cutbacks in social services within Los Angeles County. The surrounding neighborhood sustained fires and looting during the Los Angeles riots in 1992 and was near the portion of the Santa Monica Freeway that collapsed in the January 1994 Northridge earthquake. The clinic was in proximity to known "cocaine motels" and places where drugs were easily bought and sold. Sex workers also frequented the area, and crime was a major concern of the local residents and merchants. Most clients were from the surrounding neighborhood and the nearby areas of downtown and South Central Los Angeles, although some traveled from farther away, such as Hollywood and East Los Angeles, to receive free treatment.

Measures

The intake instrument was a version of the "Natural History" interview, developed by the UCLA Drug Abuse Research Center (McGlothlin, Anglin, & Wilson, 1977). Intake assessments were conducted between 30 and 60 days after treatment admission to allow for stabilization on methadone maintenance. The assessment covered a wide range of areas: drug use history, criminal activity, family history, employment history, sex behaviors, needle use, attitudes and self-perceptions regarding HIV, motivation to enter treatment, and mental health status. Five psychological tests were also administered: the Center for Epidemiological Studies Depression Scale (CES-D) (Radloff, 1977), the Suicide Probability Scale (Cull & Gill, 1988), the Luria-Nebraska Neuropsychological Screen (Golden, 1988), the Basic Personality Inventory (BPI) (Jackson, 1989), and the Social Adjustment Scale (Weissman & Bothwell, 1976). Additionally, data from clinic records were collected throughout the project on dose levels, attendance, take-home doses, urine test results, contacts with case managers, psychiatric treatment, and institutionalizations.

RESULTS

We present an overview of preliminary results in five areas: sample recruitment and characteristics, treatment retention, cocaine use and HIV risk behaviors, women's risk behaviors, and drug use and HIV risk behaviors at follow-up.

Sample Recruitment and Characteristics

A total of 500 injecting heroin addicts were recruited into the EMM Project from 1990 to 1993. Of the total sample, 46 percent were African-American, 26 percent were Hispanic, 25 percent were Caucasian, and 3 percent were classified as "other." Slightly over half of the sample (52 percent) were males. Membership in the four high-risk target groups, which were not mutually exclusive, was as follows: 15 percent were HIV-positive, 15 percent were gay or bisexual males, 36 percent were sex partners of other high-risk IDUs, and 49 percent were sex workers.

The sample was composed mainly of older addicts (median age was 40) with long-term addiction careers and associated social, economic, and psychological problems. Most had begun regular heroin use at age 19, and thus had been using for about 20 years. Almost all had used cocaine at some time; 38 percent had used cocaine or crack within the 30 days prior to intake, yet only 5 percent reported ever having received treatment for cocaine use. The other most frequently used drugs in the 30 days prior to admission were benzodiazepines (33 percent) and marijuana (32 percent). Over one-third (36 percent) had not completed high school and only 10 percent of the sample was employed at the time of intake. The most frequent source of income was from welfare (71 percent), followed by sex work (49 percent), drug dealing (46 percent), and petty theft and shoplifting (46 percent). Given their pattern of involvement in illegal activities, nearly all (96 percent) had been arrested at least once and 83 percent had been incarcerated. One-fifth of the sample was residentially unstable, either homeless or living in a motel or hotel, with an additional 9 percent doubling up with relatives. The majority of subjects (62 percent) was classified as depressed at intake on the CES-D Scale and about one-fourth (26 percent) reported a previous suicide attempt.

We examined whether individuals in the different target groups differed in their psychological profiles (Wugalter, Grella, & Anglin, 1994). Individuals who were HIV-positive scored higher on measures of depression. Sex workers were characterized by a wide range of psychological problems, including depression, suicidality, alienation, anxiety, impulse expression, and interpersonal problems. We also conducted a validity check of target group status by comparing consistency in self-reported risk behaviors across all interview points. Close to one-third of the sample initially misrepresented their behavior to gain admission into the project (Grella, Chaiken, & Anglin, 1994). Subjects who lied to gain admission were most often older males who falsely portrayed themselves as gay or prostitutes.

Although a minority of subjects admitted into the project were at relatively low risk, the vast majority exhibited a wide range of high-risk sex behaviors and needle use. Only 19 percent reported never sharing injection equipment and 69 percent reported using others' equipment subsequent to someone else's use. Over one-fourth (29 percent) reported sharing needles with strangers within the last year and only 26 percent of the sample reported that they always either used new needles or cleaned their needles with bleach or alcohol. Because we had specifically recruited sex workers into treatment, 30 percent of the men and 82 percent of the women reported receiving money for sex. Although women were more likely to report condom use, it was inconsistent among both men and women; 48 percent of the women and 74 percent of the men reported condom use half of the time or less.

Treatment Retention

Of the 500 subjects originally enrolled, 216 (43 percent) were still in treatment and 284 (57 percent) had discharged at the time of this writing (see Table 1.1). A total of 46 subjects had died, 25 of these while in treatment. We found the expected differences in retention based on demographic characteristics. Women had a higher retention rate: 47 percent were still in treatment compared with 39 percent of the men. African-Americans, who were the most numerous ethnic group, had a higher retention rate (48 percent) than either Caucasians (34 percent) or Hispanics (45 percent). Younger individuals (below the median age) were more likely to have discharged from treatment than were older individuals: 66 percent compared with 48 percent, respectively. The enhanced treatment group had a higher retention rate; 49 percent were still in treatment compared with 38 percent of the standard treatment group.

We analyzed the reasons for discharge from treatment by examining predictors of discharge for negative and circumstantial reasons in a series of logistic regressions (Grella, Anglin, Wugalter, Rawson, & Hasson, 1994). Negative reasons for discharge included discharges for noncompliance, a stated preference to return to heroin use, and nonattendance for 14 days. Circumstantial discharges included incarceration, relocation, hospitalization, and transfers to other treatment programs. The distinction between the two types of discharge was that negative discharges constituted treatment failures, while circumstantial discharges were unrelated to treatment and, theoretically, included the possibility of continued treatment.

TABLE 1.1
Treatment Retention

(*N* = 500)

	In Treatment		Discharged	
	n	%	*n*	%
All	216	43	284	57
Males	103	39	158	61
Females	113	47	126	53
Caucasian	42	34	82	66
African-American	110	48	121	52
Hispanic	58	45	72	55
Other	6	40	9	60
Enhanced Group	120	49	125	51
Control Group	96	38	159	62
40 and below	86	34	164	66
Over 40	130	52	120	48

Our findings were consistent with previous research, which has shown the important role of an individual's relationship with the criminal justice system in determining drug treatment outcome (Anglin, Brecht, & Maddahian, 1989). Individuals who had been coerced into treatment or were currently under legal supervision were less likely to discharge for either circumstantial or negative reasons. Having a greater variety of sources of legal income also conferred a protective effect by reducing the likelihood of circumstantial discharge, most likely because of the reduced probability of arrest from illegal activities. Conversely, those engaging in more types of criminal activity prior to treatment entry discharged less frequently for negative reasons and more often for circumstantial reasons, most likely because of a higher probability of arrest.

In evaluating type of discharge by membership in any of the four target groups, the strongest finding was that HIV-positive individuals were at higher probability of circumstantial, compared with negative, discharge, by a factor of eight times. In examining the specific reasons for discharge, over half (53 percent) discharged because they transferred to another methadone program or moved to another locale (although 18 percent discharged because of incarceration). Often these moves were precipitated by the need to be closer to caretakers or to programs more conveniently located when their illness progressed.

Sex workers and sex partners were both at higher risk of discharge for negative and circumstantial reasons, compared with nonsex workers and nonsex partners, respectively. This finding may reflect the highly volatile lives of these individuals and their vulnerability both to treatment failure and to changes in their life circumstances that result in leaving treatment. The most common type of discharge for individuals in both categories was because of incarceration (approximately one-fourth for each). Psychological status was also a key component in understanding the reasons why high-risk individuals left methadone treatment. Individuals who displayed more suicidal ideation and had problems with impulse control (as measured by the BPI) were more likely to have circumstantial discharges, which may reflect a chaotic and disorganized lifestyle associated with a high probability of movement or arrest. Those with problems in self-depreciation (as measured by the BPI) were more likely to have negative discharges and such individuals need to be assessed at intake and targeted for careful treatment planning because of their higher risk of treatment failure.

Participation in the enhanced treatment program appeared to reduce the likelihood of negative discharge, although this finding was only marginally significant. It is suggestive, however, and needs further exploration by examining differences in services received by type, intensity, and case manager.

Cocaine Use and HIV Risk Behaviors

Because cocaine use constitutes a major obstacle to the rehabilitation of heroin addicts in methadone treatment (Condelli, Fairbank, Dennis, & Rachal, 1991; Cushman, 1988; Des Jarlais, Wenston, Friedman, Soheran, Maslansky, & Marmor, 1992), we focused one area of analysis of cocaine use within this sample of high-risk addicts. We examined the relationship between cocaine use and HIV risk behaviors at intake into treatment, and the differences between individuals who reported crack use compared with noncrack cocaine users using discriminant function analyses (Grella, Anglin, & Wugalter, 1995).

Overall, 76 percent of the sample reported using cocaine in the 12 months prior to treatment entry. These cocaine users differed in several significant ways from noncocaine users. A profile emerged of cocaine users engaging in more high-risk behavior and more varied criminal activity and having more psychological disturbance. The greater variety of crimes reported by cocaine users may have stemmed from the need for more cash to support a cocaine habit in addition to their heroin use. As in previous studies, we found that these cocaine-using heroin addicts reported higher levels of depression and suicidality and were more likely to use alcohol.

Cocaine users were at higher risk of HIV infection and transmission in the year prior to treatment entry by virtue of several factors: they were more likely to engage in sexual exchanges for money or drugs, they were less likely to report condom use, they shared needles with a greater variety of partners, and they tended to report less frequent use of new needles. Cocaine users were also marginally more likely to be HIV-positive.

Crack smokers, who constituted the vast majority (81 percent) of cocaine users, were identified as unique from noncrack-using heroin addicts on several dimensions. Their needle-using behavior, in particular, differed from the other cocaine users who did not report crack use. Crack users were less likely to clean needles prior to injection and to use new needles but reported fewer uses per needle. This pattern may result in an overall higher risk of HIV infection or transmission, however, the needle-using behavior of heroin addicts who also use crack merits more exploration. Additionally, crack users reported more alcohol use, tended to engage in more types of criminal activities, and were marginally less likely to be either married or living with a partner.

Women's Risk Behaviors

Women constituted almost half of the subjects in the EMM Project, which is a higher proportion relative to other methadone programs in California, where women represent 43 percent of methadone clients. Most likely the high enrollment for women stemmed from our specific recruitment of sex workers as a priority target group. Capitalizing on this relatively large sample of high-risk women in treatment, we examined the relationship between individual characteristics and time-in-treatment with high-risk behaviors in a series of multiple regressions (Grella, Anglin, & Annon, 1994). We examined the following four types of risk behaviors at both intake and follow-up: risky needle usage (a composite measure of shooting gallery use, average number of uses per needle, and frequency of new needle use), needle sharing (among up to four types of partners), sex exchanges for drugs or money, and unsafe sex (lack of condom use in vaginal, oral, or anal sex).

A woman's involvement in illegal activities was the most consistent predictor of risk behavior at both intake into treatment and at follow-up. Women who scored higher on a 24-item scale of illegal activities were more likely to engage in risky needle use, needle sharing, sex exchanges for drugs or money, and unsafe sex. In addition, risky needle use prior to intake was associated with a history of either sex work or sex abuse. HIV-positive women were less likely either to exchange sex for money or to engage in unsafe sex. Women who used cocaine pretreatment or who were depressed were more likely to report unsafe sex.

Women's risk behaviors at follow-up were significantly affected by the amount of time spent in treatment. Women who spent less time in treatment between intake and follow-up were more likely to report risky needle use, sex exchanges, and unsafe sex at follow-up. Women who reported cocaine use after treatment entry were more likely to report risky needle use and unsafe sex at follow-up. Daily alcohol use was also associated with risky needle use and early discharge from treatment. Women who continued to exchange sex for money or drugs after admission also had higher depression scores at follow-up. Lastly, younger women were more likely to report unsafe sex at follow-up.

In sum, women in this sample clearly evidenced a high degree of HIV risk behavior, which was embedded in an overall pattern of risk taking in several domains, most notably criminal activity and other drug and alcohol use. Many of these behaviors formed part of their survival strategy for obtaining income, such as through sex work and property crime, and such women may lack other means for self-support. Younger women, women with a history of abuse, and women who were depressed were also at elevated risk for HIV.

Drug Use and HIV Risk Behaviors at Follow-up

To evaluate the effectiveness of the enhanced treatment program, a thorough follow-up of all EMM subjects was crucial. Our follow-up of EMM subjects has been very successful, through a combination of accessing still-enrolled clients and tracking and locating discharged clients. We conducted follow-up interviews primarily at the UCLA/Matrix Clinic, although about 10 percent were conducted in jail or prison. At the time of this writing, 405 interviews at the first follow-up point (18 months after admission) had been conducted or were in progress, which constituted 92 percent of all subjects eligible for follow-up up until this time; 6 respondents or 1 percent of the sample thus far had yet to be located for interview; and 30 subjects (7 percent) had died prior to the first follow-up. Our second follow-up (36 months after admission) is progressing at a similar rate, although the death rate has increased to 12 percent of the sample eligible for the second follow-up interview thus far.

Our analysis of changes in drug use between intake and the first follow-up showed that there were significant reductions in drug use of any kind and injection drug use in particular (see Table 1.2). As would be expected from the proven effects of methadone on reducing heroin use, heroin use within the 30 days previous to interview decreased from almost all of the sample at intake[2] to approximately half at follow-up. The proportion reporting use of powder cocaine also decreased between intake and follow-up, from 30 percent of the sample to 18 percent. Further, crack use actually increased between intake and follow-up, from

TABLE 1.2
Drug Use at Intake and Follow-up
(*N* = 316)

	Intake		Follow-up	
Drug Use	*n*	%	*n*	%
Any illegal drug use	310	98	238	75
Heroin	301	95	167	53
Cocaine	95	30	58	18
Crack	88	28	133	42
Marijuana	77	24	81	26
Speedball	74	23	60	19
Other drug*	146	46	129	41
Any injection of any drug	283	90	182	58

Note: Time frame is within 30 days prior to interview.
*Included: inhalants, hallucinogens, amphetamines, barbiturates, illegal methadone, benzodiazepines, PCP, and other opiates, including synthetic opiates.

28 percent of the sample to 42 percent, and marijuana use stayed essentially stable. There were no differences between treatment groups in drug use, hence participation in the enhanced treatment group did not result in a greater reduction in drug use.

Risk behaviors for HIV infection and transmission were reduced overall from their levels at intake, but similarly were not significantly affected by participation in the enhanced treatment group. Safe needle use (either always using a new needle or cleaning with bleach or alcohol) increased from 26 percent of the sample at intake to 34 percent at follow-up and needle sharing was reduced from 81 percent of the sample at intake to 61 percent at follow-up. High-risk sex behaviors were more resistant to change (see Table 1.3). The proportion of men who provided money or drugs for sex stayed essentially constant (and was negligible for women). Receipt of money or drugs for sex was reduced for both males and females at follow-up, however, it remained at a high level. This was especially true for women, half of whom were still engaging in sex work at follow-up. Women were more likely to report consistent condom use (more than half of the time) than were men at both intake and follow-up, although their rate of increase after treatment admission was minimal.

DISCUSSION

Our preliminary analysis of data from the EMM Project demonstrates several findings thus far. First, we were successful in recruiting into treatment a group of IDUs at high risk for HIV infection and transmission. The sample was indeed composed of those individuals who posed the greatest public health risk from unsafe sexual behavior and drug use. Their psychosocial profile also illustrated the severity of their problems, including psychological disturbance, economic instability, and criminal involvement. Of the four target groups, sex workers emerged as a group at particular risk for early discharge, psychological problems, and HIV infection.

TABLE 1.3
Sex Behavior at Intake and Follow-up
(in percent)

	Intake*		Follow-up†	
Behavior	**Males (n = 149)**	**Females (n = 151)**	**Males (n = 149)**	**Females (n = 151)**
Give money for sex	9	1	7	0
Give drugs for sex	20	3	20	0
Receive money for sex	30	82	12	50
Receive drugs for sex	29	47	13	17
Do not use condoms consistently**	74	48	62	45

*Time frame is within 12 months prior to admission.
†Time frame is since treatment admission.
**Defined as half of the time or less.

Treatment providers can use the finding that clients differed in their reasons for discharge from treatment depending on their HIV status, legal status, profile of risk behavior, psychological characteristics, primary source of income, and the treatment program they received. Clients who received the enhanced treatment program demonstrated higher levels of retention and tended to discharge less often for negative, as opposed to circumstantial, reasons. This finding is promising in terms of increasing the likelihood that high-risk addicts will stay in treatment, allowing for more opportunity for behavioral changes to take place. Treatment planning can encompass this information to target those individuals at highest risk for discharge, particularly for negative reasons, and to apply intensive counseling and other prevention techniques to forestall premature discharge.

We found that HIV-positive individuals can be successfully treated in methadone maintenance programs and that their most frequent reasons for leaving treatment have to do with changing life circumstances. Methadone programs can address the specific needs of HIV-infected individuals by ensuring that successful transfers to treatment in other areas or in other programs are easily accomplished. For those who discharge from treatment because of incarceration or hospitalization, it is imperative that methadone treatment be integrated in these other settings, and that treatment providers and public health advocates work with these other systems to increase their understanding of the role of methadone treatment within a harm-reduction strategy.

Similarly, our findings on cocaine and crack use demonstrate the need for methadone programs to target cocaine-using heroin addicts entering treatment in several areas. Since heroin addicts who also use cocaine are more likely to engage in high-risk behaviors for HIV, these individuals should be a first priority for aggressive HIV intervention, particularly regarding needle use and sex work. The greater criminal involvement of cocaine users poses an additional obstacle to their rehabilitation once in methadone treatment. Even if cocaine use is reduced after admission to methadone maintenance, and hence the impetus for criminal activity is lessened, individuals with long addiction careers and criminal histories almost certainly lack viable job skills and may also be physically or mentally incapable of working. Methadone programs must address ways to assist these clients in finding alternative sources of income, if not through vocational rehabilitation then through assistance in obtaining social services and other forms of income support. Problems associated with cocaine use, such as depression and suicidality, also must be confronted aggressively, through pharmacotherapy, psychotherapy, or both.

We found that crack smokers made up the majority of cocaine users and that they engaged in more types of criminal behavior and were more likely to engage in several high-risk behaviors, compared to other cocaine users. We also found that crack use increased after treatment admission, whereas other drug use, particularly injection drug use, declined. Coupling these two findings — the greater risk profile of crack users and the increase in its use after admission to treatment — we concluded that the problem of crack use among methadone clients should assume a first order of priority (Anglin, Grella, & Wugalter, 1994). Crack use among methadone clients may be more impervious to change, particularly among clients within a free methadone program where cash previously spent on heroin can be diverted to crack use. Crack use may be especially hard to eradicate when clients continue to live in areas where crack is widely used and easily available.

The women recruited into this project displayed a wide range of risk behaviors, which was part of a larger pattern of risk taking, criminal involvement, and other drug and alcohol use. Most of the women entering treatment lacked any legal work experience, having relied upon their own and others' criminal activities for income. Their drug use was often embedded within dependent relationships with others and consequently they continued to risk HIV infection from others' injection drug use and unprotected sexual activities. While women were more likely to report condom use than men, both at intake and follow-up, their high level of continued sex work even after treatment admission puts them at particular risk of HIV infection. Our project focused on providing a context in which these women, bereft of work skills, economic resources, social skills, and social support for behavioral change, could begin to make gradual changes in their lives. Effecting permanent changes in entrenched risk behaviors, however, will require intensive support over a long period of engagement.

Although participation in the enhanced treatment group increased retention, it failed to reduce drug use or high-risk needle behaviors for HIV beyond that observed for the standard methadone maintenance group. There are several reasons why this may be so. Because this was a demonstration project that provided subsidized treatment for all subjects, the overall impact from free treatment may have overwhelmed any possible effects from the enhanced treatment. The enhanced treatment protocol itself may not have been sufficiently differentiated from standard methadone maintenance and hence there was a dilution of possible treatment effects. The treatment provider and content of the enhanced treatment protocol changed during the course of project implementation and outcomes may be dependent on when subjects entered into the project. Further, we have only analyzed treatment effects at a fairly crude level — whether one was in one treatment group or the other. As we continue to analyze the data, we will be able to use finer measures on the type and intensity of services received (such as number of case manager visits, participation in the women's and cocaine abusers' groups, transportation assistance, and receipt of contingency-based reinforcers) and on the length of time in treatment. Based on clinical observation, we are optimistic that individuals in the enhanced group who received psychiatric intervention, in the form of assessment, crisis intervention, and medication, may show improved behavioral functioning compared with those in the control group with a similar psychiatric profile who did not have access to this treatment.

In sum, it is premature to conclude that EMM is of no additional benefit in HIV risk reduction among heroin addicts selected for their high-risk profile. A final conclusion must await the end of our follow-up efforts and data analysis. In the meantime, drug treatment providers and researchers can play an important role as advocates for changes within the health care and social services systems to increase awareness of the multiple needs of high-risk heroin addicts and the importance of intervening with this population. Our experiences in integrating HIV education and risk-reduction protocols within methadone programs can serve as a model for integrating a harm-reduction approach within other service systems as well.

ACKNOWLEDGMENTS

This research was supported by grant number R18-DA06250 from the National Institute on Drug Abuse. Anglin is also supported by research scientist development award DA00146 from the National Institute on Drug Abuse. The authors thank the staff of the UCLA EMM Project for all of their hard work on this project.

NOTES

1. State of California regulations require evidence of addiction, such as track marks or signs of withdrawal; a minimum two-year addiction history; or two prior treatment failures, one of which must have occurred within the six months prior to admission.

2. Some clients who were addicted to other opiates were admitted early in the project and hence the rate of heroin use at intake was less than 100 percent.

REFERENCES

Anglin, M. D., Brecht, M., & Maddahian, E. (1989). Pretreatment characteristics and treatment performance of legally coerced versus voluntary methadone maintenance admissions. *Criminology, 27*, 537–555.

Anglin, M. D., Grella, C. E., & Wugalter, S. E. (1994, June). Cocaine and crack use among high-risk addicts in an enhanced methadone maintenance program. Poster presented at the annual meeting of the College on Problems of Drug Dependence, Palm Beach, Florida.

Anglin, M. D., Miller, M. L., Mantius, K., & Grella, C. E. (1993). Enhanced methadone maintenance treatment: Limiting the spread of HIV among high-risk Los Angeles narcotic addicts. In J. Inciardi, F. M. Tims, & B. Fletcher (Eds.), *Innovative approaches in the treatment of drug abuse: Program models and strategies*. Westport, CT: Greenwood Press.

Ball, J. C., Lange, W. R., Myers, C. P., & Friedman, S. R. (1988). Reducing the risk of AIDS through methadone maintenance treatment. *Journal of Health and Social Behavior, 29*, 214–226.

Brettle, R. P. (1991). HIV and harm reduction for injection drug users. *AIDS, 5*, 125–136.

Condelli, W. S., Fairbank, J. A., Dennis, M. L., & Rachal, J. V. (1991). Cocaine use by clients in methadone programs: Significance, scope, and behavioral interventions. *Journal of Substance Abuse Treatment, 8*, 203–212.

Cull, J. G., & Gill, W. S. (1988). *Suicide probability scale manual*. Los Angeles, CA: Western Psychological Services.

Cushman, P. (1988). Cocaine use in a population of drug abusers on methadone. *Hospital and Community Psychology, 39*, 1205–1207.

Des Jarlais, D. C., Friedman, S. R., Choopanya, K., & Vanichseni, S. (1992). International epidemiology of HIV and AIDS among injection drug users. *AIDS, 6,* 1053–1068.

Des Jarlais, D. C., Wenston, J., Friedman, S. R., Sotheran, J. L., Maslansky, R., & Marmor, M. (1992). Crack cocaine use in a cohort of methadone maintenance patients. *Journal of Substance Abuse Treatment, 9,* 319–325.

Golden, C. J. 1988. *Screening test for the Luria-Nebraska neuropsychological battery.* Los Angeles, CA: Western Psychological Services.

Grella, C. E., & Anglin, M. D. (1994). Implementing an enhanced methadone maintenance program for HIV risk reduction in Los Angeles. In J. Inciardi, F. M. Tims, & B. Fletcher (Eds.), *Drug abuse treatment: The implementation of innovative approaches.* Westport, CT: Greenwood Press.

Grella, C. E., Anglin, M. D., & Annon, J. A. (1994, April). Reducing high-risk behavior among women in methadone maintenance. Paper presented at the National Methadone Conference, Washington, DC.

Grella, C. E., Anglin, M. D., & Wugalter, S. E. (1995). Cocaine and crack use and HIV risk behavior among high-risk methadone maintenance clients. *Drug and Alcohol Dependence, 37,* 15–21.

Grella, C. E., Anglin, M. D., Wugalter, S. E., Rawson, R., & Hasson, A. (1994). Reasons for discharge from methadone maintenance for addicts at high-risk of HIV infection or transmission. *Journal of Psychoactive Drugs, 26,* 223–232.

Grella, C. E., Chaiken, S., & Anglin, M. D. (1994, June). Validity of self-report data on risk behaviors from heroin addicts entering free methadone treatment. Poster presented at the annual meeting of the College on Problems of Drug Dependence, Palm Beach, Florida.

Jackson, D. N. (1989). *Basic personality inventory manual.* Port Huron, MI: Sigma Assessment Systems, Inc.

Jones, L. D. (1990). Working with drug users to prevent the spread of HIV: The application of an analytic framework to a range of programmes. *Health Education Research, 5*(1), 5–15.

Longshore, D., & Anglin, M. D. (1993). *HIV transmission and risk behavior among drug users in Los Angeles County.* Los Angeles, CA: Department of Health Services, AIDS Program Office.

McGlothlin, W. H., Anglin, M. D., & Wilson, B. D. (1977). *An evaluation of the California civil addict program* (National Institute on Drug Abuse Services Research Monograph Series, DHEW Publication No. ADM 78-558). Rockville, MD: National Institute on Drug Abuse.

Radloff, L. S. (1977). The CES-Scale: A self-report depression scale for research in the general population. *Applied Psychological Measures, 1,* 385–401.

Springer, E. (1991). Effective AIDS prevention with active drug users: The harm reduction model. *Journal of Chemical Dependency Treatment, 4,* 141–157.

Ward, J., Darke, S., Hall, W., & Mattick, R. (1992). Methadone maintenance and the human immunodeficiency virus: Current issues in treatment and research. *British Journal of Addiction, 87,* 447–453.

Ward, J., Mattick, R., & Hall, W. (1992). *Key issues in methadone maintenance treatment.* Kensington, Australia: New South Wales University Press.

Weissman, M. M., & Bothwell, S. (1976). Assessment of social adjustment by patient self-report. *Archives of General Psychiatry, 33,* 1111–1115.

Wugalter, S. E., Grella, C. E., & Anglin, M. D. (1994, June). Psychological characteristics of IVDU's in an enhanced methadone maintenance program. Poster presented at the annual meeting of the College on Problems of Drug Dependence, Palm Beach, Florida.

2

Outcomes of Innovations to Improve Retention on Methadone

James F. Maddux

While methadone maintenance has become well-established as an effective treatment of opioid dependence, many patients drop out of treatment and resume illicit opioid use (Ball & Ross, 1991; Dole & Joseph, 1978). Retention in treatment has become more urgent because AIDS is spread through sharing of injection equipment (Cooper, 1989). For reasons not well understood, the one-year retention rates among methadone programs have varied widely, from 89 percent (Gearing, 1974), to 34 percent (Hubbard et al., 1989). The variations in retention probably arise from variables in the patients, in the environments, and in the programs. With funding from a program of research demonstrations sponsored by the National Institute on Drug Abuse we introduced and evaluated four treatment innovations designed to improve retention on methadone. The background of the innovations and the methodology of the studies have been previously reported in detail (Maddux, 1993; Maddux, Vogtsberger, Desmond, & Esquivel, 1994) and are summarized here.

THE INNOVATIONS

The innovations were not enhancements or additions to the treatment program, but were changes designed to make the program more "user friendly," that is, to make it easier for the patient to stay in treatment. The innovations were based on clinical observation of conditions that seemed to create problems for patients. Here are brief descriptions of the innovations:

Elimination of Treatment Fees. Subjects assigned to no-fee status paid no treatment fees. Subjects assigned to fee status were required to pay a fee of $2.50 per day. Subjects in the latter group were discharged if they failed to pay the required fee.

Patient-regulated Methadone Dose. After an initial two-week period for stabilization, patients regulated their own methadone doses. They were permitted to increase or decrease the dose once a week in an amount not to exceed 10 milligrams. The maximum dose permitted was 100 milligrams. Physicians regulated the doses of subjects assigned to standard treatment.

Optional Counseling. After one month for orientation and identification of personal problems, the caseworkers provided service to the subjects only on their request. Subjects assigned to standard treatment had mandatory scheduled face-to-face counseling sessions with their caseworkers twice a month.

Rapid Admission. Admission procedures were accelerated so that the first dose of methadone was dispensed within 24 hours after registration. Subjects assigned to the control condition waited 14 days from registration to the first dose. At the time that the project started, the usual period from registration to medication was 10 to 14 days. This time was needed for efficient scheduling of professional time for the social evaluation, laboratory work, and medical evaluations.

INTRODUCING AND MAINTAINING THE INNOVATIONS

The project was conducted as a collaborative activity of the University of Texas Health Science Center at San Antonio and the Center for Health Care Services (CHCS), also located in San Antonio. The CHCS is a publicly supported community mental health center that serves a county population enumerated in 1990 to be approximately 1 million persons. The multimodal Substance Abuse Program of the CHCS was established in 1970 and has operated continuously to the present time. Methadone maintenance has always been the major part of the Substance Abuse Program. The number of patients maintained on methadone has varied, depending on funds available. In November 1989, 386 patients, excluding project patients, were maintained on methadone. Nearly all patients were required to pay a starting fee of $6.00 per day. After about six months of treatment, when a funded treatment slot became available, the fee was reduced to $2.50 per day. Pregnant women, persons receiving welfare or disability payments, and persons infected with the human immunodeficiency virus (HIV) paid reduced or no fees.

Although the treatment innovations and the research were separate activities, the aims of the project required coordinated operations of both. Before and during the project, the research staff of the University of Texas Health Science Center at San Antonio and the executive and clinical staff of the CHCS had many joint conferences to plan, implement, and maintain the innovations and to conduct the evaluations. Conferences were held with caseworkers, physicians, nurses, and others to explain the innovations, to describe the roles of clinical and research staff, to monitor the maintenance of the innovations, and to report progress and problems. All research and clinical staff were given written "Research Guides," plus one-page summaries of the procedures. The physicians and the caseworkers approved of all the interventions except optional counseling. In 1991, 15 caseworkers and 4 physicians serving research subjects completed a short questionnaire that asked for their opinions about the effects of the innovations. Only 1 of these 19 clinicians expressed a belief that optional counseling improved rehabilitation. Despite their reservations, the caseworkers cooperated in maintaining the optional counseling innovation. The entire project benefited from excellent continuing collaboration between the research staff and the clinical staff. The four innovations were introduced and maintained with only minor deviations from the research plan. Here are three examples of the deviations.

Because of a clerical error, a subject in the fee study was assigned to fee status who should have been assigned to no-fee status. The error was discovered when enrollment was completed. To equalize the numbers in the fee and no-fee groups, the next two eligible subjects were enrolled and assigned to no-fee status. A caseworker mistakenly required a subject assigned to optional counseling to report for biweekly counseling for a period of six weeks. The caseworker recognized his error and corrected it. Rapid (24-hour) admission of a subject was delayed because a newly-employed clerk made a mistake in scheduling. The subject received her first dose of methadone approximately 30 hours after registration.

EVALUATING THE INNOVATIONS

The evaluation design was that of an open clinical trial, with random assignment of subjects at the time of enrollment to an innovation or to standard treatment. The criteria for enrollment were eligible for methadone maintenance, aged 18 or over, not pregnant, intravenous drug use during at least 21 of the past 30 days, not in treatment during the past 30 days, and not enrolled in a preceding study of this project. The fee study had one additional criterion: qualified to pay $2.50 per day. All applicants were considered qualified to pay this amount unless they were in a category of patients allowed to pay reduced fees or no fees.

Nearly all eligible patients wanted to enroll because they would obtain treatment at reduced cost or no cost for one year. All project subjects received free treatment for one year except those assigned to fee status. After one year of treatment, subjects remaining in treatment could continue in treatment but were required to pay a fee of $2.50 per day.

Enrollment and random assignment were done after the admission evaluations were completed and the patient had been accepted for methadone maintenance, except that in the study of rapid admission, subjects were enrolled and assigned on the day that they applied for treatment at the CHCS. The treatment services offered were equivalent except for the innovations. All caseworkers, physicians, and nurses in outpatient services of the Substance Abuse Program served both experimental and control subjects. As subjects were admitted they were assigned in rotation to physicians and caseworkers, with adjustment for the size of caseloads.

The four innovations were evaluated in three studies that began in sequence. The first study evaluated the effects of elimination of fees. The second study simultaneously evaluated the separate effects of patient-regulated methadone dose and optional counseling. The third study evaluated the effects of rapid admission. In the fee study, 152 subjects were enrolled with half assigned to fee status and half to no-fee status. In the combined patient-regulated dose and optional counseling study, 300 subjects were enrolled; 100 were assigned to patient-regulated methadone dose, 100 to optional counseling, and 100 to standard treatment. In the rapid admission study, 186 subjects were enrolled with half assigned to rapid admission and half to slow admission. A total of 638 subjects was enrolled in the project. Enrollment started in September 1989 and ended in November 1991. Because of pretreatment attrition during the rapid admission study, only 610 were admitted to treatment.

Three data collection instruments — the initial interview, the clinical data form, and the follow-up interview — were used. The first and last of these instruments were questionnaires. The clinical data form was designed to obtain uniform information from clinical records. The questionnaires were found to have satisfactory inter-interviewer reliability (Maddux, Ingram, & Desmond, 1995). A repeat data collection with the same clinical records revealed satisfactory reliability of the clinical data form. The initial interview was completed at the time of enrollment. The clinical data form was completed from review of the clinical record one year after admission. The follow-up interview was completed as soon as possible after the first anniversary of admission. A Spanish translation of the questionnaires was prepared but it was needed for only 2 of the 638 subjects. While most Mexican-American heroin users in San Antonio speak a dialect of Spanish called Tex-Mex, nearly all also speak English.

Because the outcomes of treatment studies become increasingly difficult to interpret as the number of subjects lost to follow-up increases, special effort was made to obtain follow-up interviews with all subjects (Desmond, Maddux, Johnson, & Confer, 1995). Follow-up interviews were obtained with 599 (98 percent) of the 610 subjects admitted to treatment. Eleven subjects were not interviewed. Seven of these were dead, one had a cognitive disability, one refused, and two were not located. Most of the one-year follow-up data on the dead subjects were obtained from relatives and other sources.

FINDINGS

Like the background and methodology, the findings have also been previously reported in detail (Maddux & Desmond, 1995; Maddux, Desmond, & Vogtsberger, 1995; Maddux, Esquivel, Vogtsberger, & Desmond, 1991; Maddux, Prihoda, & Desmond, 1994; Maddux, Vogtsberger, Desmond, & Esquivel, 1993); only the principal findings are presented here.

The 638 subjects enrolled were predominantly men (78 percent), predominantly Mexican-American (70 percent), undereducated (only 47 percent completed high school), and unemployed (only 13 percent in full-time employment). Their mean age at enrollment was 36. Heroin was the primary drug used at enrollment for nearly all subjects. All were chronic users — a mean of 16 years elapsed from first intravenous drug use to enrollment. Most had been incarcerated for one or more months during the five years preceding enrollment. In all studies, the random assignment produced groups of subjects that were similar on 21 personal variables, except that in the fee study, the fee and no-fee subjects differed significantly on two variables: gender and number of heterosexual partners during the 30 days before admission. These two variables were not, however, related to retention.

Elimination of Treatment Fees

Elimination of treatment fees significantly increased retention. Only 34 percent of the fee subjects but 54 percent of the no-fee subjects were retained for one year. A no-fee subject was 1.6 times more likely than a fee subject to remain in treatment for one year. The improved retention of the no-fee subjects persisted through the second year, although all paid $2.50 per day during the second year. Only 12 percent of the fee subjects but 26 percent of the no-fee subjects were retained for two years. After one year of free treatment, some of the no-fee subjects may have become better able to pay $2.50 per day than they were at the time of admission. Payment of a fee did not lead to improved outcomes during treatment. The fee and no-fee subgroups retained in treatment for one year did about equally well on measures of intravenous drug use, crime, and incarceration. The no-fee group did better on days of productive activity during the 30 days preceding the first anniversary of admission. Days of productive activity was the sum of days worked full-time for pay, days of full-time education or training, and days of full-time homemaking.

Patient-regulated Methadone Dose

Allowing patients to regulate their methadone doses did not lead to a general escalation of doses. The mean of the maximum methadone dose during treatment of the subjects who regulated their doses, 58 milligrams, exceeded that of subjects in standard treatment, 53 milligrams, but this small difference was not significant. The increased mean dose of the subjects regulating their doses did not signify increased doses of most subjects; the increased mean was due to a small number of patients who elevated their doses to 80 milligrams or more. Fifteen percent of subjects assigned to patient-regulated methadone dose but only 6 percent of those assigned to standard treatment had maximum doses of 80 milligrams or more. During the period of this study, most program physicians tended to regulate the methadone doses partly on the basis of symptoms or need expressed by patients. Thus the subjects in standard treatment "regulated" their doses, though with less freedom than those assigned to the patient-regulated dose group. Allowing patients to regulate their methadone doses did not seem to affect retention. At the end of the year, 50 percent of the patient-regulated dose group and 50 percent of the standard treatment group remained in treatment. At the end of two years, 23 percent of the patient-regulated dose group and 21 percent of the standard treatment group remained in treatment.

Optional Counseling

Subjects allowed to choose the frequency of their counseling sessions saw their caseworkers less than half as often as those required to have two sessions per month. The mean of interviews per month with caseworker was 1.1 for optional counseling subjects and 2.5 for standard treatment subjects. This difference was statistically significant. Among the optional counseling subjects, however, the number of interviews per month during treatment varied considerably, from 0.1 interviews per month to 4.0 interviews per month. The one-year retention rate of the optional counseling group, 60 percent, exceeded that of the standard treatment group, 50 percent, but the difference was only of borderline significance. At the end of two years, the retention rates were almost the same: 25 percent of the optional counseling group and 21 percent of the standard treatment group remained in treatment. Mandatory counseling provided in standard treatment did not lead to improved outcomes during treatment. For the subgroups that remained in treatment for one year, measures of illicit drug use and of social performance during the 30 days preceding the first anniversary of admission did not differ significantly.

Rapid Admission

Rapid admission markedly reduced pretreatment attrition. Only 4 percent of subjects assigned to rapid (24-hour) admission but 26 percent of those assigned to slow (14-day) admission dropped out during the period from initial contact to first dose of methadone. The slow admission subject was six times more likely than the rapid admission subject to drop out before admission. Subjects who dropped out differed significantly in two respects from those admitted. First, they were younger; their mean age was 32, while that of subjects admitted was 37. Second, they included more Mexican-Americans; 86 percent of the dropouts but only 61 percent of subjects admitted were classified as Mexican-American.

All subjects in the rapid admission study who were admitted to treatment were followed for one year to learn whether rapid admission adversely affected retention in treatment. It did not. A slightly higher percentage of rapid admission subjects (43 percent) than of slow admission subjects (39 percent) remained continuously in treatment for one year. The two subgroups that remained in treatment for one year did about equally well on measures of illicit drug use and social performance during the 30 days preceding the first anniversary of admission.

Predictors of Retention

To evaluate the relation of 12 personal and 4 treatment variables to one-year retention in the entire cohort of 610 subjects admitted to treatment, a multiple logistic regression, with stepwise selection, was conducted. Three personal and two treatment variables were selected into the model. This means that they were significantly related to retention. The personal variables were age and two measures indicating pretreatment criminality. Age was positively related to retention: 53 percent of subjects aged 35 and over, but only 42 percent of those under 35, were retained for one year. Possibly the younger subjects found it more difficult to exchange the heroin "high" for the steady state of methadone, to conform to program expectations, or both. The two measures of criminality were days of crime during the month before admission and compulsory supervision by a probation or parole officer. Both were inversely related to retention. These two measures suggest an antisocial tendency that impaired the subject's ability to remain in methadone treatment.

The two treatment variables were maximum methadone dose and interviews per month with caseworker. The mean methadone dose of those retained, 53 milligrams, only slightly exceeded that of those not retained, 50 milligrams, but the difference was significant. Interviews per month with caseworker was inversely related to retention, meaning that increased interviews per month predicted reduced likelihood of retention for one year. The mean of interviews per month of subjects retained was 1.9, while that of subjects not retained was 2.5. It seems unlikely that interviews with caseworker impaired retention. More likely, problems of subjects that led to increased interviews also led to termination of treatment.

Admission of Referrals from Outreach

In addition to introducing and evaluating the four innovations, the project made methadone maintenance treatment available to participants in the San Antonio AIDS Community Outreach Demonstration Project. That project, supported by the National Institute on Drug Abuse, had the purpose of reducing AIDS risk behavior by providing outreach to and intervention with intravenous drug users who were not in treatment. Only small numbers of the intravenous opioid users who participated in the outreach project seemed interested in treatment. Most said that they were not addicted, or they did not need treatment, or they did not want methadone maintenance. Of 2,188 participants enrolled during three years, only 107 (5 percent) entered methadone maintenance.

IMPLICATIONS FOR CLINICAL PRACTICE AND HEALTH POLICY

The findings of the fee study suggest that retention on methadone can be improved by providing more free treatment slots. This can be done only if increased financial support is provided to the publicly supported methadone programs.

With limits imposed, patients regulated their methadone doses without marked general escalation of dose. The findings suggest that when physicians allow patients to participate in dose decisions, only small differences appear between the doses regulated by physicians and those regulated by patients.

For most patients on methadone, optional counseling seems preferable to mandatory counseling scheduled twice a month. Optional counseling led to fewer interviews per month with caseworker, a trend toward increased retention, and outcomes during treatment approximately as good as those obtained with mandatory counseling. Some patients with special problems may benefit from a period of mandatory counseling, but for most optional counseling seems preferable.

The findings of the rapid admission study indicate that waiting periods of two weeks or longer from initial contact to medication result in loss from treatment of many opioid users who could benefit from methadone maintenance. Treatment programs could accelerate the admission process, but publicly supported programs would need increased financial support to provide rapid admission for all eligible applicants.

ACKNOWLEDGMENTS

The work reported here was supported by grant number DA06128 from the National Institute on Drug Abuse. Special thanks to the research staff of the Substance Abuse Division, Department of Psychiatry, University of Texas Health Science Center at San Antonio, and to the clinical staff of the Center for Health Care Services for their assistance in the project. D. P. Desmond and B. A. Confer reviewed the manuscript and provided helpful comments.

REFERENCES

Ball, J. C., & Ross, A. (1991). *The effectiveness of methadone maintenance treatment.* New York: Springer-Verlag.

Cooper, J. R. (1989). Methadone treatment and acquired immunodeficiency syndrome. *Journal of the American Medical Association, 262,* 1664–1668.

Desmond, D. P., Maddux, J. F., Johnson, T. H., & Confer, B. A. (1995). Obtaining followup interviews for treatment evaluation. *Journal of Substance Abuse Treatment, 12,* 95–102.

Dole, V. P., & Joseph, H. (1978). Long-term outcome of patients treated with methadone maintenance. *Annals of the New York Academy of Sciences, 311,* 181–189.

Gearing, F. G. (1974). Methadone maintenance treatment five years later — Where are they now? *American Journal of Public Health Supplement, 64,* 44–50.

Hubbard, R. L., Marsden, M. E., Rachal, J. V., Harwood, H. J., Cavanaugh, E. R., & Ginzburg, H. M. (1989). *Drug abuse treatment: A national study of effectiveness.* Chapel Hill: University of North Carolina Press.

Maddux, J. F. (1993). Improving retention on methadone maintenance. In J. A. Inciardi, F. M. Tims, & B. W. Fletcher (Eds.), *Innovative approaches in the treatment of drug abuse: Program models and strategies* (pp. 21–33). Westport, CT: Greenwood Press.

Maddux, J. F., & Desmond, D. P. (1995). Rapid admission and retention on methadone. *American Journal of Drug and Alcohol Abuse, 21,* 533–547.

Maddux, J. F., Desmond, D. P., & Vogtsberger, K. N. (1995). Patient-regulated methadone dose and optional counseling in methadone maintenance. *American Journal on Addictions, 4,* 18–32.

Maddux, J. F., Esquivel, M., Vogtsberger, K. N., & Desmond, D. P. (1991). Methadone dose and urine morphine. *Journal of Substance Abuse Treatment, 8,* 195–201.

Maddux, J. F., Ingram, J. M., & Desmond, D. P. (1995). Reliability of two brief questionnaires for drug abuse treatment evaluation. *American Journal of Drug and Alcohol Abuse, 21,* 209–221.

Maddux, J. F., Prihoda, T. J., & Desmond, D. P. (1994). Treatment fees and retention on methadone maintenance. *Journal of Drug Issues, 24,* 419–443.

Maddux, J. F., Vogtsberger, K. N., Desmond, D. P., & Esquivel, M. (1994). Innovations to improve retention on methadone. In F. M. Tims, B. W. Fletcher, J. A. Inciardi, & A. M. Horton, Jr. (Eds.), *Drug abuse treatment: The implementation of innovative approaches* (p. 53). Westport, CT: Greenwood Press.

Maddux, J. F., Vogtsberger, K. N., Desmond, D. P., & Esquivel, M. (1993). Program changes and retention on methadone. *Journal of Substance Abuse Treatment, 10,* 585–588.

3

Evaluating the Effectiveness of Mobile Drug Abuse Treatment

Joseph V. Brady, Karst J. Besteman, and Lawrence Greenfield

In the fall of 1990, the Substance Abuse Center of the Institutes for Behavior Resources in collaboration with the Baltimore City Department of Health undertook a research demonstration project supported by the National Institute on Drug Abuse (NIDA) to examine the feasibility of delivering drug abuse treatment within the context of a mobile health service (Brady, 1993). In the City of Baltimore, as elsewhere, identifying fixed sites where programs can operate has become a major impediment to drug abuse treatment. It is generally the case however, that neighborhoods and communities find it less objectionable to have such services offered from mobile health units. From this perspective, the project represented an attempt to confront the obvious need to expand drug abuse treatment and respond to the concerns that drive community resistance to the opening of fixed-site drug abuse treatment clinics.

The focus of this harm-reduction initiative was on the identification and recruitment of intravenous drug abusers into a mobile methadone treatment program that provided individual and group addiction counseling as well as health education, outreach, and clinical support to inner-city communities with a high prevalence of substance abuse and other poor health status indicators (Brady, in press). This was accomplished by parking such treatment units for a few hours each day at agreed-upon locations (for example, church parking lots and city-owned facilities) and limiting the time at each location by appropriate scheduling (for example, avoiding school passage times). In addition to methadone medication and counseling for intravenous opioid abusers, the mobile units were designed to offer additional health services to the community (for example, blood pressure screening and diabetic evaluations) to insure that the program was legitimately viewed as a health initiative.

Two separate inner-city regional divisions in eastern and northwestern Baltimore were selected as sites for implementation of this mobile drug abuse treatment project (Besteman & Brady, 1993). Temporary parking locations for the vehicles were determined only after extensive consultation and agreement with the City of Baltimore planning and zoning department, local legislators, health care providers, community leaders, and especially the local clergy and church groups whose assistance proved invaluable in this sensitive process. Two 25-foot Newport motor homes were custom modified to serve as self-propelled mobile medication dispensing units to include a secure nurses station with medication safe and dispensing window, a lavatory, a small patient waiting area, and an elaborate security alarm system. In addition, two 31-foot Newmar travel trailers were custom modified to serve as counseling and general health service units to include two private individual counseling and examination areas separated by a larger centralized group meeting/waiting area, all with appropriate furnishings for seating and note-taking as required. A back-up unit was provided by a 19-foot Coachman motor home custom modified in a manner similar to the two Newport motor homes to serve as a self-propelled mobile medication dispensing unit when required.

To obtain the necessary approvals and licensing to dispense methadone, stringent requirements established by federal regulatory agencies had to be satisfied. All medications were stored in an approved security facility with no drugs permitted to remain in the mobile vehicles beyond the scheduled dispensing hours, and a facility was provided for initial screening and medical evaluation of newly enrolled patients. The implementation of effective information management procedures required mobile treatment staff to carry laptop computers containing a database providing access to essential patient records including physician's medication orders and administrative notes, as well as doses dispensed, patient absences, and reporting forms. Daily transfer of laptop information to a workstation computer accessed a local area network that refreshed the database and added administrative and demographic information on new patients. A dedicated on-screen file facilitated individual counselor record keeping (that is, urine surveillance and blood alcohol concentration), scheduling of appointments, group attendance, and the development of customized treatment plans.

The treatment program design provided for the location of one treatment unit (medication van and counseling trailer) at a single centralized site in the eastern regional division of the city, where it remained stationary throughout each day. A second treatment medication and counseling unit circulated between three or four different locations in the northwestern regional division of the city each day. After 18 months of operation under these conditions, a cross-over procedure was introduced with the eastern regional division treatment unit circulating between three or four locations in that same division each day while the northwestern regional division treatment unit remained stationary at one centralized site in that division throughout each day.

Admission for treatment required participants to have a verifiable one-year history of intravenous opioid abuse and dependence and to have attained a minimum age of 18 years. Following the initial screening interview, the Individual Assessment Profile, the Beck Depression Inventory (BDI), and a physical examination, including urinalysis and other laboratory tests, assignment was made by zip code to a mobile health treatment unit. The staff physician established the initial treatment dose for each patient and methadone was dispensed daily via solubilized diskettes by the Mobile Health Service (MHS) nursing staff upon picture I.D. verification of the patient's identity.

Weekly urine specimens were obtained from each patient and clients participated in counseling sessions at the mobile trailer units scheduled at least once per week. Within the first few weeks following admission to treatment, each patient completed a brief travel questionnaire providing comparative data on the time and money expended to attend the MHS daily medication and weekly counseling sessions on the one hand, and the time and money expended to access these same services in the client's previous fixed-site treatment program, on the other hand.

PROCESS AND OUTCOME EVALUATION

Both process and outcome studies were conducted to evaluate the feasibility, implementation, and results of the mobile treatment intervention on drug abuse and related measures. The process evaluation provided an account of all the steps required to initiate this complex undertaking. All internal staff meetings and discussions, as well as all meetings with external individuals and groups, were documented in a standardized written format and communicated expeditiously to the research evaluation team. Essential baseline information against which to evaluate outcome measures was incorporated into the individual assessment profile and other client information forms completed on each patient at intake and throughout the course of treatment.

Demographic Characteristics

During the initial three years of clinic operation, more than 300 intravenous opioid abusers were admitted for treatment by the MHS and the waiting list for admission included more than 500 individuals. A substantial database was developed relevant to both accessibility and retention in drug abuse treatment under such conditions. With regard to demographic characteristics, for example, there were but few features that distinguished MHS patients from those receiving outpatient treatment in more conventional inner-city fixed-site programs. These intravenous opioid abusers were predominantly (70 percent) African-American males (only 30 percent female), over 30 years of age (90 percent), and mostly unemployed (over 80 percent). The MHS patients were self-referred for the most part (75 percent) and they had fewer prior admissions to drug treatment programs (average under two) than patients from the fixed-site treatment programs in the City of Baltimore (average over three).

Pretreatment Criminal Justice System Involvement

We examined the extent to which the MHS attracted patients with similar pretreatment characteristics, compared with fixed-site programs in Baltimore and neighboring Washington, D.C., and how such patients managed in treatment. We also assessed the extent to which the MHS patients were involved with the criminal justice system (CJS). At intake, approximately 32 percent of MHS patients reported that they were either on probation, parole, or had criminal charges pending. Additionally, 39 percent reported that they were arrested one or more times during the past 24 months and 30 percent during the past 12 months. These percentages were found to be comparable to other programs in Washington and Baltimore. Of patients in a typical Washington clinic, 37 percent reported current CJS involvement and 31 percent said that they were arrested one or more times within the past 12 months. Data for methadone patients in six other Baltimore outpatient programs were reviewed using 1991 State of Maryland reports. The overall mean percent of patients who reported having been arrested at any time within the past 24 months was 38 percent for these programs. Thus, CJS involvement in MHS appears to be similar to other Baltimore and Washington community-based programs.

Travel Time and Travel Cost Comparisons

Figure 3.1 summarizes travel data from the reports of those patients who had participated in other outpatient drug abuse treatment programs before admission to the MHS. Some 86 percent of these patients were required to travel more than 10 minutes (average: 35 minutes) for each visit to their previous program site compared with only 54 percent required to travel that long (average: 19 minutes) to the mobile site. Figure 3.1 also shows a similar reduction in travel cost with 55 percent of the patients required to spend more than $1.00 (average: $1.37) for previous program visits compared with only 26 percent required to pay that much (average: $0.48) for travel to the mobile site. These results bear directly upon the issue of access and the overall cost of program compliance as determinants of retention and treatment effectiveness.

FIGURE 3.1
Travel Time and Travel Cost Required to Access the Mobile Treatment Service and the Previous Program Treatment Service for Those Patients Formerly Enrolled in Fixed-site Clinics

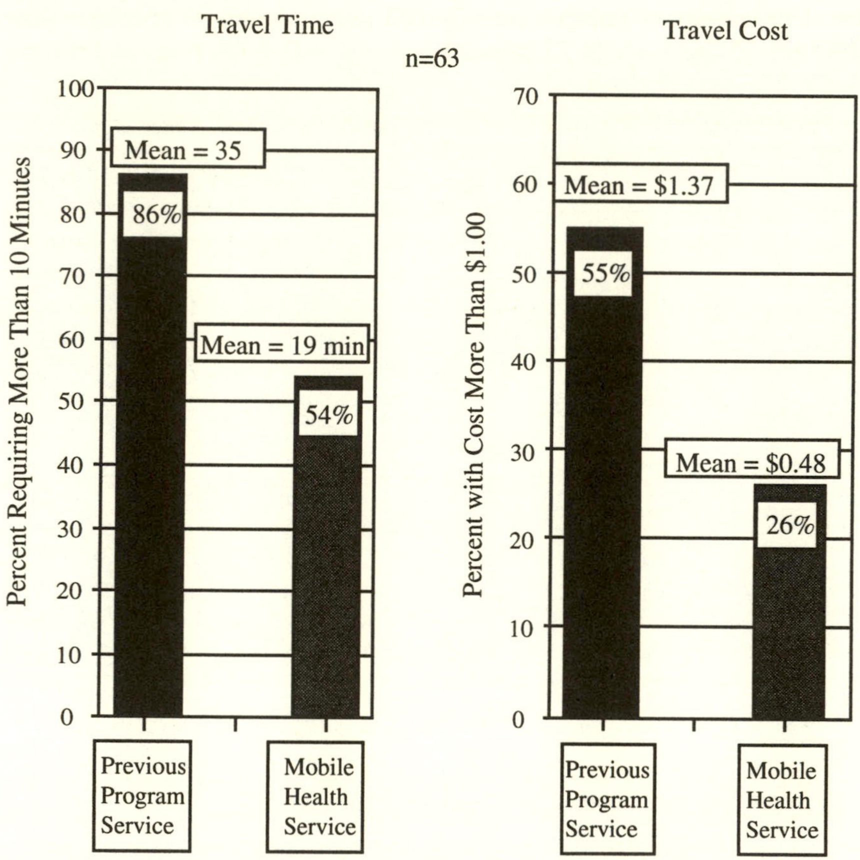

Interim Outcome Assessments

A data set developed on patients (N = 207) who completed an interim assessment after remaining in the program for six to nine months provided a basis for more directly evaluating the effectiveness of the MHS approach to drug abuse treatment. Analysis of this data showed that there was a consistent decrease in illicit drug use, particularly opiates, between intake and interim assessment, as reflected in both self-report measures and urinalysis test results. Reported illegal activity and the amount of money spent on drugs also decreased sharply between intake and interim assessments, while legitimate employment increased to at least some extent and general health status was reported to have improved. Such self-report data, especially pertaining to sensitive topics such as drug use and criminal behavior, need to be examined with caution however. Of patients who tested positive for cocaine or opiates within the past 25 days, 61 percent accurately reported past–30-day cocaine and 48 percent opiate use. Conversely, of patients who denied using cocaine or opiates within the past 30 days, about 25 percent tested positive for these substances within the past 25 days.

For a subset of these patients (N = 54), the six-to-nine-month follow-up interviews were conducted by an independent evaluation team (Treatment Research Institute, University of Pennsylvania School of Medicine) with results that were generally consistent with the indicated interim assessment outcomes. In addition, the MHS findings from the Treatment Research Institute evaluation subsample were compared with the results obtained with two other groups of previously evaluated methadone patients (McLellan, Arnt, Metzger, Moody, & O'Brien, 1993). One group of patients (Level 1, N = 42) received methadone only, and the second group (Level 2, N = 41) received the same average methadone dose plus standard drug counseling treatment. The two comparison groups and the MHS patients were generally quite similar with respect to medical and employment status, as well as drug and alcohol use. In contrast to the Level 1 and Level 2 patients, however, the MHS patients showed statistically and clinically significant increases in the percent employed ($p < .05$) and greater reductions in criminal activity ($p < .001$), as well as in drug ($p < .01$) and alcohol ($p < .05$) use. For this subset of MHS patients, the degree of correspondence between urinalysis test results and self-report results was similar to the MHS interim assessment correspondence described above.

The scores on the BDI administered at the time of admission to the program were also analyzed in relationship to reported drug usage at both intake and interim assessments. The results showed that the group with the highest BDI scores (31+) had the highest percentage of monthly cocaine users (32 percent at intake, 23 percent at interim) while the group with the lowest BDI scores (0–10) had the lowest percentage of monthly cocaine users (22 percent at intake, 13 percent at interim). To the extent that these findings suggest the participant role of a comorbid condition that may influence outcomes, they provide strong support for the integration of drug abuse treatment within the context of a general health service delivery system.

Retention in Treatment

In evaluating the effectiveness of any drug abuse treatment program, retention rate is a factor of utmost importance. Figure 3.2 shows the percentage of dropouts (that is, patients terminating treatment against medical advice) during the first year following admission to the Mobile Health Service (IBR/MHS) as compared with the percentage of first year dropouts from a model fixed-site treatment program in the District of Columbia (TOPS-DCI) and from several fixed-site outpatient programs combined as reported in the NIDA-sponsored Client Oriented Data Acquisition Process study (CODAP/NIDA). Over 50 percent of the patients from the CODAP programs and some 30 percent of the TOPS patients had terminated treatment against medical advice within the first year by comparison with a dropout rate of only 15 percent for the MHS treatment program. The enhancement of retention in drug abuse treatment by the MHS initiative is reflected as well in comparisons of length of stay for all discharges (including program transfers, hospitalization, and incarceration) during the first year following admission as shown in Figure 3.3. Within the first 90 days following admission, for example, more than 65 percent of the first year discharges from the CODAP programs had taken place while almost 80 percent of the MHS first year discharges remained in treatment at that three-month juncture. Clearly, the average number of days in treatment following admission for all patients discharged from the MHS within one year of admission can be seen to far exceed the average number of days in treatment for the CODAP first year discharges. When similar comparisons were made between the MHS program and the TOPS-DCI fixed-site clinic, as shown in Figure 3.4, almost 80 percent of the MHS patients remained in treatment nine months following admission while only 30 percent of the TOPS patients remained in treatment that long.

A survival analysis of the duration of treatment comparing CJS patients and non-criminal justice system (non-CJS) patients was carried out for both the MHS and the TOPS-DCI programs. MHS non-CJS patients (N = 215) had a median survival time in treatment of 16 months compared with 12 months for CJS patients (N = 100), a difference reaching the $p < .04$ level of significance. The TOPS clinic differences between the median survival times for 167 CJS patients (four months) and 284 non-CJS patients (six months) reached an even greater level of significance ($p < .01$) indicating clearly that CJS patients in both programs had consistently shorter stays in treatment than non-CJS patients. Although there were some differences between the way CJS and non-CJS patients were distinguished in this analysis (that is, self-report) and the way such determinations were made

FIGURE 3.2
Percentage of Patients Who Dropped Out of Treatment against Medical Advice during the First Year Following Admission to the Mobile Health Service (IBR/MHS), the Single Fixed-site Model Program in the District of Columbia (TOPS-DCI), and the Combined Programs Reported in the NIDA-sponsored Client Oriented Data Acquisition Process Study (CODAP/NIDA).

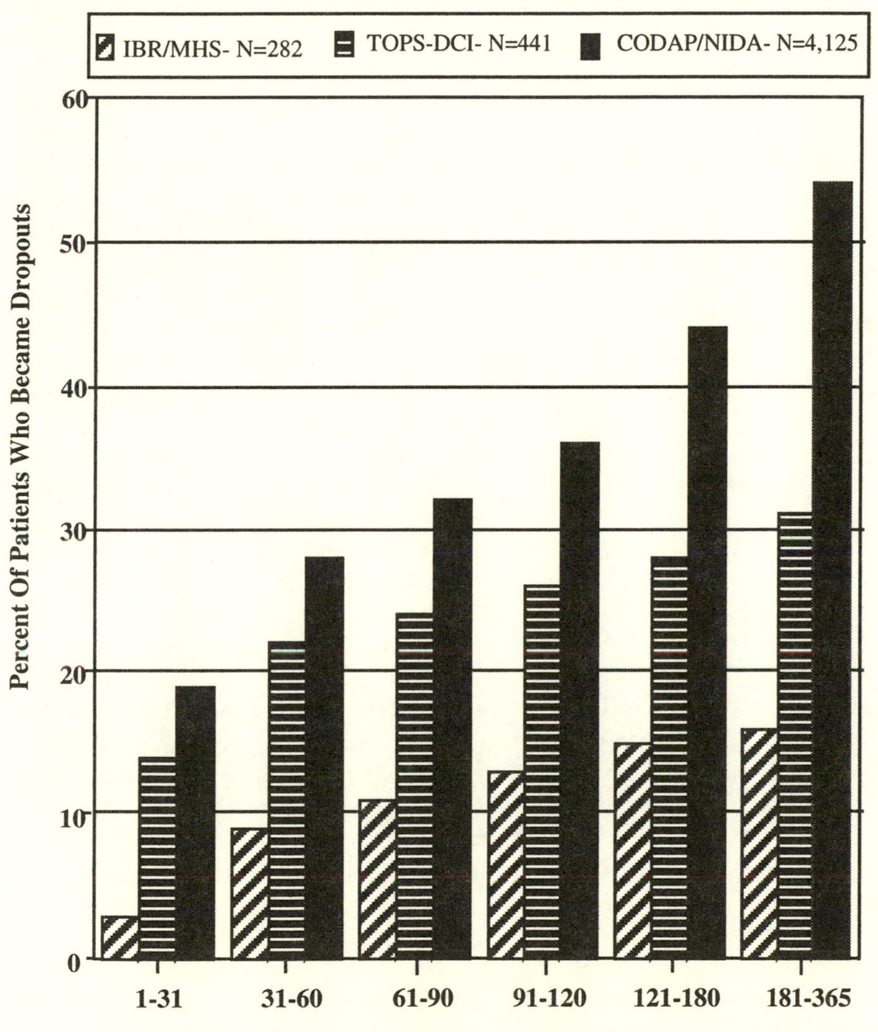

FIGURE 3.3
Percentage of All Patients Discharged within One Year Who Left Treatment Following Admission to the Mobile Health Service (IBR/MHS) and to the Combined Client Oriented Data Acquisition Process Study Programs (CODAP/NIDA).

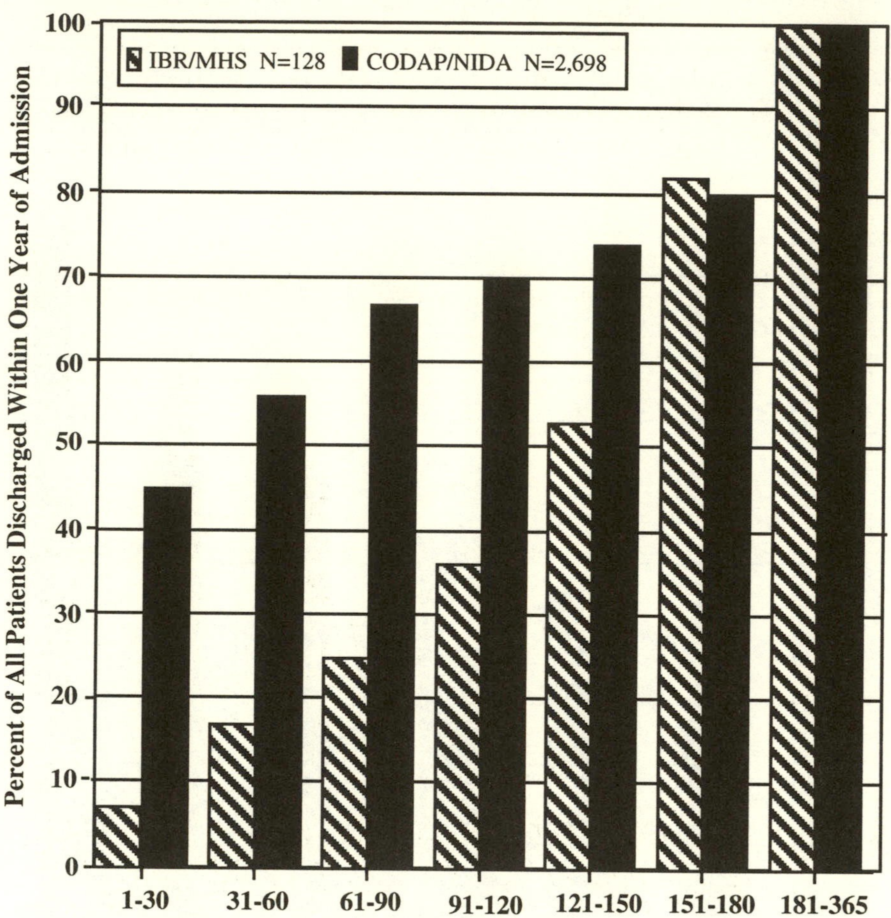

(that is, court referral) in previous studies (Collins & Allison, 1983; Hubbard et al., 1989), the present findings were not in agreement with the prevailing view that court-referred abusers tend to remain in treatment longer and therefore can be expected to have better treatment outcomes (Gerstein & Harwood, 1990). Even when the present samples were analyzed to include only those patients required or recommended for treatment by the court (MHS = 10 percent; TOPS = 18 percent), median survival times were found to be still shorter for the MHS CJS patients (9.7 months) and about the same for the TOPS CJS patients (4.2 months). Clearly, further research will be required to reconcile the contradictions between these more recent findings and earlier results that predicted more favorable outcomes with CJS patients.

Survival analysis was also used to compare retention rates for patients with and without prior methadone treatment. For the MHS program, both patients with and without prior methadone experience were found to remain in treatment for similar periods of time with median stays of

FIGURE 3.4
Percentage of Patients Remaining in Treatment during the First Nine Months Following Admission to the Mobile Health Service (IBR/MHS) and to the District of Columbia Programs (TOPS-DCI).

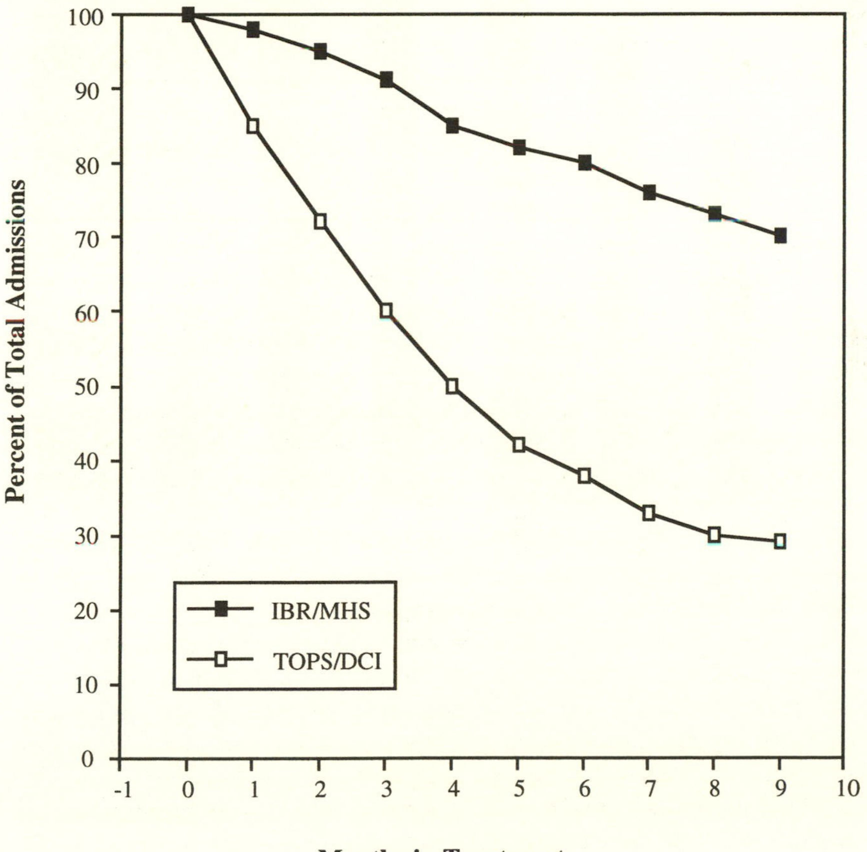

14.7 and 15.9 months respectively ($p > .10$). In the TOPS clinic however, where overall lengths of stay were consistently shorter than in the MHS program, there was a significant difference ($p > .01$) between the median length of stay for the previously methadone treated patients (5.9 months) and the median length of stay for the nonmethadone patients (4.3 months). Thus, while nonmethadone patients were attracted in similar proportions to the MHS (39 percent) and TOPS (44 percent) programs, the MHS program had better success in retaining such patients in treatment than the fixed-site TOPS clinic in the District of Columbia.

Urinalysis Assessments

Preadmission urine screens confirmed that 100 percent of the patients admitted to the MHS drug abuse treatment program tested positive for opiates while some 66 percent of the patients tested positive for cocaine upon admission. While the interim assessment profile at six to nine months following admission reflected marked reductions in opiate use confirmed by a decrease in positive urinalysis results from 100 percent to 35 percent of the patients, cocaine usage showed less of a decline from the 66 percent positive urinalysis results at intake to the 56 percent positive results at interim. When these urinalysis results for the MHS program were compared with the urinalysis finding for the model fixed-site TOPS clinic in the District of Columbia over a similar six-to-nine-month time interval following admission, a picture emerged that was in sharp contrast to the retention rate data described in Figure 3.4. The average percentage of patients with "dirty" urines (that is, positive for illicit drugs, predominantly opiates and cocaine) decreased markedly to less than 20 percent over the first nine months of treatment for the TOPS-DCI patients, as shown in Figure 3.5, while much less of a decline to approximately 60 percent was seen for the MHS patients over the same interval. As the data in Figures 3.2 and 3.4 suggest, a much higher percentage of patients were discharged from the TOPS program than from the MHS program over the indicated treatment period, and there were differences not only in the frequency of urinalysis testing and counselor feedback (that is, TOPS = weekly; MHS = monthly) but also in the more stringent requirement for "clean" urines to avoid detoxification and discharge from the TOPS treatment program. While these findings would indicate that the enhanced retention rate of the MHS program may have been maintained, at least in part, at the expense of tolerating a measure of illicit drug use, the results also suggest that the price of the clean urine outcomes attained by the TOPS-DCI clinic may have been an increased rate of treatment termination either as dropouts against medical advice or as outright noncompliance detoxification discharges.

FIGURE 3.5
Percentage of Dirty Urines (that is, Positive for Illicit Drugs) during the First Nine Months Following Admission to the Mobile Health Service (IBR/MHS) and to the District of Columbia Programs (TOPS-DCI).

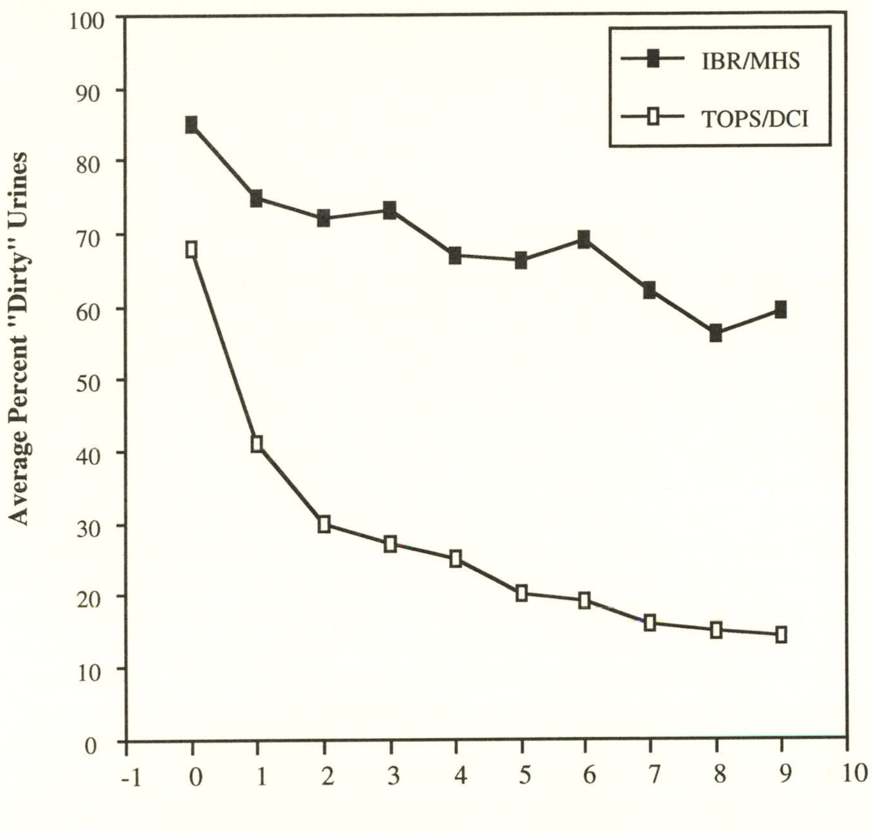

An analysis of the extent to which CJS involvement was related to urinalysis test results (with regard specifically to cocaine and opiate use) reflected clinic differences consistent with those described for the MHS and TOPS clinics in general. Urinalysis results were aggregated in a multivariate analysis of variance beginning with the intake month (0) through month eight (8) in treatment and the differences in mean percent cocaine positive urines for the MHS program (58.4 percent) and the TOPS clinic (12.5 percent) were in the expected direction. The significance of these clinic differences was confirmed in a comparison of urinalysis results over time combining data for months 0–2, 3–5, and 6–8. While TOPS mean percent positive urinalysis scores for cocaine decreased from 20 percent to 8 percent and 10 percent, respectively, over the three time periods, MHS scores declined only from 61 percent to 58 percent and 56 percent, respectively, a difference between the programs reaching the $p < .01$ level of significance. With the two clinics combined, CJS patients averaged 43 percent positive urines for cocaine compared with 35 percent cocaine positives for non-CJS patients, an 8 percent difference reaching the $p < .02$ level of significance. When the CJS and non-CJS patients were compared for each clinic separately, the MHS non-CJS patients showed a 9 percent decrease over time in the mean percent positive urines for cocaine while the mean percent positives for CJS patients increased by 6 percent over time. No such differences between CJS and non-CJS patients were found in the TOPS clinic where both groups showed similar decreases over time, and there were no differences between the CJS and non-CJS patients in percent positive opiate urinalysis results over time in either of the clinics.

When urinalysis test scores over time were examined in relationship to prior treatment experience, previously methadone treated patients were found to have a significantly higher ($p < .02$) percentage (66 percent) of positive cocaine urines than nonmethadone patients (47 percent). There was a significant difference between the previously methadone treated and nonmethadone patients at intake as well with the nonmethadone group claiming significantly less cocaine use in the prior 30 days than the previously methadone treated patients ($p < .02$). In the TOPS clinic, there were no such cocaine differences observed between previously methadone treated and nonmethadone patients and there were no significant differences between these two groups of patients in either clinic with respect to positive opiate urinalysis test scores.

The effect of program services upon treatment outcomes was evaluated using a multivariate analysis in which both counseling intensity and compliance were assessed in relationship to both cocaine and opiate urinalysis test results. As part of the interim evaluation, patients were asked the number of counseling sessions they attended since intake and the time they spent with their counselor per session. Total time in counseling was adjusted by number of months in treatment before the interview (that is, hours per month). The median adjusted number of counseling hours was 1.33 or one hour and 20 minutes per month. Patients were divided into two groups: those with more (1.33 hours per month or more) and less (below 1.33) counseling. As a proxy for compliance, we used the patient's estimate of the number of missed counseling appointments, grouping patients into those who missed (Miss) and did not miss (No-miss) appointments. Using multivariate analysis of variance, mean percent positive urinalysis scores for cocaine and opiates were examined in months 0–2, 3–4, and 5–6. For cocaine, Miss patients had greater mean percent positive scores than No-miss ($p < .01$) and differences in hours of counseling, though not statistically significant ($p < .06$), were in the expected direction. The patients with more counseling had lower mean percent positive cocaine urinalysis scores than those with less. Over time, no differences were found with either factor. The lack of such differences suggests that compliance or some other patient variable associated with counseling may have accounted for the urinalysis differences for cocaine rather than counseling per se.

With opiates, the Miss group had significantly greater mean percent dirty urines ($p < .01$) than the No-miss group. No differences were found between these patients over time. Overall, patients who reported more and less counseling did not differ significantly in urinalysis results for opiates. The data suggest, however, that such differences may have been greater later in treatment in comparison to earlier. In months 0–2, patients with more and less counseling had similar mean percent positive (54 percent versus 56 percent), respectively, while in subsequent months the differences were greater (24 percent versus 39–41 percent). To some extent at least, the results of this analysis are consistent with recent studies that have failed to demonstrate a clear dose response relationship between counseling and treatment outcomes (Hubbard, Etheridge, Craddock, & Dunteman, 1995). While the present findings would seem to indicate that increased hours of counseling were not helpful in reducing cocaine use, they do suggest that such counseling may have helped in reducing opiate use. These results are also consistent with the finding that patients who remained in treatment had decreases in percentages of dirty urines over time for opiates but not for cocaine.

Evaluation Implications

The programmatic comparisons detailed in this process and outcome analysis call attention to important differences in treatment philosophy of obvious relevance to the goals of drug policy. The early abandonment of treatment by those who fail to satisfy the abstinence demands of programs based upon a strong use-reduction philosophy is considered acceptable to the extent that limited resources are thereby preserved for those individuals who are able to comply. By contrast, the less demanding goals of programs based predominantly upon a harm-reduction philosophy tolerate a degree of illicit drug use in the interest of treatment retention and attenuation of the adverse consequences of substance abuse for both the individual and the community. Clearly, the policy choices involved must be based upon an evaluation of the short- and long-term costs and benefits of these alternative approaches to drug abuse treatment.

SUMMARY CASE FOR MOBILE DRUG ABUSE TREATMENT

The case for an MHS approach rests upon the need to expand drug abuse treatment and respond to the concerns that drive community resistance to the opening of fixed-site clinics. A mobile delivery system can also play an important role in promoting the integration of health care services and in facilitating access to and retention in treatment.

Experience over the past several years in settings where strong, politically charged community resistance continues to threaten essential treatment expansion has confirmed that urban neighborhoods find it less objectionable to have drug abuse treatment, including methadone maintenance, offered in the context of a mobile health service. Both acceptance and support are enhanced by involving community-based health service providers in the treatment and coordinating referral activities with existing mobile and fixed-site health care and social service facilities.

In confronting the multiple needs of substance abusers, a mobile treatment program can play a unique role because of its compatibility with both centralized and decentralized models of health services integration. Some mobile drug abuse treatment approaches may exemplify centralized models where clients receive medication, counseling, and health care at the same site, whereas others may follow decentralized models, using different sites for each of these services. There may even be some flexible and adaptable mobile drug abuse treatment approaches that combine both centralized and decentralized functions. Under any circumstances, the link between services (for example, general health and mental health) can be strengthened as agencies gain comfort with and confidence in the mobile modality as a stepping stone toward fully integrating drug abuse treatment into a network of services.

A mobile program may also have important advantages for administrators of community-based health service programs. The program can be adapted in ways that are consistent with an agency's mission, capabilities, and interests. A health center can offer medical services and provide administrative support for mobile units that dispense medication and conduct counseling. A substance abuse agency with experience only in drug-free treatment can offer counseling in conjunction with a medication-dispensing mobile unit. The mobile drug abuse treatment program also has many of the same advantages for a community-based health agency as those perceived by the community at large (for example, it is easier to operate on a trial basis and serve as a stepping stone for achieving the important goal of building a community-based capability for providing drug abuse services).

From a broader perspective, an effectively managed mobile program can advance the cause of institutionalizing community-based drug abuse treatment. Once the mobile program has become an accepted presence in the neighborhood, it can function as an integral part of the community's infrastructure of services. The several mobile sites in the City of Baltimore, for example, have become the focus of referral services by local clergy and other community leaders. Under such circumstances, treatment is not only more accessible but also accepted as an integral part of the fabric of the community. There is no clear and simple path to achieving these goals, but the evidence emerging from existing programs suggests that the mobile treatment approach may be an important step in the right direction.

Beyond the issues of community acceptance and health services integration, there remain abiding concerns about the conditions under which drug abuse treatment can be most effectively provided. There is convincing evidence that time spent in treatment is an important determinant of successful outcome. And "response effort" or "response cost" (that is, the time and money spent to access treatment) has a demonstrably strong influence, since clients are clearly more likely to remain in treatment programs that are easily accessed. The low dropout rates in mobile drug abuse treatment programs further reflect one of the more important strengths of these innovative efforts to enhance retention and improve effectiveness by facilitating access to treatment. Moreover, by virtue of their ability to overcome barriers to drug abuse treatment and facilitate the integration of health care services, mobile treatment programs can penetrate areas of the highest need and respond to such public health crises of alarming proportions.

REFERENCES

Besteman, K., & Brady, J. V. (1993). Implementing mobile drug abuse treatment: Problems, procedures, and perspectives. In J. A. Inciardi, F. Tims, & B. Fletcher (Eds.), *Innovative approaches in the treatment of drug abuse,* Volume 2. *Implementation issues and problems.* Westport, CT: Greenwood Press.

Brady, J. V. (in press). Drug policy and the enhancement of access to treatment. In W. K. Bickel & R. J. De Grandpre (Eds.), *Drug policy and human nature: Psychological perspectives on the control, prevention, and treatment of illicit drug abuse.* New York: Plenum Publishing Corp.

Brady, J. V. (1993). Enhancing drug abuse treatment by mobile health service. In J. A. Inciardi, F. Tims, & B. Fletcher (Eds.), *Innovative approaches in the treatment of drug abuse,* Volume 2. *Implementation issues and problems.* Westport, CT: Greenwood Press.

Collins, J. J., & Allison, M. (1983). Legal coercion and retention in drug abuse treatment. *Hospital and Community Psychiatry, 34*(12), 1145–1149.

Gerstein, D. R., & Harwood, H. J. (Eds.). (1990). *Treating drug problems,* Vol. 1. Washington, DC: National Academy Press.

Hubbard, R. L., Etheridge, R. M., Craddock, S. G., & Dunteman, G. (1995). Effects of amount of services on outcomes during treatment: Preliminary analysis from two national studies of community-based treatment programs. In L. S. Harris (Ed.), *Problems of drug dependence, 1994* (NIDA Research Monograph 152, NIH Publication No. 95-3882, pp. 71–72. Washington, DC:

Hubbard, R. L., Marsden, M. E., Rachal, J. V., Harwood, H. J., Cavanaugh, E. R., & Ginzburg, H. M. (1989). *Drug abuse treatment: A national study of effectiveness.* Chapel Hill: University of North Carolina Press.

McLellan, A. T., Arnt, I. O., Metzger, D. S., Moody, G. E., & O'Brien, C. P. (1993). The effects of psychosocial services in substance abuse treatment. *Journal of the American Medical Association, 269*(15), 1953–1959.

II

RESIDENTIAL PROGRAMS

4

Outcomes of Four Residential Treatment Models — Project IMPACT

Jane McCusker, Frances B. Garfield, Benjamin F. Lewis, and Ray Frost

Project IMPACT is a five-year treatment demonstration project that is evaluating four alternative models of residential drug abuse treatment (Lewis, McCusker, Hinden, Frost, & Garfield, 1993). Two aspects of residential drug abuse treatment are of particular interest in this study: program duration and program content. The duration of treatment needed to achieve positive outcomes is controversial. Opinions about the optimal or minimal length of residential treatment required to achieve positive outcomes are based only on observational evidence. For example, results of the Treatment Outcome Prospective Study (TOPS) suggest that beneficial outcomes are obtained only when clients stay in treatment at least six months (Hubbard et al., 1989). However, there is pressure on treatment programs to shorten treatment to increase access and accommodate increasing mandates for managed care. While some facilities are offering programs of short duration, they lack empirical evidence to support their effectiveness, either overall or in selected subgroups of clients.

Program structure and content is the second focus of the study. Traditional approaches to residential drug-free treatment have been driven by the expectation that clients would remain drug-free after reentry into the community. However, high rates of attrition and relapse to drug use are well established, and some programs have begun to apply principles of relapse prevention (Baker, Galea, Lewis, Paolantonio, & Tesser-Woupio, 1989; Marlatt & Gordon, 1985). In addition, the increasing threat of HIV has prompted many programs to incorporate AIDS education components (Galea, Lewis, & Baker, 1988; Sorensen 1991).

This study compares two residential drug-free treatment programs in New England. The first is a traditional therapeutic community (TC) and the second, a TC that was modified to incorporate relapse prevention and health education components (RP/HE). The two programs have been described previously (Lewis, McCusker, Hindin, Frost, & Garfield, 1993). The RP/HE program was delivered primarily in group sessions with the purpose of building individual skills to cope with lapses and prevent full relapse. The health education component of the RP/HE program was modeled upon the enhanced group program developed for clients of an inpatient drug detoxification program (McCusker et al., 1992).

RESEARCH DESIGN

The study design of Project IMPACT includes observational and experimental components. The observational component compares outcomes in the two different programs. The TC program is located in Rhode Island, while the RP/HE program is located in Massachusetts. It was not feasible to allocate clients randomly to one or the other program. However, within each program, clients were allocated randomly to a shorter or longer version of the same program. At the TC, clients were assigned to 6- or 12-month programs and at the RP/HE program, clients were assigned to 3- or 6-month programs.

At each site almost all (93 percent) clients were considered eligible for the study and for randomization. Reasons for noneligibility included: court stipulation to treatment of a specified duration, abuse of alcohol only, and insufficient understanding of English to complete study protocols.

At each site, randomization of clients to programs of different length occurred before admission and before approaching the client to request participation in the study. Clients who refused to participate were not placed in an alternative program. As a result, a very high percentage, 91 percent of all eligible clients, agreed to participate in the study. The final study sample of 628 represents 85 percent of all clients admitted, 91 percent of all eligible clients, and 95 percent of those asked to participate. During the two-year period of study enrollment, 184 clients were enrolled at the TC program and 444 clients were enrolled at the RP/HE program.

Extensive data were collected from clients primarily by interview during the first few weeks of treatment. Data included sociodemographics; drug abuse history; psychosocial variables; drug use and HIV risk behaviors during the 90 days prior to admission; selected psychiatric diagnoses; severity of addiction related to drug and alcohol use; and legal, employment, and psychiatric problems. Clients were also asked to participate in an exit interview scheduled for the day of exit, during which the psychosocial instruments and program satisfaction scales were administered.

At the TC program, because interviewers were not always available on site to do exit interviews, particularly for clients who left the program on short notice, arrangements were made to carry out exit interviews at the downtown offices of the treatment program, usually within two weeks of exit.

A minimum of two follow-up interviews were scheduled for all clients. The first interview (F1) was scheduled approximately three months after exit to obtain information on return to drug use shortly after leaving the program. Clients known to be in prison, in residential treatment, or at a halfway house were interviewed at those locations, if they agreed. The second follow-up interview was scheduled approximately 18 months following admission to the program. This interview was considered the time point at which the primary behavioral outcomes of the study were collected. It was considered important for decision making and policy purposes to be able to compare outcomes at a standard point from admission, because decisions regarding which treatment program a client should receive would be made at admission and would take into account varying expectations of retention and completion of the assigned program and probability of return to drug use following exit. Both follow-up interviews included many of the same behavioral and psychosocial measures as those obtained at baseline, and the same satisfaction scales administered at program exit.

To validate self-reported drug use, hair samples were taken from all consenting clients. Analyses of these data helped to substantiate the conclusions drawn from the self-report data alone.

Because standardized data collection methods were essential to allow valid comparisons between the programs, a single field coordinator supervised the interviewers at both sites and the follow-up interviewers. The field coordinator monitored forms, audited periodic taped interviews, and carried out training and refresher sessions with interviewers to improve the standardization of all data collection.

During the treatment phase of the project, the site coordinators periodically monitored groups to ensure that the programs were delivered as specified. In addition, an outside process evaluator spent time at each site, observing the milieus and selected groups. In an effort to round out the treatment picture from the program's point of view, research staff conducted a chart review for all subjects at each site after the treatment phase of the project was completed.

MAJOR FINDINGS

Client Characteristics

At admission into the study, clients were predominantly between the ages of 25 and 34, male, white, and had completed at least a high school education. The majority had previously undergone two or more episodes of drug treatment. The clientele of the two treatment program sites differed substantially with regard to drug history and other characteristics. Two-thirds of clients at the RP/HE program were prior drug injectors compared with just over half of the TC clients. More than 70 percent of RP/HE program clients reported heroin or cocaine use during the three months before admission compared to 53 percent of TC clients. The TC clients tended to have had fewer prior treatment experiences and a larger percentage had been incarcerated immediately before admission. RP/HE clients had a greater severity of drug use than the average TC client, as measured by Addiction Severity Index composite scores with regard to drug use and legal problems (McLellan et al., 1990).

Retention and Completion

Overall, about three-fourths of clients were retained to 40 days, and of these, almost three-fourths stayed to 80 days. No differences in retention through 80 days were found among the four programs. Beyond 80 days, retention could be compared only in the 6- and 12-month programs, but was very similar between these three programs. In all programs, attrition rates accelerated sharply as the end of the planned program approached. Completion rates (using program staff criteria) were 56 percent in the 3-month program, 30–33 percent in the two 6-month programs, and 21 percent in the 12-month program.

Process Evaluation

The quality of the data from the chart review was relatively good. The programs documented client sessions with primary counselors, disciplinary sessions, coercion to enter treatment by the legal and social service systems, and terminations. At one site, treatment personnel were less consistent in documenting client attendance at HIV education sessions and referrals to aftercare. Further analysis of the material from the chart review will compare retention, completion, and outcomes for different levels of coercion to enter treatment, different experiences within treatment, and different reasons for leaving treatment.

Changes in Psychosocial Variables from Admission to Exit

Overall, there were significant reductions in levels of depression and increases in self-esteem and in self-efficacy to avoid drug use. However, at each program, there were minimal differences in these changes between clients in the shorter and longer program and the changes at the two programs were also remarkably similar.

Results from First Follow-up Interviews

Substantial rates of completion of the F1 interview were achieved between two and six months following exit: 74 percent at the RP/HE program and 84 percent at the TC program. At the time of this follow-up, approximately four out of five clients were free living and the remainder were either in drug treatment, halfway house, or in prison. Half of the TC clients reported that they had used some drug other than alcohol since program exit. While this percentage was slightly smaller at the RP/HE program, it is likely that this was because of the slightly lower follow-up rate in this program. When clients who did not have an F1 interview, or who had an F1 interview later than six months from exit were included, it was estimated that 55 percent of clients of both programs had some drug use since exit. Furthermore, approximately equal percentages of clients from the shorter and the longer version of each program reported drug use. Thus, there was no evident difference in rates of return to drug use in the four alternative treatment models. Patterns of drug use (frequency and type of drug used) among those who returned to drug use were also very similar in the four programs.

We also investigated changes in HIV-risky injection and sexual behaviors at the F1 interview. These results indicated sharp reductions in the percent of clients injecting drugs at follow-up and smaller reductions in riskier injection practices (injection with shared injection equipment, and failing to bleach syringes prior to reuse) among those who continue to inject at follow-up. There were also small increases in the percent using condoms among those who were sexually active. In contrast, there was little change in numbers of sexual partners between admission and follow-up. Overall, clients were practicing somewhat less risky behaviors at follow-up compared with baseline. Once again, comparisons of these changes in the four alternative treatment models failed to find any evidence for differential behavior change: the changes were strikingly similar across the four groups of clients.

Effects of Retention and Completion on Psychosocial Changes and Return to Drug Use

In general, clients who stayed longer in treatment showed greater changes in depression, self-esteem, and self-efficacy. Furthermore, these clients were less likely to relapse or return to drug use at follow-up than those who had stayed for shorter periods in treatment. However, even among those clients who stayed for longer periods or who completed their assigned treatment program, there was no evidence of a differential effect of the alternative treatment models.

Satisfaction

Two satisfaction scales were developed using factor analysis, the first assessing general satisfaction with the program and staff and the second assessing satisfaction with the treatment facilities and family involvement. Both scales were quite stable from exit to the F1 interview. At the TC, clients who had completed their program were more satisfied with the program than were noncompleters, but this difference was not found at the RP/HE program. Completers did not differ from noncompleters in their satisfaction with the treatment facilities and family involvement at either program. However, both satisfaction scales seem to interact with completion to affect drug use during the follow-up period. These preliminary results are being analyzed further.

DISCUSSION

The study findings described above summarize our experience with Project IMPACT up to the F1 interview (that is, up to six months following program exit). As mentioned earlier, our primary study outcomes will be assessed at the second follow-up interview scheduled for completion approximately 18 months following admission to the treatment programs. The primary study outcomes include a wide range of problems and behaviors related to drug use, including time until first drug use, frequency of drug use, HIV-risky drug injection, HIV-risky sexual behaviors, and selected measures of the severity of problems related to drug use: alcohol use, legal problems, psychiatric problems, and employment problems. Only when these primary outcomes have been analyzed will we be able to draw conclusions regarding the relative effectiveness of the four alternative treatment models evaluated in this study. However, one cannot fail to be impressed by the striking lack of differential effects of the four programs upon the outcomes presented thus far. Changes in psychosocial status, return to drug use, and changes in HIV-risky behaviors seem to occur essentially independently of which program the client was treated in.

The results so far fail to provide support for several of the hypotheses we had formulated at the beginning of the study. For example, we had hypothesized that clients assigned to a shorter program might have better retention rates over similar time periods than those assigned to longer programs because of greater perceived ability to complete program requirements. We had also hypothesized that longer programs would result in greater behavior change.

Although the results to date do not support our a priori hypotheses, the study itself has been rewarding and instructive in many respects. Ours is the first study to successfully implement a randomized trial design in a TC setting. We are aware of only one prior attempt to randomize clients to residential treatment programs (Bale, Cabrera, & Brown, 1977), that was able to successfully randomize only a small percentage of clients and thus was not able to achieve its objective of comparing the effectiveness of the different treatment programs. Indeed, former commentators on the lack of controlled research in TCs have been pessimistic about the possibilities for successfully carrying out controlled trials among TC clients (Gerstein & Harwood, 1990). In spite of these concerns, we were successfully able to randomize a very high percentage of clients in the two participating programs. We believe that our success can be attributed to two characteristics of the study design. First, we were not randomizing clients to very different programs but to two versions of the same program that differed only in their length. Second, the participating programs agreed to randomize all eligible clients to a shorter or longer version of their program, regardless of whether the client agreed to participate in the research. Thus, clients who refused to participate in the research could not be transferred to another treatment program. Had this option been available, it might have been a powerful factor motivating clients to refuse to participate. Our attempts to randomize in the two participating programs were initially met with skepticism by some staff members and even by attempts to circumvent randomization and assign certain clients to the program that the staff member thought was more appropriate. Through careful monitoring of the randomization process, we were able to minimize these occurrences. These precautions resulted in very similar client characteristics in the shorter and longer version of each program, which allowed for valid scientific comparisons of outcomes between the two groups.

The nonrandomized comparison between the TC and the RP/HE programs is weaker scientifically, as there are clearly important differences between the client populations at the two programs. Thus differences in outcomes between the two programs might be because of these client characteristics rather than differences in the programs themselves. However, we have been impressed thus far in our analyses by the striking similarities in outcomes between clients in the two programs, regardless of different client characteristics. Of course, these similarities may have occurred by chance or may be because of differences between the two client populations that were not assessed or controlled in the analyses, and one must be cautious before concluding that the two types of program have similar effects upon their clients.

Based on our experience, we feel that randomized controlled trials can and should be carried out in residential treatment programs. While the results from a single study, however compelling, should not change treatment policies and options, we believe it is important that other treatment programs carry out similar research to determine the generalizability of these findings. We also feel that it is incumbent upon residential programs to demonstrate that their treatment is more effective than even shorter or minimal programs. While it is premature for us to conclude that 3-month programs can achieve as much as 12-month programs, the results thus far are certainly not as different as might have been predicted. Economic evaluations of alternative programs also need to be carried out to determine whether the costs of longer programs can be offset by a reduction in drug-related problems among clients of those programs. It is critically important that policy decisions are based on high quality scientific studies. We hope that our study and others presented in this book will open a new era of scientific investigation into the treatment of drug abuse.

ACKNOWLEDGMENTS

This work was supported by grant number R18-DA06151 from the National Institute on Drug Abuse.

REFERENCES

Baker, L. A., Galea, R. P., Lewis, B., Paolantonio, P., & Tesser-Woupio, D. (1989). Relapse prevention training for drug abusers. *Journal of Chemical Dependency Treatment, 26,* 173–192.

Bale, R.N., Cabrera, S., & Brown, J. (1977). Follow-up evaluation of drug treatment. *American Journal of Drug and Alcohol Abuse, 4,* 233–249.

Galea, R. P., Lewis, B., & Baker, L. A. (1988). AIDS education in the therapeutic community: Implementation and results among high-risk clients and staff. *International Journal of Therapeutic Communities, 9,* 9–16.

Gerstein, D. R., & Harwood, H. J. (Eds.). (1990). *Treating drug problems.* Vol. 1. *A study of the evolution, effectiveness, and financing of public and private drug treatment systems.* Washington, DC: National Academy Press.

Hubbard, R. L., Marsden, M. E., Rachal, J. V., Harwood, H. J., Cavanaugh, E. R., & Ginzburg, H. M. (1989). *Drug abuse treatment: A national study of effectiveness.* Chapel Hill: University of North Carolina Press.

Lewis, B., McCusker, J., Hindin, R., Frost, R., & Garfield, F. (1993). Four residential drug treatment programs: Project IMPACT. In J. Inciardi, F. Tims, & B. Fletcher (Eds.), *Innovative approaches in the treatment of drug abuse.* Westport, CT: Greenwood Press.

Marlatt, G. A., & Gordon, J. R. (1985). *Relapse prevention: Maintenance strategies in the treatment of addictive behaviors.* New York: Guilford Press.

McCusker, J., Stoddard, A. M., Zapka, J. G., Morrison, C. S., Zorn, M., & Lewis, B. (1992). AIDS education for drug abusers: Evaluation of short-term effectiveness. *American Journal of Public Health, 82,* 533–540.

McLellan, A. T., Patrikh, G., Bragg, A., Cacciola, J., Fureman, B., & Incmikoski, R. (Eds.). (1990). *Addiction severity index* (5th ed.). Philadelphia: Penn-VA Center for Studies of Addiction.

Sorensen, J. (1991). Preventing HIV transmission in drug treatment programs: What works? *Advances in Alcohol and Substance Abuse, 10,* 67–79.

5

CREST Outreach Center: A Model for Blending Treatment and Corrections

Dorothy Lockwood, James A. Inciardi, and Hilary L. Surratt

Since the mid-1980s, professionals from both treatment and corrections have been striving to combine their respective systems into a more effective model. Although compulsory treatment has been found effective (Anglin & Hser, 1991; Leukefeld & Tims, 1988), combining treatment and corrections has proven difficult for a variety of reasons. The primary problem has been the fundamental differences in the missions of treatment versus corrections. On the one hand, treatment aims to teach independence and self-sufficiency through increased skills and accountability. On the other hand, corrections is required to ensure punishment of the offender and safety for the community through control. Because of the dramatic increases over the past decade in the number of drug-involved offenders entering correctional settings, it has become necessary to develop effective drug treatment programs for criminal justice populations.

One of the more popular models for combining treatment and criminal justice has been the Treatment Alternatives to Street Crime (TASC) program, initiated by the Law Enforcement Assistance Administration in 1972 (Inciardi & McBride, 1991). However, most TASC programs have focused on nonincarcerated populations. As a result of the 1980s war on drugs, the nation's prisons quickly filled beyond capacity with drug-involved offenders. In fact, research shows that between 40 percent and 90 percent of arrestees test positive for drugs (Wish & Gropper, 1990) and that almost all imprisoned offenders are in need of drug treatment (Chaiken, 1989). In response, many correctional systems are now structuring appropriate drug treatment programs for their growing populations.

In 1988, the Delaware Department of Corrections established the KEY, a therapeutic community (TC) program for male inmates with histories of serious drug involvement. The KEY was originally a 40-bed program, but in the years since its inception, its capacity has more than tripled. Participants in the KEY are segregated from the general prison population and are provided intensive treatment seven days a week. Clients remain in the program for six months to two years, depending on their sentence, release date, and need for further treatment. Regardless of length of stay, most clients' treatment addresses both their drug use and their criminal involvement. In addition, clients learn and adopt new prosocial coping and life skills.

As the first cohort of clients graduated from the KEY and returned to the free community, it became evident that a community-based transitional program was necessary to ensure that treatment continued, and that relapse or return to the institution did not occur (Inciardi, Martin, Lockwood, Hooper, & Wald, 1992). To fill this gap, during the closing months of 1990 the Center for Drug and Alcohol Studies at the University of Delaware was awarded a National Institute on Drug Abuse treatment demonstration grant to develop and evaluate the effectiveness of a co-ed, work-release TC. The Center for Drug and Alcohol Studies worked with state correctional officials, the program staff at the KEY, and university administrators to establish CREST Outreach Center, the nation's first work-release TC (Inciardi & Lockwood, 1994).

While the KEY represented "primary" treatment provided in the institution, CREST was developed as a "secondary" or "transitional" stage of TC treatment for men graduating from the KEY. At the same time, CREST intended to provide primary TC treatment for both men and women from the general prison population who had no previous TC experience.

THE RESEARCH PROTOCOL

Research participants were randomly assigned to either a treatment or a comparison group. The treatment group entered CREST Outreach Center and the comparison group was assigned to the traditional state-operated work-release center for prisoners. Participation was voluntary. Because all clients were incarcerated, they were protected under the special guidelines for prisoners as research subjects established by the U.S. Department of Health and Human Services. Under these regulations, neither correctional status nor court sentences may be affected — either positively or negatively — by participation in the research project. In addition, all respondents were protected by a Certificate of Confidentiality that ensured that the information they provided would not be given to any authorities and that their participation in the research was confidential. Eligibility criteria for the study included a drug use history, work-release eligibility as defined by the Department of Corrections, and willingness to participate. Potential participants were identified by correctional counselors, prison release boards, and self-referral.

All respondents agreeing to participate in the study completed a baseline interview before leaving prison. The questionnaire was administered by a trained interviewer and assessed criminal history, drug use history, HIV risk behaviors (including needle use and sex practices), drug treatment experience, childhood experiences, mental health questions, and demographic information. Respondents were also asked to provide a urine sample for drug testing and a blood sample for HIV and hepatitis testing, however participation in the testing was voluntary. In addition, two follow-up interviews were conducted at 6 and 18 months after the baseline interview. The first follow-up interview corresponded with either the completion of work release or the CREST program, depending on research group assignment. Both follow-up interviews focused on criminal activity, drug use, drug treatment experience, HIV risk behaviors, and mental health status in the time period since the most recent interview.

CREST OUTREACH CENTER

CREST is a six-month program based on the traditional TC model, modified to serve a correctional population. It is a 60-bed program serving 12 women and 48 men, a segment of whom are graduates of the KEY. CREST is adjacent to the state-operated work-release center, and correctional officers at the work-release center also provide security to CREST. In these settings, security measures include monitoring the comings and goings of every CREST client, conducting head counts to ensure that all clients are accounted for, and securing the building at night. CREST clients spend from 7 a.m. until 10:30 p.m. in the treatment facility, returning to the work-release facility only to shower and sleep. Although CREST is adjacent to the work-release center, CREST sleeping quarters are completely separate from the other work-release quarters and clients from the two programs do not interact.

CREST was founded on a traditional TC philosophy. Drug use is considered to be a symptom of a wider behavioral disorder. As such, the reduction or elimination of drug use requires that the whole person be treated. Other symptoms of dysfunctional thinking and living are also addressed — including criminal activity and interpersonal relationships. The goal of CREST is to effect positive lifestyle changes by addressing attitudes, thoughts, and behaviors. Treatment encompasses a variety of interventions in which accountability for one's actions and attitudes, coupled with role modeling and increased responsibility, are emphasized (Hooper, Lockwood, & Inciardi, 1993).

CREST Outreach Center is a highly structured program of treatment activities that consists of five phases. The program begins with a two-week orientation period involving client assessment and evaluation, as well as an introduction to the TC process. During the second phase, clients begin to participate in treatment activities, such as morning meetings, community jobs, and group and individual counseling. After clients learn to negotiate the TC environment successfully, they move to the third phase of the program in which they begin to take on more responsibilities, such as role modeling and supervision of other clients. During the fourth phase, clients begin the process of transition to the community by working on job-seeking skills, preparing resumes, and practicing job interviewing. The fifth phase of treatment is reentry into the community. It is in this phase that clients maintain steady and acceptable employment in the community and develop an aftercare plan for continued treatment and support, including seeking an appropriate and supportive living situation. During the first three months of treatment, clients remain in the program and are not employed outside of CREST. The final three months of the program focus on transition to the community, including the development of employment skills and the establishment of support systems. During this transition phase, clients remain at CREST and participate in treatment activities when they are not working (Lockwood, 1992; Lockwood & Inciardi, 1993).

All clients, regardless of previous treatment experience, participate in all five phases. Graduates of the KEY, because of their previous TC treatment, serve as role models throughout the program. Many of the KEY clients advance quickly through the program and enter the work-release phase sooner than clients entering the program from the general prison population. Release from CREST depends on progress through the treatment program, as well as completion of the correctional sentence. Many clients progress through treatment and are ready to transition into the community before the completion of their sentence. In these cases, CREST staff work closely with correctional staff and court officials to modify sentences appropriately so that client progress does not deteriorate.

As in most TCs, CREST clients run the program, ensuring that house jobs are completed, that treatment activities are implemented, and that their peers are participating fully in the program. Each client has a job responsibility within the program. Job assignments change regularly so that all clients can be exposed to the various positions necessary to operate the program. Clients who have shown the greatest progress and growth hold positions of authority within CREST, such as facility manager. CREST staff includes both professionals and recovering persons. Staff facilitates treatment activities and monitors client progress and participation. Staff also provides both individual and family counseling.

FINDINGS

The effectiveness of CREST Outreach Center can best be evaluated by two factors. First, the number of clients completing the program and remaining drug- and crime-free indicates, in part, to what extent the program successfully provided drug treatment to its clients. Second, comparison of the status of CREST clients to a comparable group who did not participate in CREST indicates, in part, whether CREST is more effective than other programs, in this case traditional work-release.

The research design targeted 260 respondents in each of the two groups, treatment and comparison. The treatment group consisted of 288 respondents and the comparison group included 246 respondents for a total of 534 respondents. For the purposes of data presentation, three groups will be discussed:

the KEY-CREST group includes those who received primary TC treatment at the KEY program and secondary treatment at CREST;

the CREST group includes those who received primary treatment at CREST; and

the Comparison group includes respondents who participated in the regular work-release program and did not receive TC treatment.

This grouping allows for the comparison of the effectiveness of CREST with traditional work-release, as well as the examination of the outcome differences between CREST clients receiving secondary treatment and those receiving prior treatment.

Table 5.1 provides an overview of the descriptive characteristics of the study respondents. Because one purpose of the study was to test the effectiveness of a work-release TC for inmates, it was important that the research sample be representative of the general prison population. The Delaware prison population is approximately 58 percent African-American, 34 percent white-Anglo, with the remaining 8 percent classified as other. The total study sample is approximately 70 percent African-American, 25 percent white-Anglo, 3 percent Hispanic, and 2 percent other. As such, African-Americans are slightly overrepresented in the study sample. Additionally, the Delaware prison population is about 80 percent male and 20 percent female, and the study sample is comparable with 82 percent male and 18 percent female participants.

To evaluate the effectiveness of CREST as compared with traditional work release, it was important that participants in each group be similar on measures of sociodemographic characteristics, and criminal, drug use, and treatment histories. Because membership in the KEY-CREST group

TABLE 5.1
Descriptive Characteristics of Research Respondents

Variable	CREST (N = 246) N	CREST (N = 246) %	KEY-CREST (N = 42) N	KEY-CREST (N = 42) %	Comparison (N = 246) N	Comparison (N = 246) %	Total (N = 534) N	Total (N = 534) %
RACE/ETHNICITY								
Black	172	69.9	39	92.9	164	66.7	375	70.2
Hispanic	7	2.8	1	2.4	7	2.8	15	2.8
White-Anglo	65	26.4	2	4.8	67	27.2	134	25.1
Other	2	.8	1	2.4	8	3.3	10	1.9
GENDER								
Female	50	20.3	—	—	46	18.7	96	18.0
Male	196	79.7	42	100.0	200	81.3	438	82.0
AGE								
Range	18 to 52		20 to 48		18 to 53		18 to 53	
Average	29.4 years		30.3 years		29.9 years		29.7 years	
CRIMINAL HISTORY								
Previous Times in Prison:								
0 (First Incarceration)	76	30.9	10	23.8	71	28.9	157	29.4
1–2	99	40.2	20	47.6	93	37.8	212	39.7
3–5	59	24.0	11	26.2	67	27.2	137	25.7
6 or more	12	4.9	1	2.4	15	6.1	28	5.2
Previous Conviction for:								
Violent crimes	140	56.9	29	69.0	141	57.3	310	58.1
Property crimes	197	80.1	32	76.2	185	75.2	414	77.5
Drug crimes	166	67.5	30	71.4	156	63.4	352	65.9
DRUG USE AND PRIMARY DRUG OF ABUSE								
None	4	1.6	1	2.4	29	11.8	34	6.4
Alcohol	28	11.4	1	2.4	39	15.9	68	12.7
Marijuana	23	9.3	6	14.3	34	13.8	63	11.8
Cocaine	105	42.7	24	57.1	91	37.0	226	41.2
Crack	38	15.4	2	4.8	18	7.3	58	10.9
Heroin	44	17.9	7	16.7	25	10.2	76	14.2
Other	4	1.6	1	2.4	10	4.1	15	2.8
PREVIOUS TREATMENT								
	195	79.3	42	100.0	177	72.0	414	77.5

was determined by participation in the in-prison TC, and because KEY clients were selected by a different process than the other study participants, the KEY-CREST client group was not included in the comparison of the treatment and traditional work-release groups. Respondents in the CREST and comparison groups were similar in terms of sociodemographic characteristics. The CREST group was approximately 70 percent African-American, whereas the comparison group was approximately 67 percent African-American. Both groups were 2.8 percent Hispanic and approximately 27 percent white-Anglo. The average age of respondents in both groups was about 30 years, ranging from 18 to 53 years.

Importantly, both the CREST and comparison groups were similar with respect to respondents' criminal histories. More than two-thirds of the respondents in both the CREST and comparison groups had been in prison prior to the sentence they were currently serving when recruited into the research project. Almost 60 percent of the respondents in both groups had been convicted of a violent crime. Three-fourths of the respondents in the comparison group had been convicted of a property crime, as had 80 percent of respondents in the CREST group. A slightly higher proportion of the CREST group had been convicted of drug offenses (67.5 percent) than in the comparison group (63.4 percent).

At baseline, the CREST group reported a more serious drug use history than did the comparison group. Only four of the CREST group respondents reported no previous drug use problems, whereas 29 respondents, almost 12 percent of those in the comparison group, reported no drug problems. Additionally, a greater proportion of the CREST group indicated that crack, cocaine, or heroin was their primary drug of abuse than did respondents in the comparison group. With respect to previous drug treatment, more of the CREST group had been in treatment than had the comparison group, 79.3 percent and 72 percent, respectively.

The KEY-CREST group represented a slightly different population than did the CREST and comparison groups. All the respondents in the KEY-CREST group were males, 92.9 percent of whom were African-American. These respondents were slightly older than respondents in the other two groups, although the average age was also 30 years. Over three-fourths of the respondents in this group had been in prison prior to their current sentence. In addition, almost 70 percent had previously been convicted of a violent crime, 76 percent of a property crime, and 71 percent of a drug crime. Only one respondent reported no previous drug problem, while almost 60 percent and 17 percent, respectively, reported a history of cocaine and heroin use. By virtue of their participation in the KEY, all respondents in this group had had previous drug treatment experience. In summary, the KEY-CREST group was comprised of respondents with more serious criminal and drug use histories.

The preliminary follow-up data indicate that the CREST and KEY-CREST group respondents reported much lower incidences of criminal activity and drug use at the six-month follow-up than did the comparison group respondents. Of respondents from the KEY-CREST and CREST groups, 96 percent and 83 percent, respectively, remained arrest-free during the six-month period. However, only 71 percent of the comparison group had not been rearrested during the six-month period. A more stringent measure of criminal activity indicated an even stronger difference between the treatment and comparison groups. When respondents were asked if they had committed any crimes since the baseline interview, including those for which they were not arrested, 85 percent of the CREST group reported being crime-free, 97 percent of the KEY-CREST group reported no crime involvement, but only 51 percent of the comparison group reported no criminal activity. In other words, almost half of the respondents who did not receive TC treatment returned to crime within six months of release whereas only 14 percent of the respondents who received TC treatment returned to crime in the same period.

Drug use during the six-month follow-up period parallels the pattern of criminal involvement. Only 20 percent of the CREST clients and 6 percent of the KEY-CREST clients reported relapse to drug use during the six-month period. However, 45 percent of the comparison group respondents reported drug use in this period. The respondents in the CREST group who relapsed reported use of alcohol or marijuana. However, among the comparison group, respondents reported relapse to use of alcohol, marijuana, crack, and cocaine. Not only did a higher proportion of the comparison group return to drug use within six months of release from prison, they also returned to more serious drug use. In summary, 94 percent of the KEY-CREST clients and 80 percent of CREST clients remained drug-free after six months, while only 55 percent of the comparison group clients did so.

Clearly, both KEY-CREST and CREST clients reported better maintenance of drug-free and crime-free behaviors than did the comparison group clients. From this preliminary analysis, it appears that CREST, a work-release TC, is effective in reducing both criminal activity and drug use. When compared with a group similar on measures of sociodemographic status, criminal history, and drug use history who participated in a traditional work-release program, CREST clients had a significantly lower incidence of both criminal activity and drug use during the first six-month period after release. These differences have major implications for the fields of drug treatment and corrections.

First, it appears that treatment and corrections can be successfully combined in a mutually effective model. Reaching a balance between increased client responsibility and continued surveillance is a matter of coordination and cooperation. However, the TC model provides an excellent framework in which to strike this balance. The TC is structured so that both the time and activities of every client are planned and structured during the first three months of the program and are closely monitored throughout. This structure complements correctional surveillance and ensures that clients are held accountable. It is only after clients have learned and adopted prosocial behaviors that their independence and responsibilities are increased.

In fact, because clients are monitored so closely, approximately one-fourth of new admissions are returned to prison as a result of their violation of program rules. The ability of the TC structure to detect this reluctance to make positive changes in attitudes and lifestyles in the long run lowers the risk of recidivism and relapse. As such, the structure of the TC complements the correctional priority of identifying high-risk offenders and delaying their release into the community until the risk has been decreased.

The philosophy of the TC, which emphasizes treatment of the whole person, is another factor that increases the ease with which corrections and treatment can be combined. The outcome data indicate that not only is relapse to drug use reduced among CREST clients but also recidivism to criminal activity is similarly reduced. Interestingly, among the comparison group respondents who participated in the correctional work-release program, there was a high incidence of both relapse and recidivism. It appears that the TC work-release model, which treats the whole person by teaching coping and life skills, in addition to providing drug treatment, may be more effective in reducing criminal activity than the corrections-based program. From these analyses, it is clear that the TC structure is compatible with the correctional priorities of reducing recidivism to criminal activity.

Although TC treatment and corrections can be interfaced, coordination between the two systems is a necessity. The most obvious and important point of coordination is with regard to clients' correctional sentences. CREST clients' sentences vary greatly. Some clients have sentences prescribing a specific amount of time to be served, while others are sentenced until the completion of drug treatment. At CREST, as with any TC, progression through the phases of treatment is determined by the client's actions and attitudes and not by a prescribed length of time. One of the first lessons learned by clients in a TC program for criminal justice is that they are not serving time; treatment completion is not determined by a certain number of months but rather by progress and positive change. The correctional system and the courts must work with the treatment program to support this mode of completion. Frequently, clients complete treatment prior to their sentence release date. It is essential that clients are able to progress through treatment because stagnation at any phase tends to result in regression and noncompliance. CREST was quite successful in gaining the cooperation and support of the courts to reduce client sentences based on progress in treatment. Although completion of court sentences may appear to be incompatible with treatment progression, the experience at CREST proves that the two can be effectively combined.

Another point of coordination for the drug treatment and correctional systems is the determination of who has primary responsibility for the clients. CREST clients are under the custody of the Department of Corrections, which provides continuous monitoring and places priority on monitoring over and above all other activities. However, this arrangement frequently results in surveillance activities overriding the treatment process. Thus, to avoid the interruption of treatment activities, the TC program must act as the primary source of client accountability. In practice, this does not undermine or replace the surveillance responsibility of corrections. In fact, the structure and intensity of CREST, or any TC, inherently provides the monitoring and accountability necessary to fulfill the surveillance obligations of corrections.

The second major implication of this study is that compulsory drug treatment works. Although research has shown that compulsory treatment is successful (Leukefeld & Tims, 1988), an assumption prevails that successful treatment outcomes depend on motivation to seek treatment. However, the desire for treatment is not incompatible with participation in court-ordered treatment. Almost all of the CREST clients were required to complete drug treatment as a stipulation of their court sentence, yet they also volunteered to participate in CREST. Three-fourths of those choosing to go to CREST remained in the program and the overwhelming majority remained drug-free and crime-free. This suggests that compulsory treatment does work.

Compulsory treatment also provides an assurance that clients remain in treatment long enough for it to have a positive effect. In the case of CREST clients, a decision to leave treatment before completion results in return to prison. This lack of desirable options serves as an impetus for clients to remain in treatment. The drug-free and crime-free status of CREST clients indicates that remaining in treatment has a positive effect.

The TC model is an effective mechanism to impose compulsory treatment. Unlike some drug treatment modalities, it is impossible to complete TC treatment without engaging in the process and progressing. Again, the structure and intensity of the CREST program requires clients to work and become involved in their own treatment. Lack of participation and positive change results in removal from the program. As such, TC clients cannot slide through the program or in prison argot "just do time."

The final implication of this study is that a continuum of drug treatment is most effective. It is evident that the CREST clients had a lower incidence of relapse and recidivism than the respondents who did not receive TC treatment. It is also evident that clients receiving a continuum of treatment, beginning with primary treatment in prison followed by secondary treatment in the work-release setting, are less likely to relapse to drug use and return to criminal activity than the clients who received only primary TC treatment in the work-release setting.

Primary treatment in an in-prison TC also reduces the discharge rate prior to completion of the TC work-release program. About one-fourth of the CREST clients from the general prison population who had not received primary TC treatment were returned to prison before completion of CREST. However, less than 10 percent of the KEY-CREST clients failed to complete the program. Considering that, on average, the KEY-CREST clients had more extensive criminal and drug use histories, the continuum of TC treatment may be necessary for successful outcomes among the more crime- and drug-involved clients.

IMPLICATIONS

The preliminary analyses presented here indicate that TC treatment is more effective in reducing recidivism and relapse to drug use than the traditional corrections-based work-release program. Furthermore, the continuum of TC treatment appears to be most effective. The findings from this research also show that treatment and corrections can be combined and that compulsory treatment works. Thus, this research provides a tested, effective model of drug treatment for criminal justice clients. Correctional clients differ from noncriminal justice clients in that criminal justice clients must satisfy legal obligations in conjunction with treatment. In addition, they present other specific treatment needs primarily because of their criminal activity. As such, drug treatment must address the legal needs and criminal involvement of criminal justice clients. The TC offers the framework for such a drug treatment program.

The findings from this research indicate that the TC model blends corrections and treatment in an effective form to serve criminal justice clients. The structure and intensity of the TC model ensure the surveillance and monitoring necessary for criminal justice clients. In addition, the TC philosophy of treating the whole person to effect positive lifestyle changes encompasses the need to address the criminal involvement as well as the drug use of clients. The TC model allows for involvement of other organizations in ensuring appropriate treatment for criminal justice clients, such as TASC. As previously discussed, coordinating sentence completion and treatment completion is a fundamental consideration when serving criminal justice clients. On the surface, coordinating sentence and treatment completion may seem incompatible, but the experience at CREST shows that it can be accomplished. TASC case managers could serve an important role as liaison between treatment and the courts to ensure that both requirements are satisfied.

Additional findings of this study also underscore the importance and necessity of conducting research on treatment programs. Without the research component of this project, comparison data would not be available. TC treatment is expensive; however, the data provided by this research indicate that those additional costs may be justified in the long term. Intense, costly treatment at the onset may reduce costs of continued, future reincarceration. As prison populations and the cost of incarceration continue to rise, implementing programs to reduce recidivism must be a priority among criminal justice officials. Ensuring that more costly programs are also more effective is also a priority. This can only be accomplished through treatment research.

The final implication of the findings is the continued need for aftercare. The success of the KEY-CREST clients indicates the effectiveness of a continuum of treatment. However, this continuum represents only two stages. Aftercare, the final stage of the continuum, is necessary to assist clients as they return and adjust to the community. Data from the second follow-up interview will indicate the degree to which CREST clients remain crime-free and drug-free during the first year after treatment. Regardless of the outcome, aftercare must be seen as an essential component in the maintenance of a drug-free, crime-free lifestyle.

REFERENCES

Anglin, M. D., & Yih-Ing Hser. (1991). Criminal justice and the drug-abusing offender: Policy issues of coerced treatment. *Behavioral Sciences and the Law, 9,* 243–267.

Chaiken, M. R. (1989). *In-prison programs for drug-involved offenders.* Washington, DC: National Institute of Justice.

Hooper, R. M., Lockwood, D., & Inciardi, J. A. (1993). Treatment techniques in corrections-based therapeutic community. *The Prison Journal, 73*(3–4), 290–306.

Inciardi, J. A., & Lockwood, D. (1994). When worlds collide: Establishing CREST outreach center. In B. W. Fletcher, J. A. Inciardi, & A. M. Horton (Eds.), *Drug abuse treatment: The implementation of innovative approaches* (pp. 63–78). Westport, CT: Greenwood Press.

Inciardi, J. A., Martin, S. S., Lockwood, D., Hooper, R. M., & Wald, B. M. (1992). Obstacles to the implementation and evaluation of drug treatment programs in correctional settings: Reviewing the Delaware KEY experience. In C. G. Leukefeld & F. M. Tims (Eds.), *Drug abuse treatment in prisons and jails* (pp. 176–191). Rockville, MD: National Institute on Drug Abuse.

Inciardi, J. A., & McBride, D. C. (1991). *Treatment alternatives to street crime: History, experiences and issues.* Rockville, MD: National Institute on Drug Abuse.

Leukefeld, C. G., & Tims, F. M. (Eds.). (1988). *Compulsory treatment of drug abuse: Research and clinical practice.* Rockville, MD: National Institute on Drug Abuse.

Lockwood, D., & Inciardi, J. A. (1993). CREST outreach center: A work release iteration of the TC model. In J. A. Inciardi, F. M. Tims & B. W. Fletcher (Eds.),

Innovative approaches in the treatment of drug abuse (pp. 61–70). Westport, CT: Greenwood Press.

Lockwood, D. (1992, March 10–14). Modeling a modified TC design for work release. Paper presented at the annual meeting of the Academy of Criminal Justice Sciences, Pittsburgh, Pennsylvania.

Wish E. D., & Gropper, B. A. (1990). Drug testing by the criminal justice system: Method, research and applications. In M. Tonry & J. Q. Wilson (Eds.), *Drugs and crime* (pp. 321–390). Chicago, IL: University of Chicago Press.

6

Homeless, Mentally Ill, Chemical Abusing Men in Different, Community-based, Treatment Programs

Michael Rahav, James J. Rivera, Larry Nuttbrock, Daisy Ng-Mak, Elizabeth L. Sturz, Bruce G. Link, Elmer L. Struening, Bert Pepper, and Benjamin Gross

In a society where services and treatment are fragmented and are usually rendered on the basis of a single predominant problem, homeless, mentally ill, chemical abusers (HMICAs) have been an underserved and relatively unstudied population. In what has been referred to as "ping pong therapy" (Ridgely, 1991), HMICAs have been bounced from homeless shelters to psychiatric hospitals to substance abuse facilities, utilizing scarce resources of each of the three systems, yet with poor results (Drake, Osher, & Wallach, 1989; Hellerstein & Meehan, 1987; Kofoed, Kania, Walsh, & Atkinson, 1986; Lehman, Myers, & Corty, 1989; McLellan, 1986; Osher & Kofoed, 1989; Ridgely, Osher, & Talbott, 1987). Estimates of the size of the HMICA population in the United States vary widely (Fischer, 1991). The number of homeless people in the United States in a given week in 1989 was estimated to be between 567,000 and 600,000 (Burt & Cohen, 1989). Extrapolating from this figure, we estimate the number of HMICAs in the United States in a given week to be between 82,215 and 87,000 (Rahav & Link, 1995). Adopting Jencks' (1994) estimate of 1.2 million homeless people in the United States in any given week, the derived estimate of HMICAs is raised to 168,000. Because of this sizable and probably growing population and its impact on society, the treatment system and the afflicted individuals, it is critical that we develop a body of research data about the characteristics and treatment of this population.

The scarcity of mentally ill, chemical abuser (MICA)-specific treatment programs in institutional settings also prevails in the community. Despite the considerable overlap between mental illness and substance abuse

(Regier et al., 1990), until recently, there have been virtually no community-based programs in the United States that cater to MICAs. To the best of our knowledge, Harbor House, a modified therapeutic community (TC) in the South Bronx, operated by Argus Community Inc., since 1989, is the first MICA-specific community-based program in New York City. Community-based programs may typically be categorized as either TC, which treat substance abuse, or community residence (CR), which care for the mentally ill. TCs were established in the United States for substance abusers in the 1960s by recovering heroin addicts seeking to live in self-help/peer support residences. The TC aims at a global change in lifestyle, including abstinence from illicit substances, elimination of antisocial activity, acquisition of work skills and prosocial attitudes and values (De Leon, 1985, 1986), which may characterize the TC as a "high expectations environment." The daily schedule during the entire treatment regimen is rigidly and tightly structured, with movement through the TC stages and standards for graduation clearly defined.

CRs were started and privately funded in the 1960s in the United States by middle-class families who could not deal at home with their recently deinstitutionalized relatives. In comparison with the TC, the CR may be referred to as a "low expectations environment," allowing for a great deal of personal freedom and gentle counseling. The CR seeks to provide the least restrictive alternative to the psychiatric hospital, separating the housing and psychiatric functions from each other. The CR staff provide housing, assistance, and training in the activities of daily living and monitoring medication compliance and day program attendance.

Recognizing the need to develop MICA-specific treatment programs, TC and CR programs in New York City have been modified and enhanced with additional therapeutic amenities to treat specifically HMICA men (Rahav et al., 1993, 1994). Because of the lack of established protocols for treating MICAs (Ridgely, Osher, & Talbott, 1987) and the paucity of research-based knowledge regarding the efficacy of various MICA treatment approaches (Thacker & Tremaine, 1989), a study to evaluate the treatment of MICAs in community-based programs is urgently needed.

The aims of the study described here were to evaluate the efficacy of two treatment modalities — modified TC and modified CR in treating HMICAs — and to identify psychiatric, substance abuse, sociodemographic, and family history characteristics of this population. Such data are extremely rare and the data that do exist come from highly select populations. The study we report is based on a comprehensive effort, through the use of an extensive community referral network in the New York City metropolitan area, to identify men who are homeless, mentally ill, and chemical abusers. It differs sharply from past studies of men in treatment because it includes any man who possesses these characteristics, whether he is eventually accepted into a treatment program. Thus, the sample is far less biased by factors influencing selection into treatment (for example, "creaming" — a practice where the easy-to-treat candidates are accepted and the more difficult-to-treat cases are rejected) (Rahav & Link, 1995) and is much more likely to represent the full population of HMICA men. The remainder of the chapter describes briefly the methodology of the study, summarizes some of its initial findings, and concludes with a discussion of these findings.

METHODS

The sample consists of 652 HMICA men recruited for placement in community-based treatment programs in New York City between 1991 and 1994. The city-wide recruitment involved advertising treatment opportunities to facilities in contact with HMICA clients around New York City. More than 100 facilities referred HMICA clients to this study, including 13 state psychiatric hospitals, 41 city and other hospitals, 16 homeless shelters, clinics, drug rehabilitation programs, and the criminal justice system. Although referred clients do not constitute a probability sample of the New York City HMICA male population, they offer a broad-based profile of men who suffer from a major psychiatric illness with at least two psychiatric hospitalizations and chronic, persistent substance abuse and who sought or were referred to community-based treatment.

The treatment settings consist of one modified TC and four modified CR programs. The modified TC is represented by Harbor House, a 45-bed, modified TC program that was developed by Argus Community Inc., for the treatment of homeless, severely mentally ill, chemical abusing men. Harbor House staff includes psychiatrists, psychologists, psychiatric social workers, and substance abuse counselors who together have developed an integrated model for the treatment of MICAs. In Harbor House, the rigorous TC structure is modified only enough to protect fragile residents (Sturz, 1992). All treatment takes place under one roof, ensuring that treatment is integrated and that residents do not manipulate it by pitting outside mental health professionals against TC professionals. Harbor House also offers its residents treatment through the New Identity Process (Casriel, 1972) and an extensive work program. Harbor House emphasizes similarity in background and culture between staff and residents. At least 30 percent of the direct care staff are recovering addicts. Harbor House emphasizes mutual self-help and community theme. Residents are taught to bond with others, to trust others and themselves, and live engaged with others in a community. Many activities are run by the residents themselves, and as they advance through the different treatment phases, responsibilities as well as privileges increase.

The enhanced CR is represented in this study by two organizations and a variety of programs they run in New York City. Services for the Underserved operates two of these programs: Montrose Community Residence (Montrose) and Patchen Avenue Community Residence (Patchen). Montrose is a co-ed, 48-bed, supervised residence program in Brooklyn that provides group living arrangements with around-the-clock staff supervision. Patchen is a 24-bed facility in Brooklyn for men who meet the homelessness criteria according to the New York, New York agreement (Dennis, Buckner, Lipton, & Levine, 1991).

The Bowery Residents Committee operates the two other CR programs that participated in the study: Fulton House and the Metropolitan Apartment Program. Fulton House is a fully supervised residence program in the East New York section of Brooklyn. The Metropolitan Apartment Program is an intensive supportive community residence that operates apartments in various sites in Manhattan and provides daily staff supervision, counseling, and assistance in activities of daily living.

The study design was determined with the goal of comparing the efficacy of HMICA treatment between TC and CR. Such a comparison requires perspective over time, leading this study design to be longitudinal. It also requires comparability of the subjects of treatment, dictating an experimental research design. The fact that the research is taking place in the "real world" of hospitals, clinics, shelters, and community-based treatment programs, dictates a naturalistic design of minimal interference in the daily routines of treatment and referral. The study design is therefore longitudinal, experimental, and naturalistic.

Random assignment of clients into either TC or CR was accomplished by an agreement between the researchers and the TC/CR programs that they refrain from recruiting clients to their programs on their own. Instead, all referrals of clients to the TC/CR programs were sent to the researchers, who then prescreened and randomly assigned clients deemed suitable for treatment to either the TC or CR programs. Suitability for treatment was determined by integrating the minimal entry requirements of the TC/CR programs. Criteria on suitability fell into three areas: demographic, diagnostic, and behavioral risk. Demographically, clients had to be male, 21 years or older, and homeless or at risk for homelessness. Clients had to have dual diagnoses of alcohol or drug dependence and a psychiatric disorder with at least two psychiatric hospitalizations. In addition, clients were assessed at the prescreening interview for severe psychopathology and impairment in cognition and judgment and might be temporarily excluded on those grounds. Finally, recent history of assaultive behavior, arson, rape, or suicide attempts could deem a client unsuitable for referral to treatment (Rahav et al., 1993).

Measures of treatment outcomes aimed at collecting data before, during, and after treatment were: baseline measures (referred to as CPU for central prescreening unit) instruments including:

Existing Data Questionnaire (EXIST): Developed by Argus Research Department (ARD) to extract existing data from clients' referral charts (for example, DSM III-R diagnosis, homelessness status, suicidality, hallucinations, and so on);

Personal History Form (PHF): Developed by ARD to measure early childhood family experiences, feelings about and relationship with parents;

Addiction Severity Index (ASI): (McLellan, Luborsky, O'Brien, & Woody, 1981);

CES-Depression Scale (CES-D): (Radloff, 1977);

Psychotic Ideation (P.I.): (Dohrenwend, Shrout, Egri, & Mendelsohn, 1980);

Pepper Anxiety Scale (PEP): Developed by Bert Pepper of ARD;

Brief Psychiatric Rating Scale (BPRS): (Overall & Gorham, 1962); and

Global Assessment of Functioning (GAF): (Endicott, Spitzer, Fleiss, & Cohen, 1976).

Treatment course measures were administered at specific times and consisted of the following instruments:

Treatment Related Events Questionnaire: Designed by ARD and used tri-monthly by program staff to report such events as urine tests results, relapse, rehospitalization, changes in treatment status, attainment of treatment goals, and so on;

Short Michigan Alcohol Screening Test (SMAST): (Selzer, 1971);

Short Michigan Drug Screening Test (SMDST): Prepared by ARD based on the SMAST;

Drug and Alcohol Dependence (D&A): (Skinner, 1982);

Stigma Questionnaire: Developed by Bruce Link (Link, Cullen, Streuning, Shrout, & Dohrenwend, 1989);

Rosenberg Self Esteem Scale (RSE): (Rosenberg, 1979);

Dropout Questionnaire: Developed by ARD to tap correlates of dropout before dropout actually occurs;

Specific Level of Functioning Scale (SLOF): (Schneider & Struening, 1983);

Community Oriented Programs Environment Scale (COPES): (Moos & Otto, 1972);

ASI: (abbreviated); and

CES-D, PI, PEP, BPRS, GAF.

Follow-up measures, based on the list of instruments above, were used to tap various posttreatment outcomes.

FINDINGS

HMICA Characteristics

Sociodemographic Characteristics

Sociodemographic characteristics of the 652 HMICA men who were prescreened by the researchers between 1991 and 1994 are shown in Table 6.1.

TABLE 6.1
HMICA Sociodemographic Characteristics
(N = 652)

Characteristic	Percent
Ethnicity	
African-American	57.6
Hispanic	22.8
Caucasian	17.3
Other	2.0
Religion	
Catholic	35.7
Baptist	14.3
Protestant	12.9
Jewish	2.3
Islamic	2.2
Other/no data	32.5
Marital Status	
Never married	76.9
Separated	10.1
Divorced	8.0
Married	2.0
Age (in years)	
Mode = 29	
Median = 32	
Mean = 32.99	
SD = 7.29	
Education (years completed)	
Mode = 12	
Median =11	
Mean = 10.87	
SD = 2.22	

The data show that 80.4 percent of the HMICA men sampled were ethnic minority. Only 2.0 percent were married, even though half of them were age 32 or older. Over half of them did not finish high school.

Employment

Only 20.3 percent reported a full-time job in the three years prior to the prescreening interview. During the 30 days prior to the prescreening interview, 94.4 percent earned no money from employment.

Family Background

Based on a sample of 551 HMICA men who were interviewed with the Personal History Form, 36.5 percent reported that, by the time they reached the age of one year, their fathers were neither living at home with them nor involved in any part of their upbringing. Many of them had never met their fathers. By age 13, 54.1 percent did not have their fathers around. For 12.7 percent of the sample, their mothers were not around by the time they were one year old. This proportion rose to 20.3 percent by the time they were 13 years old. For those HMICA men whose parents were present, many of these parents were substance abusers themselves: 52.7 percent of the fathers were reported to have a history of a drug or alcohol problem; 3.1 percent had a psychiatric problem; and 8.8 percent had a psychiatric, drug, and alcohol problem. Among their mothers, 23.1 percent were reported to have had alcohol or drug problems; 8.0 percent had psychiatric problems; and 5.3 percent had alcohol, drug, and psychiatric problems.

Prevalence of alcohol, drug, and psychiatric problems was reported to be very high among the HMICA men's siblings. For those who had at least one brother, 40.0 percent of their brothers were reported to have alcohol or drug problems; 2.9 percent had psychiatric problems; and 8.9 percent had alcohol, drug, and psychiatric problems. Among those who reported having at least one sister, 23.0 percent of their sisters were reported by the HMICA men to have had alcohol or drug problems; 5.0 percent had psychiatric problems; and 3.0 percent had alcohol, drug, and psychiatric problems.

Psychiatric Characteristics

The study participants were chronically mentally ill and seriously impaired psychiatrically. The mode and median number of psychiatric hospitalizations was four, with a mean of five, and standard deviation of 5.1. The majority were diagnosed with schizophrenia or other psychotic disorders (55.5 percent), mood disorders (8.0 percent), and substance abuse/dependence (8.1 percent). The majority reported present or past hallucinations (65.9 percent), delusions (56.7 percent), and severe depression (50.4 percent).

Substance Abuse Characteristics

The major substances of abuse for the 652 men were crack (44.9 percent), cocaine (13.3 percent), alcohol (20.8 percent), marijuana (9.5 percent), and heroin (6.8 percent).

The HMICA men started using different illicit substances at different stages in their lives. The mean age of first using alcohol (97.0 percent have used it) was 14.02 (SD = 4.23); marijuana (93.0 percent have used it), 15.73 (SD = 4.34); heroin (41.0 percent have used it), 19.51 (SD = 5.1); cocaine (86.0 percent have used it), 21.58 (SD = 6.76); crack (80.0 percent have used it), 27.54 (SD = 7.08).

Admission Processes

Out of 589 HMICA men determined suitable for referral to the participating programs, 313 (53.0 percent) were randomly assigned to TC treatment. Only 170 of them (54.0 percent) actually entered treatment however. The other 143 (46.0 percent) either dropped out before admission (N = 68, 22.0 percent) or were rejected by the TC intake staff (N = 75, 24.0 percent). Of the 276 (47.0 percent) HMICA men randomly assigned into CR treatment, only 119 (43.0 percent) actually entered treatment. One hundred and one (37.0 percent) dropped out before admission, and 56 (20.0 percent) were rejected by the CR staff.

These findings highlight the difficulties in enrolling HMICAs in treatment. A large proportion who were deemed by the researchers as possibly appropriate candidates were regarded by the programs' intake staffs as unsuitable to enroll in treatment. An even larger proportion dropped out either before they were seen by the programs or after being seen and accepted by the programs. The problem of preadmission dropout was particularly noticeable at the CR programs, where 37 percent dropped out before admission.

A possible corollary of the high preadmission dropout rate may be the length of time it took programs to admit clients to treatment. The average number of days between referral of a client to a program and admission of that client was 22.5 (SD = 17.4) for the TC, and 53.6 (SD = 32.7) for the CR.

Random assignment assured the comparability of clients referred to the TC with those referred to the CR. Once referred however, each program had full autonomy to accept or reject clients as it deemed appropriate. Indeed, there were significant differences in the selection and rejection of candidates between TC and CR. The TC accepted younger clients (TC mean age = 31.5; CR mean age = 34.9, $p < .001$); more depressed (TC mean CES-D score = 24.2; CR = 21.0, $p = .028$); more chronically addicted (56.7 percent versus 33.0 percent, $p < .01$), and more clients referred from the court (13.1 percent versus 3.4 percent, $p < .01$). Paradoxically, there were more clients admitted to CR with mood disorders and more admitted to TC with "other" diagnoses consisting mainly of psychoactive substance dependence/abuse, alcohol dependence/abuse, and organic disorders. Both programs were comparable on the proportion of clients diagnosed with schizophrenia, about 53.0 percent.

Comparisons between the two modalities were statistically corrected, as appropriate, to adjust for the initial differences between the two samples.

Treatment Services

A comparison between TC and CR was conducted with regard to hospitalizations for medical reasons, hospitalizations for psychiatric reasons, detoxification, changes in psychiatric medications, total number of days on any medication at program exit, prevocational training, vocational training, employment during treatment, education, and urine testing.

Statistically significant differences were found with regard to:

CRs administered a greater number of urine tests ($p < .05$) with a greater proportion of positive results ($p < .00$);

CRs sent more clients to detoxification ($p < .05$);

CRs were generally less successful in reducing the number of residents on medication during treatment; and

CRs had a smaller proportion of residents in General Educational Development classes.

Treatment Outcomes

The TC and CR have different treatment goals and treatment schedules, and may not be compared along "final outcomes." Instead, the two modalities are being compared here on differences in clients' status at various stages of treatment.

Measures of Psychiatric Symptoms and Social Functioning

At the point of their random assignment to either TC or CR, the TC and CR samples were similar on all psychiatric symptoms and social functioning scales. However, because of differences in admission criteria and preadmission dropout, the TC and CR samples differed significantly from each other by the time treatment began. Comparison of 41 HMICA men who completed one year of treatment in the TC with 28 who completed one year treatment in CRs shows that the TC sample was:

more depressed (TC CES-D = 27.95; CR CES-D = 16.86);
more psychotic (TC P.I. = 9.85; CR P.I. = 6.54);
more anxious (TC Pepper = 6.22; CR Pepper = 3.71);
more impaired (TC BPRS = 33.05; CR BPRS = 29.07);
more impaired (TC GAF = 40.85; CR GAF = 43.43); and
had lower self-esteem (TC RSE = 26.02; CR RSE = 27.64).

After one year in treatment, comparison of the 41 TC clients with the 28 CR clients shows that the TC clients were:

less depressed (TC CES-D = 13.63; CR CES-D = 16.54);
less psychotic (TC P.I. = 2.02; CR P.I. = 3.07);
less anxious (TC Pepper = 1.85; CR Pepper = 2.89);
less impaired (TC BPRS = 24.49; CR BPRS = 26.39);
less impaired (TC GAF = 56.73; CR GAF = 52.30); and
had higher self-esteem (TC RSE = 30.41; CR RSE = 29.36).

Differences between TC and CR were tested by regression analysis (dependent variable: one year change in the various measures above; independent variables: TC versus CR, age, level of addiction, and whether client was a court referral). Differences between TC and CR were significant with regard to depressive symptoms ($p < .01$), anxiety ($p < .05$), BPRS total impairment ($p < .05$), and GAF impairment ($p < .01$).

We conclude that TC clients, although starting their treatment more psychiatrically impaired than their CR counterparts, were significantly better off on most psychopathology scales after one year in treatment.

Dropout from Treatment

Dropout from treatment is probably the most significant problem in treating HMICAs. Out of 170 HMICA men who were admitted to the TC program, 114 (67.0 percent) dropped out or were discharged by the program before completing treatment. Only 56 (33.0 percent) completed or are still in treatment. In the CRs, out of 119 HMICA men who entered into treatment, 65 (55.0 percent) dropped out or were discharged. The other 54 (45.0 percent) either completed or are still in treatment. CR programs retained their clients longer than the TC did (CR: mean number of days = 272.9, SD = 256.1, median = 166; TC: mean = 199.7, SD = 204.1, median = 123). Nevertheless, the large difference between the two means is reduced to a much smaller difference when the two medians are compared, suggesting differences in the skew of the two distributions. The differences between TC and CR were particularly marked for the early stages of treatment: By 30 days, 26.6 percent of all the TC clients dropped out of treatment, compared with only 12.9 percent of the CR clients. By 60 days, 36.1 percent of all TC clients dropped out of treatment, compared with 21.8 percent of the CR clients.

For preadmission and postadmission dropout data, regression analysis was conducted with various psychopathologies as independent variables. Due to nonlinearity of CES-D and P.I. scales with dropout, the two scales were quartiled into four equal ordinal categories. The highest three were regressed on dropout with the low quartile as the reference category. Both multinomial logit and Cox proportional hazards analyses were used in estimating the role of various psychopathologies in explaining dropout. The multinomial procedure incorporates both administrative discharge and dropout because of splitting (the client's own decision to leave against medical advice) as the outcome variable. The base category was defined as currently in or completed treatment. The Cox procedure explains splitting only, with administrative discharge treated as nonsplitting. Results of this analysis suggest that different factors account for dropout in the TC from those in the CR, and different factors were related to preadmission dropout from those related to dropout from treatment. Specifically:

HMICAs diagnosed with substance abuse/dependence (DSM III-R), were less likely to drop out prior to admission to the TC than those diagnosed with depression.

HMICAs who started treatment with history of serious symptoms of depression (based on clinical report), were more likely to be discharged from the TC, and more likely to split from the CR, than those without the severe symptoms.

HMICAs who scored high on CES-D were less likely to split from the TC than those who scored low.

HMICAs who had a history of suicidal ideation and cognitive impairment were more likely to split from the CR than those who did not have those histories.

HMICAs with a history of chronic addiction were less likely to split from the TC than those without such a history.

DISCUSSION

The research described in this chapter examined various characteristics of HMICA men and their treatment in different, community-based programs. From the findings, HMICA men appear to be severely impaired on multiple psychiatric and psychological indicators and to occupy multiple deviant roles. They all had multiple psychiatric hospitalizations and most of them were diagnosed with schizophrenia or other psychotic disorders. They scored high on various measures of psychopathology and the majority had a history of severe psychopathology (for example, hallucination, delusions, depression, and so on). Sociologically, they seem to be placed outside the boundaries of society, with little or no affiliation with any social groups or organizations. Virtually all of them live alone, outside of social organizations like the workplace or the family. They deviate from most major social codes and norms: they are homeless, they are mentally ill, they abuse drugs and/or alcohol, and the majority have a criminal record. HMICAs' family background might suggest some possible clues to their situation. Based on extensive interviews with the HMICA men about their feelings and relationship with their parents and other family members and about their early childhood background, many appear to have been deprived of normal social development and socialization (Rahav & Link, 1995). They grew up without the needed support structures and social controls generally provided by families in the forms of love, guidance, role models, and definitions of cultural values and goals. From reviewing the early family history and characteristics of the HMICA men, a hypothesis emerges that the seeds of the HMICA syndrome were sowed at a very early age and proliferated with the perseverance of deleterious social, emotional, and physical conditions.

The multiplicity of impairments on so many fronts makes the treatment and rehabilitation of these men a heroic task. Two community-based types of programs, TC and CR, representing radically different approaches and philosophies, were modified to treat, specifically, HMICA men. Thirty-nine months of longitudinal evaluation of the TC and CR, through a carefully implemented experimental research design, has provided initial data on the differences between the two modalities. From our initial data, TC and CR programs appear to differ from one another in virtually all aspects of screening and selecting candidates for treatment and treatment itself. It took CR programs an average of 53.6 days to admit a client from the day that client was referred to them. The corresponding average in the TC was only 22.5 days. The difference in admission time may account for the sizable difference in preadmission dropout between CR and TC: 36.0 percent and 21.5 percent of all referrals dropped out before admission to the CR and TC, respectively. The difference in preadmission dropout between CR and TC may partially explain differences in dropout from treatment between CR and TC (21.8 percent of all admissions dropped out from the CR in the first 60 days of treatment, compared with 36.1 percent from the TC). The delayed admission causes the most severely impaired candidates to drop out. Having to wait so many days to enter treatment (53 days in the case of the CR) may lead those who need help the most (and they need this help urgently and immediately) to drop out. They may relapse and resume the use of illicit substances, decompensate mentally, or become involved in criminal activities and arrested. The delayed admission operates, ostensibly, as a filter that screens out the most clinically vulnerable and frail candidates. In programs where admission is rapid (for example, the TC) HMICAs are admitted who would have been preadmission dropouts had they been referred to the CR. These vulnerable-to-dropout men who were not filtered out by the (rapid) admitting program are the first ones to succumb to the pressures of the new treatment environment and drop out.

Our findings call attention to a relatively unknown and unstudied problem: preadmission dropout. There were more clients dropping out before admission than there were clients dropping out in the first 60 days of treatment. Dropout begins from the point when recruitment to treatment starts. Our data demonstrate the importance of widening the scope of studying dropout, to include preadmission dropout.

TC and CR also differed in the way they selected their clients into treatment. TC clients scored higher (that is, were more impaired) on all scales of psychopathology and more of the TC clients had chronic drug abuse/dependence problems.

Despite their initial disadvantage, after one year in treatment TC clients improved more than their CR counterparts and surpassed them on all measures of psychopathology. One possible explanation to the higher efficacy of the TC in reducing psychopathology may be that it is an artifact of differential dropout: more clients dropped out of treatment in the TC than in the CR and they might have been the most impaired, leaving the healthiest clients in the TC. Our data, however, do not give credence to this hypothesis. In the TC the most impaired tended to stay in treatment. In the CR the most depressed and suicidal tended to drop out.

In sum, from reviewing their clinical, substance abuse, psychosocial, and family background characteristics, HMICAs may be the ultimate epitome of the ills of the postindustrialized modern society. From our data HMICAs appear impaired, dysfunctional, and socially deviant in a number of major areas and social roles, requiring treatment on multiple fronts. Only a few of them were able to go through a prolonged treatment course. For those few who did, our initial data suggest that, in comparison with the CR approach, the TC modality may be better equipped to treat HMICAs and their complicated symptomatology.

REFERENCES

Burt, M. R., & Cohen, B. E. (1989). *America's homeless: Number, characteristics, and programs that serve them*. Washington, DC: Urban Institute Press.

Casriel, D. (1972). *A scream away from happiness*. New York: Grosset and Dunlap.

De Leon, G. (1986). The therapeutic community for substance abuse: Perspective and approach. In G. De Leon & J. T. Ziegenfuss (Eds.), *Therapeutic communities for addictions*. Springfield, IL: Charles C. Thomas.

De Leon, G. (1985). The therapeutic community: Status and evolution. *The International Journal of the Addictions, 20*, 823–844.

Dennis, D. L., Buckner, J. C., Lipton, F. R., & Levine, I. S. (1991). A decade of research and services for homeless mentally ill persons. *American Psychologist,*

46(11), 1129–1138.

Dohrenwend, B. P., Shrout, P., Egri, G., & Mendelsohn, F. (1980). Measures of nonspecific psychological distress and other dimensions of psychopathology in the general population. *Archives of General Psychiatry, 37,* 1229–1236.

Drake, R. E., Osher, F. C., & Wallach, M. A. (1989). Alcohol use and abuse in schizophrenia: A prospective community study. *Journal of Nervous and Mental Diseases, 177,* 408–414.

Endicott, J., Spitzer, R. L., Fleiss, J. L., & Cohen, J. (1976). The global assessment scale: A procedure for measuring overall severity of psychiatric disturbance. *Archives of General Psychiatry, 33,* 766–771.

Fischer, P. J. (1991). *Alcohol, drug abuse and mental health problems among homeless persons: A review of the literature, 1980–1990.* Rockville, MD: National Institute on Alcohol and Alcoholism.

Hellerstein, D. J., & Meehan, B. (1987). Outpatient group therapy for schizophrenic substance abusers. *American Journal of Psychiatry, 144,* 1337–1339.

Jencks, C. (1994). *The homeless.* Cambridge, MA: Harvard University Press.

Kofoed, L. L., Kania, J., Walsh, T., & Atkinson, R. M. (1986). Outpatient treatment of patients with substance abuse and co-existing psychiatric disorders. *American Journal of Psychiatry, 143,* 867–872.

Lehman, A., Myers, C. P., & Corty, E. (1989). Assessment and classification of patients with psychiatric and substance abuse syndromes. *Hospital and Community Psychiatry, 40*(10), 1019–1025.

Link, B. G., Cullen, F. T., Struening, E. L., Shrout, P., & Dohrenwend, B. P. (1989). A modified labeling theory approach to mental disorder: An empirical assessment. *American Sociological Review, 54,* 400–423.

McLellan, A. T. (1986). Psychiatric severity as a predictor of outcome from substance abuse treatment. In R. E. Mayer (Ed.), *Psychopathology and addictive disorder.* New York: Guilford.

McLellan, T., Luborsky, L., O'Brien, C. P., & Woody, G.E. (1981). An improved evaluation instrument for the substance abuse patients: The Addiction Severity Index. *Journal of Nervous and Mental Disorders, 168,* 26–33.

Moos, R. H., & Otto, H. (1972). The Community Oriented Programs Environment Scale: A methodology for the facilitation and evaluation of social change. *Community Mental Health Journal, 8*(1), 28–37.

Osher, F. C., & Kofoed, L. L. (1989). Treatment of patients with psychiatric and psychoactive substance abuse disorders. *Hospital and Community Psychiatry, 40*(10), 1025–1030.

Overall, J. E., & Gorham D. R. (1962). The brief psychiatric rating scale. *Psychological Reports, 10,* 799–812.

Radloff, L. S. (1977). The CES-D Scale: A self report depression scale for research in the general population. *Applied Psychological Measurement, 1,* 365–401.

Rahav, M., Guagenti-Tax, E., Rivera, J. J., Raskin, R., Gross, B., Sturz, E. L., Struening, E. L., Pepper, B., & Link, B. G. (1993). Dually diagnosed men in different community treatment programs: A longitudinal evaluation study. In J. A. Inciardi, F. M. Tims, & B. W. Fletcher (Eds.), *Innovative approaches in the treatment of drug abuse* (pp. 71–83). Westport, CT: Greenwood Press.

Rahav, M., & Link, B. G. (1995). When social problems converge: Homeless, mentally ill, chemical abusing men in New York City. *The International Journal of the Addictions, 30*(8), 1019–1042.

Rahav, M., Rivera, J. J., Collins, J., Ng-Mak, D., Sturz, E. L., Struening, E. L., Pepper, B., Link, B. G., & Gross, B. (1994). Bringing experimental research designs into existing treatment programs: The case of community based treatment of the dually diagnosed. In B. W. Fletcher, J. A. Inciardi, & A. M. Horton (Eds.), *Drug abuse treatment: The implementation of innovative approaches*. Westport, CT: Greenwood Press.

Regier, D. A., Farmer, M. E., Rae, D. S., Locke, B. Z., Keith, S. J., Judd, L. L., & Goodwin, F. K. (1990). Comorbidity of mental disorders with alcohol and other drug abuse: Results from the epidemiologic catchment area study. *Journal of the American Medical Association, 264*(19), 2511–2518.

Ridgely, M. S. (1991). Creating integrated programs for severely mentally ill persons with substance disorders. In K. Minkoff & R. E. Drake (Eds.), *Dual diagnosis of major mental illness and substance disorders*. San Francisco: Jossey-Bass.

Ridgely, M. S., Osher, F. C., & Talbott, J. A. (1987). *Chronic mentally ill young adults with substance abuse problems: Treatment and training issues*. Rockville, MD: Alcohol, Drug Abuse and Mental Health Administration.

Rosenberg, M. (1979). *Conceiving the self*. New York: Basic Books.

Schneider, L. G., & Struening, E. L. (1983). SLOF: A behavioral rating scale for assessing the mentally ill. *Social Work Research and Abstracts, 41*, 9–21.

Selzer, M. L. (1971). The Michigan Alcoholism Screening Test: The quest for a new diagnostic instrument. *American Journal of Psychiatry, 126*, 1653–1658.

Skinner, H. A. (1982). The Drug Alcohol Screening Test. *Addictive Behavior, 7*, 363–371.

Sturz, E. L. (1992) *Dealing with disruptive adolescents and drugs*. New York: Argus Community Inc.

Thacker, W., & Tremaine, L. (1989). System issues in serving the mentally ill substance abusers: Virginia's experience. *Hospital and Community Psychiatry, 40* (10), 146–149.

III

CASE MANAGEMENT PROGRAMS

7

The Effectiveness of Case Management in Working with Intravenous Drug Users

Cheryl L. Mejta, Peter J. Bokos, E. Michael Maslar, Judith H. Mickenberg, and Edward C. Senay

Intravenous drug users (IDUs) are plagued with repeated relapses and multiple, complex, and often life-threatening problems. The substance abuse treatment system, already burdened by increased demands for treatment and by under-funding, is frequently unable to respond to the multiple needs of IDUs in a comprehensive manner. As an approach designed to orchestrate, coordinate, and integrate services for client populations experiencing chronic and multiple problems, case management offers promise as a means to improve and enhance treatment services for IDUs. This chapter presents initial findings from a study examining the effectiveness of case management in improving treatment access, retention, and outcome and in reducing drug-associated problems among IDUs. The most dramatic findings to date indicate that the case management approach used in the current study significantly increased clients' admission to treatment, reduced the amount of time to get clients into treatment, and increased the amount of time clients spent in treatment. Reductions in clients' drug use and drug-associated problems also were found.

Ridgely and Willenbring (1992) noted that urban drug injectors frequently have multiple, chronic problems in different life domains, such as housing, medical, mental health, legal, educational, and vocational. They cited the fragmentation of public service systems encountered by multiproblem drug injectors as an impediment to the development of effective substance abuse interventions. It is commonplace in the drug treatment community that many primary care, mental health, and social service systems range from indifference to frank hostility to addicts. Dennis, Karuntzos, and Rachal (1992), in a study examining the use of case managers to link methadone maintenance clients with community services, observed that community agencies employed a variety of mechanisms, such as delays, misuse of eligibility criteria, or implicit exclusionary policies to avoid multiproblem methadone maintenance patients.

Methadone maintenance clinics historically have been isolated from mainstream primary care and mental health service systems and are not linked with each other in any functional way; most cogently, they have not had, and have no prospect of having, the resources to assist with problems in other domains. Problems in multiple domains often aggregate and overwhelm the adaptive striving of multiproblem drug injectors leading to dropout from treatment or to relapse. The need for a mechanism to sustain and to integrate care in multiple domains for this population would appear to be beyond dispute.

Case management has been explored as a possible solution. A number of studies indicate that case management is successful in enhancing the accessibility and effectiveness of drug treatment. In a study examining case management as an approach to link primary care and substance abuse providers, Schlenger, Kroutil, and Roland (1992) found that case-managed subjects were successfully linked with a variety of services. The authors noted that these findings were consistent with the notion that case management leads to more effective service delivery and may play a role in providing comprehensive service delivery. Dennis, Karuntzos, and Rachal (1992) found that case managers were effective in linking methadone maintenance patients to needed services with associated reductions in drug use. Lidz, Bux, Platt, and Iguchi (1992) found that case management led to improved access to needed services for IDUs while Bokos, Mejta, Mickenberg, and Monks (1992) and Mejta, Bokos, Mickenberg, and Maslar (1994) found that case-managed IDUs entered treatment faster, in greater numbers, and had longer time in treatment compared to randomly assigned controls. In the future environment of managed care, the case manager may be able to make important contributions to the integration of services for multiproblem drug injectors.

In the age of HIV, rapid entrance into treatment and improved retention in treatment may have far-reaching effects in preventing individuals from acquiring and spreading HIV. Data from a number of studies indicate that positive effects from treatment, such as reductions in drug use and criminal activity, are related to time in treatment (Ball, Lange, Myers, & Friedman, 1988) and that methadone treatment, particularly for those performing well in it, has preventive effects with respect to HIV (Barthwell, Senay, Marks, & White, 1989; Novick et al., 1990). IDUs constitute 32 percent of all AIDS cases and they constitute a rapidly growing faction of persons affected by HIV (Centers for Disease Control, 1991). The Chicago metropolitan area appears to be part of these national trends as "heroin purity has continued to escalate to the highest levels seen in over twenty years. The incidence of heroin use has also skyrocketed predominately among black males age 25–34 as the popularity of snorting the drug has emerged as a major new trend" (Weibel, Ouellet, & O'Brien, 1993). Historically, we have observed that many heroin snorters turned to injection as their heroin careers matured; in any event, the need for improving treatment for this growing population is urgent. Case management, thus, appears to be an intervention urgently needing further exploration.

OVERVIEW OF THE CASE MANAGEMENT STUDY

Study Design

Using a three-year, longitudinal study design, the effects of a generalist case management intervention were explored in relationship to IDUs' access to treatment, retention in treatment, participation in HIV high-risk activities, completion of treatment, coexisting problems, and long-term recovery status. A total of 316 IDUs seeking treatment through a central intake facility participated in the study. Clients providing written informed consent to participate in the study were matched according to gender, ethnicity, and age. Within the matched pairs, clients were randomly assigned to the case-managed intervention or to "treatment as usual condition." In the case-managed condition, clients were assigned a case manager who assisted clients with identifying and locating service resources. In the treatment as usual condition, clients were provided the names of clinics in their geographical area. Clients were contacted monthly for three years by a research interviewer who administered a series of research instruments to assess clients' substance use, associated problems, HIV risk behaviors, and treatment status. A detailed description of the study design appears in Bokos, Mejta, Mickenberg, & Monks (1992) and Mejta, Bokos, Mickenberg, & Maslar, (1994).

Client Population

Clients who participated in the study were chronic, multiproblem, substance abusers in need of diverse and long-term health, mental health, and other social services. Clients were primarily minority males over 40 years old. All clients were intravenous and multiple drug users whose primary drugs included opiates, cocaine, alcohol, and marijuana. Many clients had used drugs for more than 16 years and most had several previous unsuccessful treatment episodes. In addition to their drug use, clients entered the study with housing, financial, employment, legal, familial, and medical problems. A more detailed description of the client population appears in Mejta, Bokos, Mickenberg, & Maslar, (1994).

Case Management Model

Case management approaches can vary along several dimensions including the goals of the case management intervention, the functions performed by the case manager, the roles assumed by the case manager, the size of the case manager's caseload, the processes used to accomplish case management goals, the characterization of the provider network, and the organizational setting and structure within which case management is provided. A variety of case management models currently are in use with substance-abusing populations (Dennis, Karuntzos, & Rachal, 1992; Falck, Siegal, & Carlson, 1992; Inciardi, Isenberg, Lockwood, Martin, & Scarpitti, 1992; Lidz, Bux, Platt, & Iguchi, 1992; Mejta et al., 1994).

This study used a case manager "generalist" model in which the case manager functioned in differing capacities according to the client's need, stage of recovery, and success in achieving independence. Table 7.1 outlines the case management model used in the study. The goals of the case management intervention emphasized rapid access to treatment, increased treatment retention, improved treatment outcomes, reduced drug use, and reduced high-risk behaviors for contracting HIV. To enable case managers to work with clients and service providers effectively, case managers maintained a maximum caseload equivalence of 15 clients.

The case management project functioned independently of treatment provider organizations, relying instead on the development of referral arrangements with a wide variety of providers. Within this model, the case manager's ability to negotiate different systems of care and to access resources are emphasized. In concert with the client's stated and assessed needs, case managers established and implemented a case management plan that included but was not limited to identifying and referring subjects to appropriate services and service providers; facilitating access to treatment by eliminating financial, transportation, housing, and other personal and administrative impediments; facilitating completion of treatment by monitoring the client's progress, providing ancillary support services, and reassigning the client, if necessary, to a different type of service, level of service, or service provider; and developing and implementing modified case management plans as clients' service needs or provider service capabilities changed.

TABLE 7.1
Interventions Case Management Model

Program Goals
- Rapid treatment access
- Increased treatment retention
- Improved treatment outcome
- Reduced drug use
- Abstinence through linkage
- Reduced high-risk behaviors for the contraction of HIV

Characterization of Model
- Broad spectrum
- Generalist case manager
- Client focused and driven versus system focused and driven
  - Developmental
  - Strength focus
  - Growth model
  - Problem solving
  - Empowering

Function of Case Manager
- Accessing
- Planning
- Linking
- Monitoring
- Advocacy

Role of Case Manager
- Facilitate opportunities for client
- Service broker
- Advocate
- Service network expert
- Service coordinator

Caseload
- Caseload equivalence of 15

Setting
- Independent of treatment provider

Character of Network
- Wide variety of providers

Supportive Services
- Transportation assistance
- Treatment subsidy
- Gap-filling in service delivery system

Discharge Criteria
- Three years

CLIENT OUTCOMES

As previously noted, clients are followed for three years. The 18-month follow-up has been completed on 73 percent of the total sample. Preliminary analyses of the data demonstrate the efficacy of the case management intervention in improving treatment admission and retention and in enhancing treatment outcomes.

Treatment Admission and Retention

Case-managed clients entered treatment in greater numbers, entered treatment more quickly, and stayed in treatment longer than the comparison group clients. As seen in Table 7.2, a greater number of case-managed clients entered a substance abuse treatment program. Within the case-managed group, 97 percent of the clients entered a substance abuse treatment program (155 of 160). Within the comparison group, 53 percent of the clients entered a substance abuse treatment program (83 of 156). Chi-square analysis yielded a statistically significant between-group difference in the number of clients who entered treatment ($\chi^2 = 79.75$, $df = 1$, $p < .01$).

TABLE 7.2
Admissions to Substance Abuse Treatment by Experimental Condition

Treatment Condition	Entered Treatment	Did Not Enter Treatment
Case-managed	155	5
Comparison	82	74

Case-managed clients also entered treatment more quickly than did the comparison group clients. For case-managed clients, the average time for treatment admission was 16.8 days, with a minimum wait of 0 days and a maximum wait of 829 days. Within one week of entering the study, 63 percent of the case-managed clients were in a treatment program. Within one month of entering the study, 87 percent of the case-managed clients were in a treatment program. For the comparison group clients, the average time for treatment admission was 101.7 days, with a minimum wait of 1 day and a maximum wait of 798 days. Within one week of entering the study, only 8 percent of the comparison group clients were in a treatment program and within one month of entering the study, only 22 percent of the comparison group clients were in a treatment program. The between-group difference in the number of days to enter a substance abuse treatment program was statistically significant ($F = 35.16$, $df = 1$, $p < .001$).

At the 18-month follow-up, the case-managed group spent an average of 432 days in treatment while the comparison group spent an average of 211 days in treatment; this represents a statistically significant between-group difference ($F = 84.83$, $df = 1$, $p < .01$). When considering only those comparison group clients who entered treatment, the case-managed clients still averaged more treatment days than did the comparison clients (432 treatment days for case-managed clients compared to 318 treatment days for comparison clients); this between-group difference approached statistical significance ($t = 4.78$, $df = 1$, $p < .07$). Further examination of the number of days spent in treatment showed that case-managed clients spent 80 percent of their time in treatment while comparison group clients spent only 40 percent of their time in treatment (Figure 7.1). Chi-square analysis yielded a statistically significant between-group difference in the number of days spent in a treatment program ($\chi^2 = 183.78$, $df = 1$, $p < .001$).

FIGURE 7.1
Percentage of Time in Treatment at 18-month Follow-up

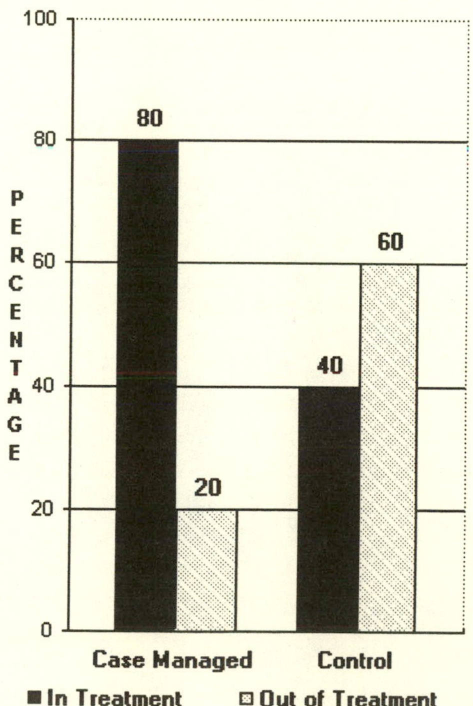

Treatment Outcomes

Treatment outcomes examined at 18 months included drug use, drug injection behaviors, and drug-associated problems. Drug use was measured through self-reports to items on the Addiction Severity Index and a drug and alcohol use questionnaire. Both case-managed clients and comparison clients showed reductions in drug use across time. However, case-managed clients showed greater reductions in their drug use. Case-managed clients were more likely than comparison clients to be drug-free at the 6-month (46 percent versus 30 percent), 12-month (51 percent versus 36 percent), and 18-month (59 percent versus 44 percent) follow-up periods (Figure 7.2).

Statistically significant between-group differences were obtained at each follow-up interval: $\chi^2 = 7.63$, $df = 1$, $p < .01$ at 6 months; $\chi^2 = 5.31$, $df = 1$, $p < .02$ at 12 months; and $\chi^2 = 5.69$, $df = 1$, $p < .02$ at 18 months.

Opiates were the primary drug of choice for all clients. The findings showed reductions in opiate use for both groups across time. Again, however, case-managed clients were more likely than comparison clients to be opiate-free at each follow-up interval (Figure 7.3). At the 6-month

FIGURE 7.2
Drug-free Subjects at Follow-up

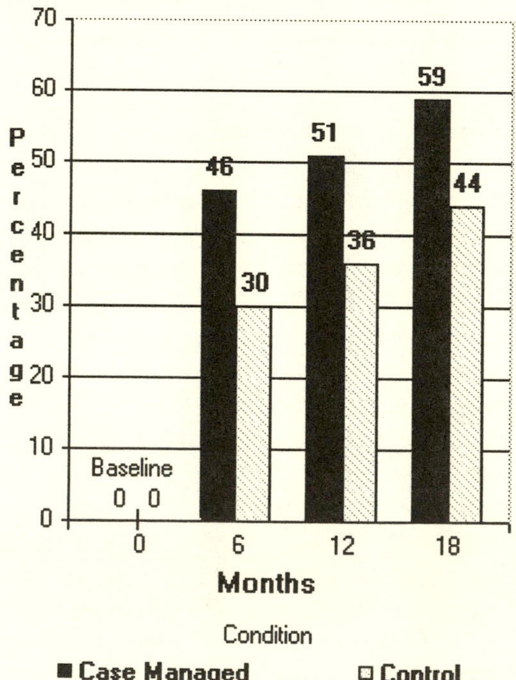

FIGURE 7.3
Opiate-free Subjects at Follow-up

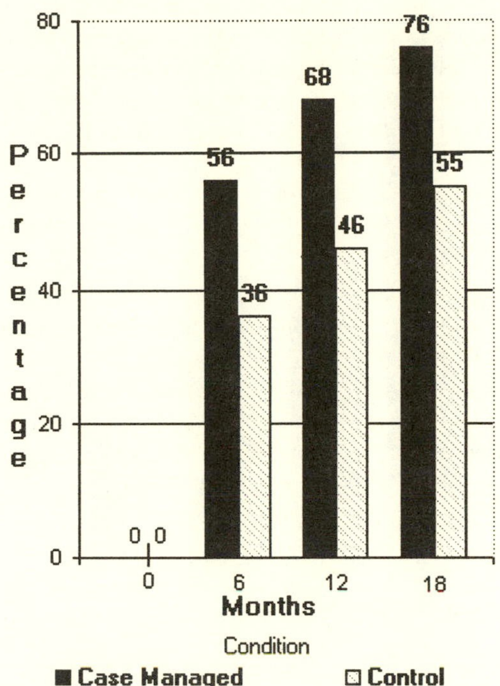

follow-up, 56 percent of the case-managed clients versus 36 percent of the comparison group were opiate-free ($\chi^2 = 11.36$, $df = 1$, $p < .01$). At the 12-month follow-up, 68 percent of the case-managed clients versus 46 percent of the comparison group clients were opiate-free ($\chi^2 = 12.36$, $df = 1$, $p < .01$). At the 18-month follow-up, 76 percent of the case-managed clients and 55 percent of the comparison group clients were opiate-free ($\chi^2 = 11.13$, $df = 1$, $p < .01$). Reductions in the use of other drugs also were found across time, but these differences were not as dramatic.

The client population served in the study was at risk for HIV infection through use of injection drug equipment. In addition to their drug use, drug-injection behaviors were examined. Related to their greater reduction in opiate use, the case-managed group also showed greater reductions in drug-injection behaviors than did the comparison group (Figure 7.4). At the 6-month follow-up, 49 percent of the case-managed clients versus 67 percent of the comparison group reported needle use in the past 30 days ($\chi^2 = 7.4$, $df = 1$, $p < .01$). At the 12-month follow-up, 36 percent of the case-managed clients and 53 percent of the comparison

FIGURE 7.4
Percentage of Subject Needle Use at Follow-up

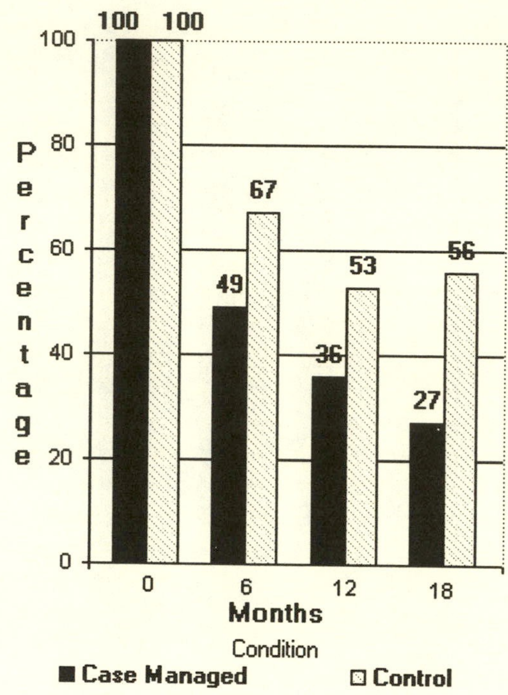

clients reported needle use in the previous 30 days ($\chi^2 = 6.58$, $df = 1$, $p < .02$). At the 18-month follow-up, 27 percent of the case-managed clients and 56 percent of the comparison clients reported needle use ($\chi^2 = 12.61$, $df = 1$, $p < .01$).

Additional analyses are underway to assess changes within groups and between groups in drug-associated problems as measured through the Addiction Severity Index and Substance Abuse Problem Checklist, such as medical problems, legal problems, family and social problems, and psychological problems. Service utilization patterns and costs attached to the case management intervention are also being analyzed. These results will be reported in subsequent publications.

DISCUSSION

The results of the present study demonstrate that a case management intervention may help injection drug users to access needed services, especially substance abuse treatment, and reduce or eliminate their use of illicit substances, thereby reducing their risk of contracting HIV from sharing needles. Improved access to substance abuse treatment was achieved primarily through access to existing treatment slots and the generation of new slots, enabled by the use of funds administered through the case management program. Although assistance with transportation, acquisition of necessary records from prior treatment experiences, and other actions by the case manager helped to speed access, the existence of long waiting lists at virtually every public clinic in the Chicago area proved to be a formidable problem (W. Watkins, personal communication, September 1992). This problem could be surmounted consistently through the use of funding as a means of providing temporary placement until public treatment became available. This practice of capitation may be an important function of case management. Some have asserted that the control of resources by the case manager is critical to the success of the case management process (Roberts-DeGennaro, 1987). The success of capitation also has been demonstrated in the mental health field (Harris & Bergman, 1988).

Time in treatment is an important predictor of future positive outcomes from treatment (Ball & Ross, 1991; Hubbard et al., 1989; Sells & Simpson, 1976). Novick and colleagues (1988) and Senay and colleagues (1993) have data indicating that being in treatment is associated with a substantial reduction in HIV risk. Clients often encounter several common problems that may impede completion of treatment. One involves problems with access to ancillary services already identified as being needed by the client. Another involves the occurrence of unpredictable life crises that place a burden on the client. Both of these problems, made worse by the unresponsiveness of an overburdened social services system, may reduce the client's motivation and often precipitates relapse and dropout from treatment.

In the current study, case-managed clients spent significantly more time in treatment resulting in greater reductions in their drug use and HIV risk behaviors compared with their control group counterparts. Case managers worked to sustain clients' involvement in treatment by working toward filling gaps in service delivery to address clients' needs better. In particular, case managers addressed clients' needs for stable living situations, financial support, medical and psychiatric assistance, and employment skills. Left unaddressed, each of these factors has been found to contribute to relapse (Catalano, Howard, Hawkins, & Wells, 1988). In addition, the sustained positive relationship between the client and the case manager served to provide important social support frequently missing from clients' lives.

The case manager concept is accompanied by controversy despite positive effects, such as those demonstrated above (Ashery, 1992; Bagarozzi & Pollane, 1984; Harris & Bergman, 1988; Roberts-DeGennaro, 1987). Some of this controversy revolves around the lack of a clear definition of case management and the variety of models involved in current research (Dennis, Karuntzos, & Rachal, 1992; Falck, Siegal, & Carlson, 1992; Inciardi, Isenberg, Lockwood, Martin, & Scarpitti, 1992; Lidz, Bux, Platt, & Iguchi, 1992). Roberts-DeGennaro (1987) noted that a successful case manager empowers clients to control their own lives and that the case manager must develop or have access to an existing network of available resources to use on behalf of the client. The ability of the case manager to negotiate different systems of care and to have access to the resources required to do so also should be stressed. In the present study's definition of case management, the case manager had funds to purchase treatment from the private sector until there were openings in the public systems and the case manager had resources to facilitate travel and other common impediments to access needed services for multiproblem IDUs.

REFERENCES

Ashery, R. S. (1992). Case management community advocacy for substance abuse subjects. In R. S. Ashery (Ed.), *Progress and issues in case management* (DHHS Publication No. (ADM) 92-1946, pp. 383–394). Rockville, MD: National Institute on Drug Abuse.

Bagarozzi, D., & Pollane, L. (1984). Case management in mental health. *Health and Social Work, 9,* 201–211.

Ball, J. C., Lange, W. R., Myers, E., & Friedman, S. R. (1988). Reducing the risk of AIDS through methadone maintenance treatment. *Journal of Health and Social Behavior, 29,* 214–226.

Barthwell, A., Senay, E., Marks, R., & White, R. (1989, October). Patients successfully maintained with methadone escaped human immunodeficiency virus infection. *Archives of General Psychiatry, 46,* 956–957.

Bokos, P. J., Mejta, C. L., Mickenberg, J. H., & Monks, R. L. (1992). Case management: An alternative approach to working with intravenous drug users. In R. S. Ashery (Ed.), *Progress and issues in case management* (DHHS Publication No. (ADM) 92-1946, pp. 92–111. Rockville, MD: National Institute on Drug Abuse.

Catalano, R. F., Howard, M. O., Hawkins, J. D., & Wells, E. A. (1988). Relapse in addictions: Rates, determinants, and promising strategies. In *1988 Surgeon General's report on health and consequences of smoking*. Washington, DC: U.S. Government Printing Office.

Centers for Disease Control (1991). *HIV/AIDS surveillance: U.S. AIDS cases reported through July 1991.* Atlanta, GA: Centers for Disease Control.

Dennis, M. L., Karuntzos, G. T., & Rachal, J. V. (1992). Accessing additional community resources through case management to meet the needs of methadone subjects. In R. S. Ashery (Ed.), *Progress and issues in case management* (DHHS Publication No. (ADM) 92-1946, pp. 54–78). Rockville, MD: National Institute on Drug Abuse.

Falck, R. S., Siegal, H. A., & Carlson, R. G. (1992). Case management to enhance AIDS risk reduction for injection drug users and crack cocaine users:

Practical and philosophical considerations. In R. S. Ashery (Ed.), *Progress and issues in case management* (DHHS Publication No. (ADM) 92-1946, pp. 167–180). Rockville, MD: National Institute on Drug Abuse.

Harris, M., & Bergman, H. D. (1988). Capitation financing for the chronic mentally ill: A case management approach. *Hospital and Community Psychiatry, 39,* 68–72.

Hubbard, R. L., Marsden, M. E., Rachal, J. V., Harwood, H. J., Cavanaugh, E. R., & Ginsburg, H. M. (1989). *Drug abuse treatment: A national study of effectiveness.* Chapel Hill: University of North Carolina Press.

Inciardi, J. A., Isenberg, H., Lockwood, D., Martin, S. S., & Scarpitti, F. R. (1992). Assertive community treatment with a parolee population: An extension of case management. In R. S. Ashery (Ed.), *Progress and issues in case management* (DHHS Publication No. (ADM) 92-1946, pp. 350–367). Rockville, MD: National Institute on Drug Abuse.

Lidz, V., Bux, D. A., Platt, J. J., & Iguchi, M. Y. (1992). Transitional case management: A service model for AIDS outreach projects. In R. S. Ashery (Ed.), *Progress and issues in case management* (DHHS Publication No. (ADM) 92-1946, pp. 112–144). Rockville, MD: National Institute on Drug Abuse.

Mejta, C. L., Bokos, P. J., Mickenberg, J. H., & Maslar, E. M. (1994). Case management with intravenous drug users: Implementation issues and strategies. In J. A. Inciardi, F. M. Tims, & B. W. Fletcher (Eds.), *The implementation of innovative approaches to drug abuse treatment.* Westport, CT: Greenwood Press.

Mejta, C. L., Bokos, P. J., Mickenberg, J. H., Maslar, E. M., Hasson, A. L., Gil, V., O'Keefe, Z., Martin, S. S., Isenberg, H., Inciardi, J. A., Lockwood, D., Rapp, R. C., Siegal, H. A., Fisher, J. H., & Wagner, J. H. (1994). Approaches to case management with substance abusing populations. In J. Lewis (Ed.), *Current concepts in addictions.* Gaithersburg, MD: Aspen Publishers.

Novick, D. M., Joseph, H., Croxson, T. S., Salsitz, E. A., Wang, G., Richman, B., Poretsky, L., Keefe, J. B., & Whimbey, E. (1990). Absence of antibody to human immunodeficiency virus in long-term socially rehabilitated methadone maintenance patients. *Archives of Internal Medicine, 150,* 97–99.

Novick, D. M., Pascarelli, E. F., Joseph, H., Salsitz, E. A., Richman, B. L., Des Jarlais, D. C., Anderson, M., Dole, V. P., & Nyswander, M. E. (1988). Methadone maintenance patients in general medical practice. *Journal of the American Medical Association, 259(2),* 3299–3302.

Ridgely, M. S., & Willenbring, M. L. (1992). Application of case management to drug abuse treatment: Overview of models and research issues. In R. S. Ashery (Ed.), *Progress and issues in case management* (DHHS Publication No. (ADM) 92-1946, pp. 12–13). Rockville, MD: National Institute on Drug Abuse.

Roberts-DeGennaro, M. (1987). Developing case management as a practice model. *Journal of Contemporary Social Work, 68,* 466–470.

Schlenger, W. E., Kroutil, L. A., & Roland, E. J. (1992). Case management as a mechanism for linking drug abuse treatment and primary care: Preliminary evidence from the ADAMHA/HRSA linkage demonstration. In R. S. Ashery (Ed.), *Progress and issues in case management* (DHHS Publication No. (ADM) 92-1946, pp. 316–330). Rockville, MD: National Institute on Drug Abuse.

Sells, S. B., & Simpson, D. D. (1976). *Studies of the effectiveness of treatments for drug abuse.* Vol. 5. Cambridge, MA: Ballinger.

Senay, E. C., Barthwell, A. G., Marks, R., Bokos, P., Gillman, D., & White, R. (1993). Medical maintenance: A pilot study. *Journal of Addictive Diseases, 12*(4), 59–76.

Weibel, W., Ouellet, L., & O'Brien, M. U. (1993, June). Nature and scope of substance abuse in Chicago. *Community Epidemiology Work Group*. Rockville, MD: National Institute on Drug Abuse.

8

Case Management for Drug Involved Parolees: It Proved To Be a Hard ACT to Follow

Steven S. Martin, James A. Inciardi,
Frank R. Scarpitti, and Amie L. Nielsen

The Assertive Community Treatment Program (ACT) for Delaware parolees was a research driven initiative, designed to assess the delivery and impact of a program of primary treatment and case management services for inmate clients who would be leaving prison and reentering the outside world. The original plan called for 400 parolees with histories of injecting drugs or other drug-related HIV risk behaviors to be randomly assigned upon release to either the ACT program (N = 200) or to conventional parole (N = 200). Data from a variety of interviews and from HIV and urine tests were used to determine outcome. If the program failed to produce discernible improvements in reducing relapse and recidivism, it would suggest looking elsewhere for more promising treatment alternatives for drug-involved prison releasees.

The ACT program in Delaware targeted an especially hard-to-reach group: parolees with histories of HIV risk-related drug involvement. Most of the clients in this program had been in prison more than once (average 3 times), had been arrested numerous times (average 10 times), and had been using drugs for many years (median age of first use of drugs other than alcohol or marijuana = 16). Nevertheless, these individuals had shown some success in prison, as evidenced by the fact that they were being released before serving their entire sentence. However, they still faced the potential for relapse to drug use and HIV infection, as well as the myriad disadvantages associated with having been incarcerated, including the stigma of a prison record and associated disruptions in work, school, and family activities. In most cases, the clients were not actively seeking treatment, although participation in the program was voluntary. Under these circumstances, most treatment programs would be particularly taxed and likely to have limited successes in the face of the combined stresses of recovery and reentry into society.

The ACT program also proved to be a difficult program to implement as originally planned, because of a combination of factors within and outside the control of the program. Although the target number of recruits into the ACT program (N = 218) and comparison group (N = 237) were both exceeded, the number of clients who actively engaged in the ACT program was much smaller, and the number who could be said to have completed the entire program was only a fraction of the recruits. Nevertheless, the ACT program did achieve some modest program successes, and, where it did not succeed, it provided important information for changes in programming, some of which have already been implemented by the treatment provider. ACT should be a useful case study for other programs using an outpatient approach for the seriously drug-involved.

This chapter begins with a brief overview of material that has been presented in detail elsewhere: the ACT program and how clients were recruited (Martin, Isenberg, & Inciardi, 1993), followed by discussions of the issues and obstacles to implementing the program and the strategies developed to deal with them (Scarpitti, Inciardi, & Martin, 1994). The chapter then looks at what the numbers suggest about program outcome, followed by qualitative results from ACT clients and staff concerning what worked and what did not work about the intervention. The chapter ends with a discussion of four major issues surrounding the ACT program and the treatment needs of drug-involved offenders.

CASE MANAGEMENT WITH DRUG-INVOLVED CLIENTS

The case management approach to rehabilitation found in both the social work and mental health fields has only recently been applied to substance abusing clients (Graham & Birchmore-Timney, 1990; Martin & Inciardi, 1993a; Mejta et al., 1994). The basic case management approach is to assist clients in obtaining needed services in a timely and coordinated manner. The key components of the approach are assessing, planning, linking, monitoring, and advocating for clients within the existing nexus of treatment and social services (Bagarozzi & Pollane, 1984). As a treatment tool, case management has been increasingly employed in a variety of fields for clients who have chronic, multiple problems; whose treatment and service needs are quite complex; and where the available social service delivery systems are highly bureaucratized and fragmented.

In theory, the linkages between treatment and other primary services needed by the client can best be accomplished when case management takes on both treatment and linking functions. This has been attempted in the mental health field with the continuity of care model for the community treatment of the chronically mentally ill. This model originated in Madison, Wisconsin, during the early 1970s (Test, Knoedler, & Allness, 1985), and it is often referred to as "assertive case management." The program's focus is proactive — to go out to help the client reenter the community by providing "*in vivo* treatment" in small client-staff ratios (Bond, Witheridge, Dincin, & Wasmer, 1991). Evaluations of case management approaches with the mentally ill are limited (Fisher, Landis, & Clark, 1988), but the results are generally positive (Bond, Miller, Krumwied, & Ward, 1988; Goering, Farkas, Wasylenkl, Lancee, & Ballantyne, 1988; Olfson, 1990; Rapp & Chamberlain, 1985; Stein & Test, 1980; Test, 1981).

The similarities between the chronic mentally ill and chronic drug users led to this demonstration project to assess the use of assertive case management in the drug abuse field. Both populations require treatment and a comprehensive network of continuing support to interrupt the relapse cycle and allow the client to remain stabilized in the community. Mental health clients and substance abusers in treatment both need a variety of rehabilitative services to treat the multiple areas of their lives affected by their disorders, and both groups are likely to have problems accessing and negotiating on their own to get the services they need.

Despite the promise of applying case management to drug users, there were also major differences in translating the case management model from the mental health field to treating chronic drug abusers. Most obvious was the expectation that, although drug use may be considered a chronic relapsing syndrome, drug users can and should improve. Eventually, they should cease to need case management assistance. As such, with the exception of programs for the dually diagnosed, case management applications in the drug field needed to have success goals within a certain time, rather than the continuous availability of help envisioned for the mentally ill. A second major difference was the difficulty of getting treatment staff to expand the concept of drug treatment beyond the confines of their offices and clinics. This was a difficult barrier to overcome in the mental health field. It was even more difficult in dealing with drug users where counselors felt clients were responsible for their situation and could only be helped if they sincerely wanted to be helped. There is some evidence that substance abusers are less likely to receive the array of rehabilitative services available to the chronically mentally ill (Solomon, 1986).

CASE MANAGEMENT AND DRUG-INVOLVED PRISON RELEASEES

With the many instrumental needs of prison releasees and the correctional mandate to monitor and supervise them in community settings, the use of assertive case management in drug treatment appeared to have great promise. There has been a general movement in corrections toward community-oriented programs (Chavaria, 1992). The most visible and enduring of these efforts is the Treatment Alternatives to Street Crime (TASC) program. Under TASC, community-based supervision is made available to drug-involved individuals who would otherwise burden the system with repeated drug-associated criminality (Inciardi & McBride, 1991). Yet, the TASC model does not directly provide treatment, nor does it highlight the advocacy function of assertive community treatment as was attempted in the Delaware ACT program.

OVERVIEW OF THE ACT MODEL FOR TREATMENT OF PRISON RELEASEES

The assertive/advocacy capacities of case management initiatives were explicitly incorporated into the treatment research demonstration project funded by the National Institute on Drug Abuse that targeted prison releasees. This effort applied an ACT model for parolees released from the Delaware prison system (Inciardi, Isenberg, Lockwood, Martin, & Scarpitti, 1992). Clients had a history of chronic drug use that placed them at increased risk for HIV infection. The program was developed by NorthEast Treatment Centers (NET) and the University of Delaware, with service delivery provided by NET. NET is a nonprofit social service organization headquartered in Philadelphia that operates over 25 programs in the Delaware Valley. NET provides a continuum of care for both substance abusers and troubled adolescents, including short- and long-term residential treatment, outpatient and intensive inpatient treatment, case management services, group homes, foster care, and in-home detention. NET also offers a variety of specialized programming for women, adult and juvenile criminal justice clients, and other high-risk populations. The ACT regimen integrated an intensive outpatient biopsychosocial model of drug treatment with the community support system approach to assertive case management.

The Delaware program provided drug treatment and case management in five stages, with the fifth and final stage occurring after approximately six months. The first stage involved intake evaluation and assessment; the second, intensive drug treatment, including group counseling, drug and AIDS education and discussion groups, individual counseling, and family therapy; the third stage included group counseling and life skills planning, with an emphasis on educational and vocational training; the fourth stage focused all facets of the program on the prevention of relapse; and the fifth stage, case management, was designed to support the client's transition into normal community life with instrumental support from case managers. More details on the theoretical rationale, planned stages of the program, and its implementation are available in an earlier volume in the "Contributions in Criminology and Penology" series (Martin, Isenberg, & Inciardi, 1993).

PROBLEMS IN IMPLEMENTING THE ACT PROGRAM WITH PRISON RELEASEES

A number of problems occurred in implementing the ACT program that limited the potential for successful outcomes. Although the program put into place all of the planned components of assertive case management (Martin, Isenberg, & Inciardi, 1993) and the program director felt all the pieces were in place at program implementation, subsequent process evaluation identified some significant implementation shortcomings (Scarpitti, Inciardi, & Martin, 1994), which are summarized here.

Since the ACT study was a federal research demonstration project, special protections for prisoners as research subjects were mandated. Among these was the requirement that participation in treatment be voluntary. As such, clients could not be offered treatment as either a means for early parole or as a condition of parole. This inability to require participation in treatment severely affected retention (Martin & Scarpitti, 1993). ACT clients were free to leave the program at any time; no form of coercion and only the benefits of treatment could be offered to induce prolonged participation.

In point of fact, some of the clients assigned to the program never made contact with it, others failed to connect fully and engage with it, and many others dropped out prematurely, particularly when they were no longer subject to work-release requirements. The data also indicate that voluntary participation did lead to differences between the ACT assignees and the comparison group. Comparing baseline data on the ACT assignees and the comparison group, those who did agree to participate in ACT were more likely to be African-American, more likely to be male, more likely to have been heavy drug users in the six months prior to prison, less likely to have a high school education, and less likely to have had prior treatment. To some extent these differences can be statistically controlled in the multivariate analyses, but they do point out the difficulty of establishing equivalent comparison groups in such naturalistic experiments.

Second, there was the matter of the random assignment itself (see Inciardi, Isenberg, Lockwood, Martin, & Scarpitti, 1992; Scarpitti, Inciadri, & Martin, 1994) in drug treatment research, particularly in environments where releasing high-risk people from prison by parole was politically unpopular. There aws a variety of ethical and practical considerations as well. For example, some inmates wishing to be in the ACT program were assigned to the control group; many inmates assigned to the ACT intervention were not those whom clinical personnel would normally classify as ready for treatment; and some of those assigned to the control group sought treatment on their own or were referred to separate programs by correctional officials and parole officers.

In practice, it can be argued that random assignment actually undermined any practical evaluation of the ACT treatment initiative. In the real world of drug abuse treatment, NET program staff members choose the clients they feel are ready for treatment and are appropriate for the particular modality. Random assignment does not allow for client selection. As a result, clients unready or unwilling for treatment were assigned to ACT, often undermining the effects of treatment and contaminating the treatment environment. Consequently, conclusions made about treatment conducted within the context of controlled research may not necessarily apply to treatment conducted with clinically selected and appropriate clients. Conversely, a bias in client selection by treatment staff creates circumstances where one is never sure if treatment success is more a function of client selection rather than the treatment experience itself. If one can select clients likely to succeed, the program is likely to appear successful.

A final problem was that the intervention was less assertive than planned. At the outset, ACT counselors and case managers were less willing to reach out to clients who, because of the random selection, were not actively seeking treatment (Scarpitti & Pan, 1992). Moreover, treatment and managerial personnel experienced more difficulty in dealing with drug users compared with the mentally ill or the homeless. It proved even more problematic for ACT case managers to work with prison releasees because of their fears of greater physical risk and, at times, their stated feelings that the clients were in great part responsible for their precarious situations. As one staff member stated: "It's different than working with people who really want help. These people, many of them are here involuntarily. And, to begin with, many of them are angry and hostile, many of them have a bad-ass don't-mess-with-me attitude, and it's intimidating." The staff found the target population difficult to work with because these clients were, in the words of one staff member, "the most slippery souls on the face of the planet."

OUTCOMES FROM THE ACT INTERVENTION

Earlier published analyses from six-month follow-up data (retention rate was 71 percent) found very limited support for the effectiveness of the ACT program (Inciardi, Martin, & Scarpitti, 1994; Martin & Inciardi, 1993b; Martin & Scarpitti, 1993; Scarpitti, Inciardi, & Martin, 1994). Using the incomplete data then available, we looked at four outcomes in logistic regression analyses: relapse to drug use, relapse to injection drugs, significant involvement in unprotected sex, and rearrest. There were no significant differences between the ACT assignees and the comparison group for each of these four outcomes when no other variables were taken into account. When the analyses controlled for the effects of other variables — age, gender, ethnicity, previous drug use, previous treatment history, previous arrest record, and length of time in treatment between baseline and the six-month follow-up — some small differences were observed. Without going into the analysis in detail, the results for program outcome can be summarized as follows: assignment to the ACT program was associated with small but significant reductions in the likelihood of relapsing to illegal drugs or injection drugs when contrasted with the comparison group, but there was a small but significant increase in the likelihood of rearrest among the ACT assignees relative to the comparison group. An examination of the relative risk ratios suggests that none of the effects of the ACT assignment are very significant. A summary of these analyses is presented in Table 8.1.

TABLE 8.1
Significant Predictors of Logistic Regression Outcomes for ACT Clients and Comparison Group

	Outcome Variables			
Independent Variables	**Relapse**	**Injection Drugs**	**Unprotected Sex**	**Rearrest**
ACT Group	–	–	NS	+
African-American	NS	NS	–	+
Female	NS	+	NS	NS
Age	–	+	NS	–
Previous Arrests	+	+	NS	+
Drug Use Before Prison	+	+	NS	+
Past Drug Treatment	NS	NS	NS	NS
Treatment since Prison	–	NS	NS	NS

Note: A minus (–) indicates a significant negative effect, a plus (+) indicates a significant positive effect, and NS indicates that the effect is not significant ($p < .10$).

One explanation for the lack of program effect is evident when we compare mean days of treatment for the ACT assignees and the comparison group between baseline and follow-up. The ACT assignees have more days in treatment (mean = 31.2 days) compared to the comparison (mean = 22.7 days) group, but this difference is only marginally significant ($p < .10$). It appears that any meaningful comparison of the two groups and any tacit assessment of ACT effectiveness using the entire database is not possible.

Analyses with the 18-month follow-up data are still in progress; however, the preliminary data available from 18 months indicate no large changes from what the 6-month data revealed. There is a nonsignificant reduction in drug use and, now, a nonsignificant reduction in rearrest at 18 months among the ACT assignees, relative to the comparison group. The only significant reduction among the ACT clients is for cocaine use, and it is modest, at the .05 level of significance.

ACT CLIENTS' EVALUATION OF THE PROGRAM

A representative group of 15 ACT clients who participated in the ACT program for a short period (less than two weeks), medium period (one to two months) and long period (five months or more) were interviewed about their experiences with ACT. These interviews followed a structure but were essentially open-ended. Interviews were tape recorded and transcribed.

In general, the clients interviewed found ACT helpful to them, even those clients who had not participated in the program very long. Only 1 of the 15 reported ACT was "not helpful." One client said ACT was "not really harsh . . . its not . . . too light, you know, its just right." Another client felt that "most of it was all in all, it was pretty good," and another said that ACT "really helped me. It helped a lot." The most helpful thing derived from ACT, for still another client, was becoming less impulsive and thinking before acting; ACT "mellowed him out." One client who stayed with the program found ACT to be helpful in three ways: in identifying his addiction; in realizing that relapses do not have to be disastrous; and in dealing with life in general (that is, his parents' deaths). One person who had attended several treatment programs prior to ACT thought ACT was the most helpful of all of the programs.

Program Strengths

In describing ACT, clients provided a range of responses. For some, the program helped them to decide how to live their lives, in addition to increasing motivation, insight, and awareness to remain drug-free and not recidivate. Clients said ACT accomplished this through the talking, discussions, and projects. Another client said that the program helped one better her conditions, taught about drugs, and allowed clients to "just get into" themselves while simultaneously helping others by talking about oneself and one's addiction. Another person said ACT was "very educational . . . it was for real . . . you could be yourself, voice your opinions, your thoughts, your feelings. There was a sense of being cared for." One client described the program as a combination of therapy and education about drugs that had an extensive carry-over with clients after they left ACT.

ACT was useful in different ways to different clients. The program was most helpful to some in dealing with their substance abuse problems through its straightforward approach to treatment without medication. For others, ACT helped them deal with their attitudes, primarily through group sessions. Others received assistance with family relationships through ACT. Still others were most helped with employment, housing, and medical needs. Clients appreciated the variety of services and the fact that different services could be emphasized depending upon their particular needs.

Program Weaknesses

A few clients indicated that the program was not altogether helpful. One client reported that ACT made him into a better manipulator: he learned to manipulate small quantities of time by going home after he left ACT in the afternoons and before returning to the work-release center. One client was critical of the urine screenings. According to him, "I partied while I was in there, and never got caught . . . they check you for pot, and speed, and the normal piss test. They never check you for booze!" Another client cited the program format and clientele as least helpful. He thought he needed a different treatment setting (for example, a residential therapeutic community) with more positive clients who had already started their recoveries. He also felt that the staff undermined employment efforts because they did not approve of the jobs clients obtained ("They want you at McDonalds, you want to make the money to pay the bills").

Clients disliked the educational focus of the program, saying it involved too much discussion and describing it "like sitting in a classroom all day, you know, like going to school." Another complaint was that clients were not transitioned to a new phase when the staff said they would be. Another client said ACT needed to retain its staff better, because turnover was problematic for clients in the program. For those who left or graduated and considered returning, if their counselor was no longer there, it discouraged them from returning for assistance.

One factor that may have affected clients' willingness to share in groups was confidentiality, particularly for clients living at the work-release facility. According to one person, when ACT clients from work-release relapsed, as a means of not returning to prison they sometimes informed on others, based on information heard in group sessions. This hindered the treatment of some clients because, according to this respondent, "You [were] supposed to have confidentiality . . . there was a few of them, that oh man . . . you wouldn't say nothing, cause you know — it'd get back to the guards at the Plummer House, and next thing you know, they'd have you — pulling urines on you."

Changes Recommended

Clients made a number of suggestions about how they would change or redesign the program. Some recommendations focused on increasing the intensity of the program. One interviewee thought the program should be tougher on clients, although "staff did all they could do." Another recommended that the length of treatment before graduation be increased. Recommended changes also centered on making the program more interesting. Suggestions included adding components that hold clients' interest, such as showing films about substance abuse and its effects on families, bringing in successful recovering people to talk, or allowing clients to help other addicts. According to one client, the program needed to incorporate "Some type of opportunity, you know, something that will hold a person's interest, and make them want to help themselves." Another recommendation was to take time, when clients first enter the program, to match them with case managers to facilitate good relationships between them.

Other suggested changes revolved around the nature of the sessions offered. Clients suggested that individual counseling sessions occur more frequently and that the first sessions consist mostly of one-on-ones until they were more comfortable discussing their pasts. Clients stated that incarcerated persons needed individual counseling prior to entry into treatment so they could decide if they wanted to attend, begin to deal with themselves to trust people, and start preparing for the transition back into society. Another suggestion was to introduce the job component earlier in treatment while concurrently providing assistance with budgeting income.

Overall, despite a number of individual complaints, the clients had more positive than negative things to say about the ACT program. From the clients' viewpoint, it would appear that the putative benefits of the ACT program were not salient to clients' immediate needs and desires. Or, as one client clearly put it: "Gettin' out of prison and then goin' into a treatment thing like this isn't something I would do unless someone made me. I was inside [in prison] for a long time, and I have too much catchin' up to do. I gotta be out here and breathin' a while, with my kids, my friends, my world. I just couldn't be doin' your program. I just couldn't."

ACT STAFF EVALUATIONS OF THE PROGRAM

All of the current and several of the former ACT staff employed by NET were interviewed after the completion of the treatment intervention. As with the client group, these interviews were semistructured, eliciting open-ended responses, and they were tape recorded and transcribed.

If success for the ACT program was measured by the number of drug-free people, staff felt that ACT was not successful, with one person considering ACT to be an "abysmal failure." By other standards, however, the staff assessed ACT as successful. On the basis of spreading information about the availability of treatment, as well as being "a step in the right direction," ACT was considered successful. In providing a learning experience for clients regarding treatment modalities, ACT had some long-term impact on clients. In giving birth to other, more focused, outpatient treatment programs at NET that use components of assertive case management, ACT was also a success.

The primary reasons cited by staff to explain why more clients did not complete the program included: continued substance use, lack of attendance at ACT, and, in particular, the client selection process, which resulted in a preponderance of clients not interested in treatment. Some ACT staff members felt that the clients selected for the program were the "hardest of the hard." These clients were not interested in treatment but were interested in the $50 incentive received for completing the interviews and tests requested by the researchers. If clients who wanted help had been selected for treatment, the staff felt that the program could have been more successful. In addition, if more time had been available for work with clients in prison greater success may have been achieved in retaining clients.

The goals of the program were met in the relatively small number of cases with which the program kept contact. These goals included: reduced drug use, risk of HIV infection, and recidivism rates; increased educational levels, vocational marketability, and trainability; and helping clients become self-sustaining. According to one staff person, "I don't think we were able to work with most of the people long enough toward those goals to attain any level of success, but the ones we did I think we were successful in."

Program Strengths

The staff cited a variety of strengths of the ACT program. The assertiveness of the program, the ability to go into the community to look for clients, and the emphasis on being a community-based rather than an office-based program were specified by several staff members as program strengths. The ability to meet clients in prison to build rapport, the continuity in treatment from prison to the streets, and providing hope and the opportunity for treatment the clients would not have received otherwise were other strengths indicated by the ACT staff. The staff itself, with its talents and strengths, support for the population, and team staffing approach were considered strengths of the program. Other program strengths cited by staff members included: the flexibility to discard ineffective parts of the program and retain effective elements; the availability of material resources with which to aid clients; the intensive outpatient component; the HIV education element with its prevention and risk-reduction components; and the attempt to "look at individualized treatment."

Program Weaknesses

The staff members felt that the weaknesses overshadowed the strengths in the ACT program. Some staff were less willing than others to enter the community in search of clients or to see them in prisons. These staff made the program too facility-based, and too little contact occurred between case managers and incarcerated clients. Some staff members' lack of experience dealing with criminal justice clients was also cited as a liability, as was having the same counselor provide both the assertiveness component and the intensive outpatient treatment. The lack of diversity among staff members was also mentioned as a program weakness. The inability to motivate clients to be interested in treatment was perhaps the biggest program frustration. This frustration was accentuated by the initial assumption of support from the probation/parole department and the subsequent weak relationship with parole officers.

Staff felt that clients viewed ACT as another component of the criminal justice system. Most clients had been incarcerated many times and were "system-wise" and abused. As a result, the staff had difficulty developing trust with the clients, which led to problems with them in treatment. These clients did not necessarily respond well when ACT staff attempted to locate them in the community, particularly when they did so with the assistance of the client's parole officer.

Changes Recommended

The staff recommended changes to the overall design of ACT that they felt would make future, similar programs more successful. Several of these recommended changes have already been implemented by NET in its programming.

1. More contact. More contact between the case manager and clients while clients are incarcerated was suggested. More contact would lead to strong

initial rapport and would allow the development of treatment plans before clients' release from prison. It was recommended that case managers perform the intake evaluations and testing of clients assigned to them, rather than having a special intake worker.

2. Get the appropriate clients. A screening system to determine readiness for treatment, more information provided to clients before participation in the program, and elimination of the random selection process and the monetary incentive for participation in treatment were additional changes suggested. Clients not interested in treatment should be discharged from the program more quickly than they were in the ACT program.
3. Contacts with the criminal justice system. Changes were suggested in the area of relations with parole officers. It was recommended that parole officers be contacted as soon as clients are released from prison. Another staff member suggested improved relationships with parole officers by providing officers with greater knowledge and understanding of the program while another recommended obtaining written support for compulsory treatment from the parole officers.
4. Programmatic changes. The staff recommended several ways to improve the ACT program design. These included: greater attention to adjustment [to being free] issues; providing five days of treatment per week instead of three; greater staff diversity; more communication between case managers and management; clients separate from clients from other NET programs; smaller caseloads for case managers as the size of the area they cover increases; and greater involvement with clients' families to provide a more team approach to treatment.

DISCUSSION

In evaluating the overall impact and lessons to be learned from the Delaware ACT program, four questions need to be addressed: Were the clients appropriate for the intervention? How and with whom should the program have been assertive? Did the innovation of combining treatment and case manager roles in one counselor work? What is the potential role of compulsory treatment for criminal justice clients?

Overall, the ACT staff felt that, for treatment to be effective, clients must be ready for treatment or want treatment. The ACT clients, in general, were not interested or personally invested in treatment, factors that several ACT staff cited as important for treatment. While still in prison, clients appeared to be interested and motivated to be in the ACT program. Following release, however, the number of clients still interested in the program declined markedly, as evidenced by the many clients who avoided contact with ACT once they got out of prison. Staff estimated that only 5–25 percent of clients who originally agreed to participate in ACT were ready for treatment. While the ACT model itself was considered "fine," one staff member stated that, "I don't feel like we've made a big dent in the substance abuse problems by the approach that we've taken."

Ironically, many of those who stayed with the ACT program were those most in need of help, often requiring assistance that went beyond even an intensive day treatment program. Many of these clients who remained with ACT did not do so for treatment per se; rather, clients were interested in other components ACT offered, such as living skills and referrals to job training. According to one staff person, "We have people that their habilitation was totally dysfunctional, so I have no place to take them back to. What I have to do is start teaching them social skills from the beginning." Staff felt that the ACT clients lacked responsibility, understanding, and skills that most people take for granted. In sum, the ACT program never successfully engaged many assignees who were unready for and even hostile toward treatment, and those they did engage often were in need of more services and help than could be provided in a three-times-a-week outpatient program.

Second, as noted earlier in the chapter, staff were at first unwilling to take an assertive role in engaging the clients in treatment. When requested to be more assertive by research staff, based on the preliminary process analysis findings, the ACT treatment staff did take a more active role with clients. As one staffer put it, "The clients that we were working with were not real responsive to what we were trying to do. We chased them more than worked with them. . . . We chased them on paper, we chased them by phone, we went out and looked for them." This was a necessary step but only captured part of what was intended in ACT. The model called for assertiveness to be directed mostly toward accessing needed services for the client. This was difficult for counselors to do with their seemingly ungrateful clients. According to another ACT staff member, "Many of them — it didn't matter what you did for them . . . they didn't care — they weren't at a point where they wanted to do something themselves." Another said, "We would literally drag them to treatment. . . . I've come to think that no matter how hard a counselor works to help somebody, if that person doesn't have it within themselves that they want that help, and they're willing to work at least as much as the counselor, it's not going to help."

The notion of assertiveness led to a fundamental conflict with what many clinicians believe about treatment: the necessity of avoiding enabling the client. With the assertiveness of the program, and the variety of services offered, it was difficult to determine the boundaries between enabling and helping. Because clients remained in the program for an extended period of time and were pursued by the case managers as part of the ACT program, the program model itself led staff to enable clients. According to one staff member, "Sometimes we did too much, we gave too much, we enabled clients to continue in their addiction because we didn't cut them off fast enough. . . . It felt like sometimes we weren't doing the best thing for the client, but we were doing what we were supposed to do for the ACT project."

Third, the study found that combining assertive case management with intensive outpatient treatment was difficult to implement. Contrary to initial expectations, it proved more problematic than helpful to combine the roles of treatment counselor and case manager in one person. Rather than getting the best of both positions in one person working with the client, the relative strengths and biases of the counselor toward treatment or case management seemed to produce a synthesis where neither the treatment needs nor case management needs of the client were best served. According to one staff member, "You can't both be out in the community and man an intensive outpatient program with the same staff." Another staff member felt that the assertive case management and intensive outpatient treatment components were complementary functions but that they should have been performed separately and not by the same person as in the ACT program. The combination of roles produced a program that was too generic and worked against tailoring an individual treatment and case management regimen for clients.

Finally, the federal limitations on the ability to require or even actively encourage participation in ACT precluded an ideal test of the intervention. The possibility of treatment (with appointments, obligations, and regulations), all voluntary, and with no effective carrot or stick to encourage participation, simply did not appeal to most parolees upon release from prison. Most offenders, upon release from prison, are more interested in resuming their lives and enjoying their freedom than in voluntarily participating in an intensive treatment program with, at best, a delayed and amorphous benefit. Clients felt they had already "done their time." In the words of one staff member: "I wouldn't see it as that difficult a population if we had some of the supports we counted on going in. . . . I still believe that ACT would be effective with this population if we had the leverage that we thought we would have . . . but at some point you have to have a wall to back them against, and there was no wall. . . . These people actively avoid being involved with anything. . . . The better they are at being fugitives, the more successful they are in that counterculture or that subculture."

Counselors agreed that the backing of the criminal justice system was necessary to compel clients into treatment. Although staff believed that clients must be motivated for treatment to work, that motivation initially could come from the criminal justice system. According to one counselor: "Although motivation starts out as external, the goal is to get people to internalize that motivation. Without an external force making sure they attend when first released from prison, there is little that can be done to help clients internalize the motivation to stay in treatment and to stay clean." According to another staff person, forced treatment "may be good in the sense that just being there, after a while you end up behaving in a certain way and not even intending to behave that way only because you've been exposed to it." Still, even the threat of probation and parole officers was not sufficient to compel many clients into treatment. According to one staffer, "Consequences meant nothing to those clients. If they missed group and you sent a letter to their probation officer which jeopardized their probation, they didn't care. . . . Nothing seemed to faze them, as opposed to clients who were not involved in the criminal justice system."

From both a research and a treatment perspective, this points to the need to develop means to retain criminal justice clients in treatment, even if it means making clear to clients that doing treatment is part of doing time. One consensual finding from treatment research is the longer a client stays in treatment, the better the outcome in terms of decline in drug use and criminality (Anglin & Hser, 1990). One of the few advantages of dealing with criminal justice clients is the potential to coerce treatment. Studies consistently demonstrate that success in treatment is a function of length of stay (Collins & Allison, 1983) and that those coerced into treatment do at least as well as voluntary commitments (Hubbard et al., 1989; Leukefeld & Tims, 1990).

The population targeted for ACT was a difficult group to work with. However, as a treatment modality, staff felt that ACT was feasible for a criminal justice population. This was because "If you show them that you're not going to give up on them, that they are worth working with, the clients are going to realize 'Hey, I think you care.' I don't think you can pacify that population and sit back and wait for them to come see you. They're not going to do it."

It is possible that under better conditions than those encountered with ACT, case management can encourage substance abusers to stay in treatment and to reach treatment goals (Kofoed, Tolson, Atkinson, Toth, & Turner, 1986). If case management is combined with legal sanctions to enforce participation and monitoring (such as parole and probation stipulations), the potential to retain prison releasees in treatment and to obtain services for them will be greatly increased. Despite the limitations of being unable to mandate or encourage participation by clients in the full Delaware ACT program, the project did modestly help reduce client injection drug use and some other drug use within a particularly difficult treatment population — criminal justice clients under parole supervision. However, these limited successes do not justify the use of an intensive outpatient program as a primary care mechanism for prison releasees. Rather the small quantitative improvements measured and the reports from both staff and clients lend support to the conclusion drawn by Simpson, Savage, and Lloyd (1979) some years ago: outpatient case management is not the best alternative for the "primary" treatment of prison releasees with extensive histories of substance abuse.

Data from this study and from other projects suggest that drug-involved offenders are a highly troubled population (Inciardi & Martin, 1993; Leukefeld & Tims, 1992). There is evidence that many of the drug offenders in U.S. jails and prisons are victims of child abuse (Glantz & Pickins, 1992; Levy & Rutter, 1992; Roth, 1991; Wallace, 1991, 1992) and/or have cognitive problems, psychological dysfunction, or deficits in educational and employment skills (Blume, 1989; Christie et al., 1988; Clark & Zwerben, 1989; Cloninger & Guze, 1970). As such, drug abuse may be a response to a series of social and psychological disturbances.

Treatment that does not address the root causes may be ineffective. Long-term residential treatment, rather than case management, would appear to be the more appropriate approach for these clients. Assertive case management holds better promise as an aftercare approach for drug involved offenders following more intensive and extensive primary treatment.

REFERENCES

Anglin, M. D., & Hser, Y. (1990). Treatment of drug abuse. In M. Tonry & J. Q. Wilson (Eds.), *Drugs and crime* (pp. 393–460). Chicago: University of Chicago Press.

Bagarozzi, D. A., & Pollane, L. P. (1984). Case management in mental health. *Health and Social Work, 9*, 201–211.

Blume, S. (1989, April–June). Dual diagnosis: Psychoactive substance abuse and personality disorders. *Journal of Psychoactive Drugs, 21*, 135–138.

Bond, G. R., Miller, L. D., Krumwied, R. D., & Ward, R. S. (1988). Assertive case management in three CMCHs: A controlled study. *Hospital and Community Psychiatry, 39*, 411–418.

Bond, G. R., Witheridge, T. F., Dincin, J., & Wasmer, D. (1991). Assertive community treatment: Correcting some misconceptions. *American Journal of Community Psychology, 19*, 41–51.

Chavaria, F. R. (1992, March). Successful drug treatment in a criminal justice setting: A case study. *Federal Probation*, 48–52.

Christie, K. A., Burke, J. D., Regier, D. A., Rae, D. S., Boyd, J. H., & Locke, B. Z. (1988, August). Epidemiologic evidence for early onset of mental disorders and higher risk of drug abuse in young adults. *American Journal of Psychiatry, 145*, 971–975.

Clark, H. W., & Zwerben, J. E. (1989, April–June). Legal vulnerabilities in the treatment of chemically dependent dual diagnosis patients. *Journal of Psychoactive Drugs, 21*, 251–258.

Cloninger, R., & Guze, S. B. (1970). Psychiatric illness and female criminality: The role of sociopathy and hysteria in antisocial women. *American Journal of Psychiatry, 127*, 79–87.

Collins, J. J., & Allison, M. (1983). Legal coercion and retention in drug abuse treatment. *Hospital and Community Psychiatry, 34,* 1145–1149.

Fisher, G., Landis, D., & Clark, K. (1988). Case management service provision and client change. *Community Mental Health Journal, 24,* 134–142.

Glantz, M., & Pickins, R. (Eds.). (1992). *Vulnerability to drug abuse,* Washington, DC: American Psychological Association.

Goering, P. N., Farkas, M., Wasylenkl, D. A., Lancee, W. J., & Ballantyne, P. (1988). Improved functioning for case management clients. *Psychosocial Rehabilitation Journal, 12,* 3–17.

Graham, K., & Birchmore-Timney, C. (1990). Case management in addictions treatment. *Journal of Substance Abuse Treatment, 7,* 181–188.

Hubbard, R. L., Marsden, M. E., Rachal, J. V., Harwood, H. J., Cavanaugh, E. R., & Ginzburg, H. M. (1989). *Drug abuse treatment: A national study of effectiveness.* Chapel Hill: University of North Carolina Press.

Inciardi, J. A., Isenberg, H., Lockwood, D., Martin, S. S., & Scarpitti, F. R. (1992). Assertive community treatment with a parolee population: An extension of case management. In R. Ashery (Ed.), *Case Management in Drug Abuse Treatment* (pp. 350–367). Rockville, MD: National Institute on Drug Abuse.

Inciardi, J. A., & Martin, S. S. (1993). Drug abuse treatment in criminal justice settings. *The Journal of Drug Issues, 23,* 1–6.

Inciardi, J. A., Martin, S. S., & Scarpitti, F. R. (1994). The appropriateness of assertive case management for drug-involved prison releasees. *The Journal of Case Management, 3,* 145–149.

Inciardi, J. A., & McBride, D. C. (1991). *Treatment alternatives to street crime (TASC): History, experiences, and issues.* Rockville, MD: National Institute on Drug Abuse.

Kofoed, L., Tolson, R., Atkinson, R., Toth, R., & Turner, J. (1986). Outpatient treatment of patients with substance abuse and coexisting psychiatric disorders. *American Journal of Psychiatry, 143,* 867–872.

Leukefeld, C. G., & Tims, F. M. (1992). The challenge of drug abuse treatment in prisons and jails. In C. G. Leukefeld & F. W. Tims (Eds.), *Drug abuse treatment in prison and jails* (pp. 1–7). Rockville, MD: National Institute on Drug Abuse.

Leukefeld, C. G., & Tims, F. M. (1990). Compulsory treatment for drug abuse. *International Journal of the Addictions, 25,* 621–640.

Levy, S. J., & Rutter, E. (1992). *Children of drug abusers.* New York: Lexington Books.

Martin, S. S., & Gossweiler, R. S. (1993, March). *Alcohol use and treatment success among injection drug users.* Paper presented at the annual meeting of the Eastern Sociological Society, Boston, Massachusetts.

Martin S. S., & Inciardi, J. A. (1993a). Case management approaches for criminal justice clients. In J. A. Inciardi (Ed.), *Drug treatment and criminal justice* (pp. 81–96). Newbury Park, CA: Sage.

Martin S. S., & Inciardi, J. A. (1993b). A case management treatment program for drug involved prison releasees. *The Prison Journal, 73,* 319–331.

Martin, S. S., Isenberg, H., & Inciardi, J. A. (1993). Assertive community treatment (ACT): Integrating intensive drug treatment with aggressive case management for hard to reach populations. In J. A. Inciardi, F. M. Tims, & B. W. Fletcher (Eds.), *Innovative approaches in the treatment of drug abuse: Program models and strategies* (pp. 97–108). Westport, CT: Greenwood Press.

Martin, S. S., & Scarpitti, F. R. (1993). An intensive case management approach for paroled IV drug users. *Journal of Drug Issues, 23,* 43–59.

Mejta, C. L., Bokos, P. J, Mickenberg, J. H., Maslar, E. M., Hasson, A. L., Gill, V., O'Keefe, Z., Martin, S. S., Isenberg, H., Inciardi, J. A., Lockwood, D., Rapp, R. C., Siegal, H. A., Fisher, J. H., & Wagner, J. H. (1994). Approaches to case management with substance abusing populations. In J. A. Lewis (Ed.), *Addictions: Concepts and strategies for treatment* (pp. 301–319). Gaithersburg, MD: Aspen Publishers.

Olfson, M. (1990). Assertive community treatment: An evaluation of the experimental evidence. *Hospital and Community Psychiatry, 41,* 634–641.

Rapp, C. A., & Chamberlain, R. (1985). Case management services for the chronically mentally ill. *Social Work, 30,* 417–422.

Roth, P. (Ed.). (1991). *Alcohol and drugs are women's issues.* Metuchen, NJ: Women's Action Alliance.

Scarpitti, F. R., Inciardi, J. A., & Martin, S. S. (1994). Assertive community treatment: Obstacles to implementation. In B. W. Fletcher, J. A. Inciardi, & A. M. Horton (Eds.), *Drug abuse treatment: The implementation of innovative approaches* (pp. 115–129). Westport, CT: Greenwood Press.

Scarpitti, F. R., & Pan, H. (1992). *Preliminary report: Process evaluation of the ACT program.* Unpublished paper. Newark, DE: Center for Drug and Alcohol Studies.

Simpson, D. D., Savage, J., & Lloyd, M. R. (1979). Follow-up evaluation of treatment of drug abuse during 1969 to 1972. *Archives of General Psychiatry, 36,* 772–780.

Solomon, P. (1986). Receipt of aftercare services by problem types: Psychiatric, psychiatric/substance abuse and substance abuse. *Psychiatric Quarterly, 58,* 180–188.

Stein, L. I., & Test, M. A. (1980). Alternative to mental hospital treatment. *Archives of General Psychiatry, 37,* 392–412.

Test, M. A. (1981). Effective community treatment of the chronically mentally ill: What is necessary? *Journal of Social Issues, 37,* 71–86.

Test, M. A., Knoedler, W. H., & Allness, D. J. (1985). The long-term treatment of young schizophrenics in a community support program. In L. I. Stein & M. A. Test (Eds.), *Training in community living — ten years later* (pp. 17–27). San Francisco: Jossey-Bass.

Wallace, B. C. (1991). *Crack cocaine: A practical treatment approach for the chemically dependent.* New York: Brunner/Mazel.

Wallace, B. C. (Ed.). (1992). *The chemically dependent: Phases of treatment and recovery.* New York: Brunner/Mazel.

9

Treatment Induction and Case Management: Two Promising Drug Treatment Enhancements

Harvey A. Siegal, Richard C. Rapp, James H. Fisher, Phyllis A. Cole, and Joseph H. Wagner

Dropping out of treatment and noncompliance with therapeutic activities are two persistent problems affecting the treatment of drug abusers. For example, a published report from a short-term (two-week) drug rehabilitation and detoxification program offered by a Veterans Affairs Medical Center described a dropout rate routinely ranging between 50 and 70 percent (Craig, 1985). Regarding longer term treatment modalities, such as methadone maintenance and therapeutic communities, the findings are even less optimistic. A study of heroin addicts randomly assigned to either of these modalities (Bale et al., 1980) found that therapeutic communities retained only 39 percent of those initiating treatment, while a scant 31 percent were retained by the methadone program. Dropping out or quitting treatment seems to occur rapidly as well. A classic research study of a large treatment database found that many — almost one-third — quit before their first month and more than one-half left within 90 days (Joe & Simpson, 1975). Clearly, for drug abuse treatment to have any effect at all, patients need to be able to receive the service.

In 1989, using resources provided by the National Institute on Drug Abuse, Wright State University's Substance Abuse Intervention Programs initiated the Enhanced Treatment Project (ETP). The project was designed to address the thorny issues of quitting and longer term therapeutic noncompliance by augmenting a conventional, drug-free treatment program. The program, known as the Polysubstance Rehabilitation Program (PRP) is operated by the Department of Veterans Affairs Medical Center at Dayton, Ohio. PRP was selected as a performance site because of the strong relationship between the Wright State University School of Medicine and the medical center. Of great interest as well was that most of PRP's drug abusing patients were primarily crack cocaine abusers. This population of drug abusers is one about which little is known and one that has been particularly difficult to retain in treatment and successfully manage.

The planned treatment enhancements were designed to address early-stage quitting and noncompliance with program activities. To address the former, we looked to role induction, believing that if drug abusers would recognize that they, indeed, have a problem, and then learn that there were certain definitions, behaviors, and rewards associated with being a patient in a drug treatment program, they would be less likely to drop out of treatment, than those drug abusers simply thrust into treatment. The second issue of longer term noncompliance would be addressed through the implementation of an innovative case management modality. Our hypothesis was that by offering clients case management activities, it would help keep them focused on the substance abuse treatment regimen they were receiving.

In the next section we will briefly describe these treatment enhancements. Some of our preliminary observations concerning their efficacy follow. Let us stipulate, however, that because of the project's late start — because of the 1990–91 Persian Gulf conflict and the effect this had on activities at many of the nation's VA hospitals — we are still admitting research subjects and just beginning the analysis of our efficacy data. The data to date are very encouraging. We will conclude with a brief discussion of the implications of these findings and their relevance to future substance abuse services research.

PROJECT ENHANCEMENTS

A crucial task of substance abuse treatment involves introducing patients to the process, content, and culture of treatment. To succeed, a supportive environment must allow patients to start the process of self-diagnosis, observe others engaging in their own self-assessment, and begin considering a lifestyle free of alcohol and other drugs. Such an environment exists in the form of the Weekend Intervention Program.

The Weekend Intervention Program

The Weekend Intervention Program (WIP) is an intensive, three-day residential education/intervention program based on substance abuse counseling using a cognitive-behavioral model. Developed nearly 15 years ago as an interdisciplinary effort linking the Dayton area's courts and substance abuse treatment agencies, the WIP has served as a therapeutic response to the community's concerns about the problems of drug- and alcohol-impaired driving. WIP participants, most of whom are convicted of driving under the influence (DUI), are encouraged to explore their own relationship with alcohol and drugs. A comprehensive evaluation of the individual is completed by WIP staff and a recommendation for treatment is given to each client and to the referring court.

Operating as a brief, intensive, residential program, WIP can deliver its educational lectures and group counseling activities with greater intensity than would be found in a conventional treatment program. Through its supportive environment and gentle educational confrontation, WIP clients acknowledge their own problematic relationship with drugs and alcohol. These elements combine to create an experience that leads to a positive perception of treatment.

The Strengths Perspective of Case Management

While WIP may be an effective means of preparing patients for the early phases of treatment, the benefits would be, at best, short-lived. We hypothesized that additional services would be useful in improving longer term treatment. Such services could help keep the patient focused on therapeutic activities by addressing the personal, social, and environmental problems that continue to affect the substance abuser, even in treatment. A strengths-based approach to case management was chosen as an enhancement to complement the treatment induction accomplished by WIP.

The model of case management used in this demonstration project is based on a strengths approach developed by Rapp and Chamberlain (1985). In its original application, the Strengths Perspective of Case Management/Advocacy was employed to assist persons with mental illness in making the transition from institutionalized care to independent living. The model is predicated on five principles, two of which allow individuals direct control over their search for crucial resources and assisting individuals in using their strengths and assets to acquire those resources. This view of working with patients is in opposition to problem-oriented models based on an individual's perceived pathologies, problems, or deficits. These problem-oriented perspectives have dominated substance abuse programming.

Using the principles inherent in the Strengths Perspective, the project's case managers worked with the patient in reestablishing an awareness of internal resources, such as intelligence, confidence, and problem-solving skills, by arranging for contact between the patient and external resources and by serving as an advocate to assist the patient in acquiring needed services. The patient actively directed the intervention, with the case manager serving in the role of "traveling companion, not a travel agent" (Deitchman, 1980).

The case managers for this project received a month-long training program under the direction of the project staff. Three case managers were employed and their caseloads were kept to no more than 15 patients at any time to permit them to deliver services with the intensity necessary to accomplish their objectives.

RESULTS OF INTERVENTION

A four-group, random-assigned design was used to evaluate the efficacy of the two enhancements on treatment outcome. Extensive baseline data was collected on each participant and then data relevant to the specific program enhancement was obtained. Two types of data will be presented. First, we will discuss process data, emphasizing specific activities of the WIP and the Strengths Perspective of Case Management, and client attitudes about these interventions. Second, a summary of the attitudinal and behavioral changes exhibited by clients over a six-month period following the initiation of treatment will be presented. Analyses will highlight differences that appear to be attributable to receiving the enhanced treatment services, either WIP alone, strengths-based case management alone, or WIP and case management together. The results are based upon interviews collected from 363 clients at the initiation of treatment and again six months later. This represents approximately 85 percent of all clients who were eligible for follow-up during this period. Fifteen percent of eligible clients could not be located during their follow-up window (one month pre- and one month post-entry into treatment). Preliminary analysis of the intake data does not indicate significant differences for the persons lost to attrition.

Process Data — Weekend Intervention Program and Strengths Perspective

Process data were gathered from the WIP at four stages: at the beginning of the weekend, at the end of the weekend, a few days after returning to the medical center and six months later. Self-administered instruments (for example, the Michigan Alcoholism Screening Test) were employed to assess client involvement with alcohol and drugs as well as self-appraisal of their life circumstances. During the weekend, counselors assessed clients with respect to their use of alcohol and drugs through individual and group sessions. Not surprisingly, most ETP clients were identified as exhibiting moderate or severe dependence on drugs or alcohol and as experiencing generally difficult life circumstances. Psychological problems were noted in a minority of cases, while social and occupational problems were noted for a majority.

Client attitudes about WIP were generally very positive. Most clients responded that they participated actively in group discussions, often encouraging each other to reexamine their lives. Clients reported that they believed their counselors were empathetic listeners, were interested in helping them, and were knowledgeable in the field. Clients often noted that group sessions and a lecture on the medical effects of alcohol and drug abuse were especially beneficial. Criticisms were rare and fell into a few observable patterns focusing on the food and lodging provided. More ETP clients focused their criticisms toward other clients who attended WIP as a result of a DUI conviction, observing that DUI clients would continue to deny having a drug or alcohol problem, even when one existed.

Process data were collected for case-managed clients as well. These data were collected continuously during the client's participation in case management activities and assessed the actual implementation of strengths-based case management and its role in improving treatment. Specifically, areas examined included:

client self-evaluation of functioning, especially during the past year;

goal-setting activities in various life domains; and

client-perceived, beneficial aspects of case management.

Client Self-evaluation

Of all inpatient clients assigned to case management (as the sole treatment enhancement or in combination with the WIP), more than 90 percent engaged in a first contact with case managers. A somewhat lower percentage (67 percent) of outpatients began this process. During the first meeting with a case manager, clients are asked to rate themselves (initial rating) in each of nine life domains: life skills, finance, leisure, relationships, living arrangements, occupation and education, health, internal resources, and recovery. Specific behavioral anchors, which define functioning on a nine-point scale in each of the life domains, comprise the ETP Progress Evaluation Scales.

Comparisons of the two client rating points for all clients reveal that, as a group, clients view themselves as functioning at a higher level in all life domains after completion of the strengths-based assessment. Most notably, the "relationship" life domain showed the effects of assisting clients in examining the constructive aspects of a particular area of their life. After initially rating themselves as "seldom able to get along with others without quarreling," many clients in effect, created an inventory of abilities in this area. This inventory would seem to provide a more hopeful foundation from which clients can address their current substance abuse problems. The significance of identifying and reinforcing strengths and assets in a disease-oriented treatment environment continues to be an area of considerable interest.

Goal-setting Activities

Numerical goal ratings are translated into specific plans through use of the ETP Case Management Plan. The first step in identifying goals is the creation of broad goal statements. By definition, these goal statements are sweeping and never really fully attainable. Objectives are then identified that are measurable and that lead individuals toward completion of their goals. Strategies, which are specific steps that lead to accomplishment of an objective, are then created. The establishment of target and review dates prompt regular review of the progress made toward completion of specific objectives and strategies and, hence, the client's overall goal.

The client-driven nature of the Strengths Perspective is demonstrated by an examination of case management plans created by clients and case managers. Fully two-thirds (66.8 percent) of the 868 objectives created across the nine life domains were completed, as were 66.1 percent of the strategies. Goals relating to tangible needs are most frequently identified for work by clients. These goals are included in life domains including living arrangements (the life domain most often pursued by clients), employment and education, and recovery.

Beneficial Aspects of Case Management

Six months after entry into the project all clients were asked to respond to the open-ended question: What was the single most helpful topic that you worked on with your substance abuse counselor (and, if applicable, your case manager)? Of those clients who had case managers, 16 percent responded that setting goals was the single most helpful topic on which they worked with case managers. In contrast, 1 percent of clients responded that setting goals was the most helpful topic they worked on with their substance abuse counselors.

Those clients who were case-managed also identified a wide range of topic areas as being "most helpful," in contrast to opinions about topics that they worked on with their substance abuse counselor. Five areas — relationships, occupational and educational, internal resources, recovery, and learning to set goals — were identified at least 10 percent of the time by case-managed clients as most beneficial. Only two areas — recovery and internal resources — were identified as most beneficial in work with substance abuse counselors.

While process data relevant to both the WIP and case management are important in establishing and identifying the relationship between interventions and outcomes, they are not sufficient. The following section will examine data from six-month follow-up interviews conducted with project participants.

Outcome Data — Weekend Intervention Program and Strengths Perspective

Client assignment to WIP was chronologically clustered. Clients who entered treatment within one week of a scheduled WIP were assigned, while clients entering during off-weeks were not. The result was the creation of approximately two cohorts per month that were random with respect to client attributes. Most clients assigned to WIP attended within two weeks of entering treatment. However, participation was optional and approximately 26 percent of inpatients and 53 percent of outpatients assigned to attend WIP elected not to attend. Thus, while assignment was virtually random, self-selection came into play and must be considered in analyzing results.

To test the effects of self-selection, or alternatively, the possible effects of WIP as a gating mechanism, baseline data for three groups (persons who attended, persons who refused, and persons not assigned) were compared. Comparisons of preweekend, baseline data indicate no significant differences between any of the three groups.

The primary objective of sending clients through WIP was to motivate active participation and retention in treatment at the PRP. Data at six months indicate that WIP provided few statistically significant boosts in treatment retention, with only modest differences between persons who attended, persons who refused, and the control group. Attendance in Alcoholics Anonymous self-help meetings was notably higher for WIP participants, with an average of 18 additional meetings over the six-month period when compared with the control group. Many clients reported enjoying the two Alcoholics Anonymous meetings sponsored in the course of the weekend and may have established contacts for future meetings during this brief exposure.

Attitudinal responses of clients at six months reflect very positively on WIP, with fewer than 10 percent offering any criticism of WIP. Most respondents felt that WIP was a beneficial enhancement to their treatment program and that others would also benefit by attending. The paradox of very positive, persistent, attitudinal responses with weak observed behavioral changes suggests that the effects of WIP had a short half-life, and that additional reinforcement would be required. Case management was one such reinforcement mechanism.

Assignment to case management was strictly random and was based on computer-generated random numbers. Willingness to engage in case management was much better than with WIP, with only 13 of 181 persons assigned to case management (7 percent) not meeting at all with case managers. Of the 13 nonengagers, approximately one-half never engaged in core drug treatment activities either. Another 24 percent of assigned persons met with their case managers four weeks or less; most were inpatients who stopped meeting with case managers at the end of their 30-day inpatient stay. The remaining 69 percent of clients continued to meet with case managers beyond four weeks, with some continuing throughout the entire six-month follow-up period.

Baseline data indicate few significant differences between persons who engaged four weeks or less, persons who engaged longer, and persons not assigned to case management. Excluding the 13 persons who never met with their assigned case managers, persons assigned to case management showed somewhat greater problems with respect to criminal activities and drug use.

Two significant objectives of case management were to improve retention in treatment and improve various related outcomes, such as sobriety, employment, and legal behavior. Case managers were encouraged to meet clients in a variety of settings and to actively persist in arranging meetings and other activities with clients. Because case management was designed as an open-ended, individually-tailored process, clients showed considerable variation in the degree to which they engaged in this enhancement and the type of benefits they reaped. As a result, the simple comparisons of group means between assigned groups will understate the effect that individually-tailored case management had on clients.

After six months, there appeared to be numerous differences between persons who engaged at all (less than one week) with case management and the control group. Most notable was the finding that reported days of cocaine use were approximately 50 percent less for persons who engaged in case management. Their Addiction Severity Index drug composite scores and drug severity ratings were also significantly lower ($\alpha = .05$). With lower drug use, other covariates were also improved for the case-managed clients. Reported family, social, and mental health problems were also significantly lower. Comparison of persons who engaged in case management for more than four weeks indicate even stronger improvements over the control group, although the issues of self-selection certainly become more important in quasi dose-response comparisons. In no instance did the case-managed clients appear significantly worse off than the control group ($\alpha = .05$).

Finally, this research project hypothesized the potential for positive, synergistic effects of combining treatment induction using the WIP model and individualized case management. Although the thorny issues involved in client self-selection cannot be set aside, there is some suggestion of positive interaction effects. After excluding all persons who elected not to participate in their assigned enhancement, analysis comparing six-month data for all four treatment groups reveals that the combined

WIP and case management clients frequently displayed lower levels of pathology than single enhancement groups, while the control group often displayed the highest levels of pathology. For instance, the combined enhancement group ranked lowest on six out of seven Adiction Severity Index composite indexes, including those for health, employment, alcohol abuse, drug abuse, legal involvement, and mental health.

These findings must still be considered preliminary but suggest that both WIP and case management contribute to substance abuse treatment; the two combined may provide an added boost. As our sample increases, it will be subjected to more sophisticated statistical analysis to more adequately control for potential biases resulting from client self-selection and other factors. Additional research into the role of case management, especially during outpatient and aftercare treatment phases, will be a key focus for future analyses.

DISCUSSION

These preliminary results, although certainly encouraging, must be offered with some qualification. Our concerns, naturally, center on the as-yet-incomplete sample, as well as the issues presented by client self-selection. The sample will, of course, complete itself — to one degree or another — with time. Given the nature of our research and those we study when using the presumed "gold standard" of random assignment imposed upon us, we have to expect to qualify any findings obtained.

Our data suggest that the enhancements do indeed improve treatment outcomes. These preliminary data seem to say that those patients who actually received the enhancements of (pre)treatment induction and strengths-based case management were less likely to be involved in subsequent criminality and used (as a group) less cocaine less frequently than those who did not receive these therapeutic enhancements. Furthermore, these same data suggest a positive interaction between the amount of case management received and reduced criminality and lessened drug use.

Regrettably, the fact that clients randomly assigned to our experimental group elected not to receive the enhancement makes it impossible to offer definitive, defensible conclusions about the actual efficacy of these activities. The results are, however, tantalizing. As flawed as the rigorous methodologically-driven data may be, the process measures are clear in their message that the clients not only liked the enhancement activities they participated in but also were convinced that they aided and continued to support their recovery. Again, the findings that these clients did, in fact, do better than the others who did not receive the enhancements encourages us to conclude that they certainly did not carry a negative or harmful impact.

Perhaps the most valuable lesson learned from this study is also the most obvious: people reaching out to each other in a positive, caring way can make a difference. As treatment enhancements, the WIP and strengths-based case management have indeed demonstrated that they do offer additional support to patients needing more than core substance abuse treatment. The challenge remains to continue using research designs that are both scientifically sound and hold practical value. We must not only examine the relative effect of these kinds of enhancements on treatment but also look at for whom they appear to work best, under what conditions, and then understand the mechanisms of their actions.

REFERENCES

Bale, R., VanStone, W. W., Kuldau, J. M., Engelsing, T. J., Elashoff, R. M., & Zarcone Jr., V. D. (1980). Therapeutic communities vs methadone maintenance: A prospective controlled study of narcotic addiction treatment: Design and one-year follow-up. *Archives of General Psychiatry, 37*, 179–193.

Craig, R. (1985). Reducing the treatment drop out rate in drug abuse programs. *Journal of Substance Abuse Treatment*, 2, 209–219.

Deitchman, W. S. (1980). How many case managers does it take to screw in a light bulb? *Hospital and Community Psychiatry, 31*(11), 788–789.

Joe, G., & Simpson, D. (1975). Retention in treatment of drug users: 1971–1972 DARP admissions. *American Journal of Drug & Alcohol Abuse*, 2(2), 63–71.

Rapp, C. A., & Chamberlain, R. (1985). Case management services for the chronically mentally ill. *Social Work, 30*, 417–422.

IV

MULTIMODALITY AND OTHER ECLECTIC PROGRAMS

10

Therapeutic Community Methods in Methadone Maintenance (Passages): An Empirical Evaluation

George De Leon, Graham L. Staines, Stanley Sacks, Theresa E. Perlis, Karen McKendrick, Robert Hilton, Ronald Brady, and Ronald Melchionda

Reviews of relevant empirical studies have documented the effectiveness of methadone in reducing heroin use and criminal behavior, improving health status, and increasing employment among methadone clients (for example, Hubbard et al., 1989; Lipton & Magura, 1991; McLellan, 1983; Senay, 1985). As with other treatment modalities, methadone treatment outcome is positively related to retention in the program: the longer one stays in treatment the better the outcome. Despite the evidence of the utility of methadone, there is ample evidence that numbers of methadone-treated clients continue to use other nonprescribed drugs, participate in HIV-related high-risk behaviors (for example, unprotected sex and needle use) and have problems in psychological functioning (Chaisson et al., 1989; Hubbard, et al., 1989; Kang & De Leon, 1993; Lipton & Magura, 1991; Rosenbaum, 1981). Methadone treatment is thus in need of other strategies that increase its overall effectiveness, especially with methadone-maintained clients whose general level of life functioning is poor. One approach to enhancing methadone treatment involves a day treatment model modified from therapeutic community (TC) residential treatment.

THE PASSAGES MODEL

The perspective and approach of the traditional TC on drug abuse and recovery have been systematically described (De Leon, 1986, 1994). Briefly, drug abuse is seen as a disorder of the whole person, reflecting problems in conduct, attitudes, moods, emotional management, and values. For many people there are chronic deficits in social, educational, and marketable skills. The specific goal of treatment is the development of a prosocial lifestyle marked by alcohol and drug abstinence and the elimination of antisocial behavior and attitudes. The psychological goal is to change the negative patterns of behavior, feeling, and thinking that predispose the individual to drug use. A critical assumption of the TC is that stable recovery depends on an integration of the social and psychological goals. Rehabilitation, therefore, involves a multidimensional effort that requires an intensive mutual self-help process in a 24-hour residential setting.

To be practical and effective with methadone clients, modifications to traditional TC methods are needed. This chapter reports on an enhanced day treatment program (Passages) based on TC methods that were suitably adapted for opiate addicts in methadone clinics (De Leon, Sacks, & Hilton, 1993). Passages was implemented as an intensive day treatment program that meets four days a week. Each day begins with a morning meeting followed by other group meetings (that is, administrative, informational, accountability, and general discussions). In short, much of the Passages regular program consists of group sessions. Clients also prepare and eat a community lunch and complete daily job assignments. One day each week includes a special recreational event.

Most of the key components of residential TCs are retained in the Passages model. Modifications to the TC approach that were implemented included greater emphasis on outreach and advocacy, reduction in the intensity of personal and interpersonal interactions, graduated and guided implementation of all new expectations, and greater responsiveness to individual differences. Furthermore, flexibility in the phase format inherent to residential TCs was increased to allow clients greater variability in both responsibility and freedom as part of the treatment process.

In addition, the nonresidential nature of the program led to the development of several innovations, including the Client Action Plan, the Passages Fellowship, the Stipend Trainee Program, and Self-government. The Client Action Plan, a special goal-oriented treatment plan, is a clinical tool that integrates individual client goals and objectives within the group context. The Passages Fellowship is a weekly evening group meeting that provides some clients with extended program hours, others with primary treatment hours, and many with opportunities for accelerated movement through the phases of recovery. The Stipend Trainee Program seeks to develop a new cadre of trained staff to work with methadone or other special substance-abusing populations in other TCs or other programs. Finally, Passages Self-government includes a peer-managed legislative process to define rules and boundaries, a judicial system to enforce these rules, and an executive function to oversee the structure.

Notwithstanding these four innovations, the central TC feature remains: Passages, like all TC programs, seeks to develop a culture where clients learn through a self-help process to foster change in themselves and others.

EVALUATING THE PASSAGES PROGRAM

This nonrandom open clinical trial of the Passages program was conducted at two methadone maintenance treatment programs (MMTP): a free-standing urban clinic (Bridge Plaza Treatment and Rehabilitation Services PC [BP]) and a hospital-based clinic located in the suburbs (the Substance Alternative Clinic at the Nassau County Department of Drug and Alcohol Addiction [NC]). Clients eligible for a daytime program were recruited through the use of clinic rosters, counselor recommendations, and word of mouth. A total of 326 clients participated at BP and 130 at NC. Prior to the baseline interview, clients were informed about the Passages clinical program and were encouraged to join. Of the 456 clients who completed baseline and six-month follow-up interviews, 176 clients joined the Passages clinical program (Passages clients). The remaining 280 clients elected to participate in the research (that is, agreed to be interviewed) but chose not to enter the clinical program (nonPassages clients). All participants received $25 for completing each interview (baseline, six-month follow-up, and one-year follow-up). Passages and nonPassages clients received identical interview protocols including structured face-to-face interviews and self-administered psychological scales. Data, which included urine toxicological information, were also collected from both clinic and Passages administrative records.

The structured interview obtained information on basic demographic variables (for example, age, race, and education), HIV risk-related behavior (drug use, needle use, and sexual activity), and criminal activity for several time periods. All self-report data presented reflects activity in the last 30 days from the time of the interview. Questions on drug use asked clients to indicate the frequency of their use of various drugs. Composite measures of self-reported drug use were developed from the original drug items. For example, the overall measure for cocaine was defined as the highest frequency reported for crack, cocaine powder, cocaine injected, speedball snorted, or speedball injected. Composite measures were not independent of each other. Clients were also asked how many times they had used needles (clean or dirty) to inject drugs. Sexual activity was measured by the number of different partners (men or women) with whom clients had engaged in sex (safe or unsafe).

Interviewers asked clients about the nondrug-related criminal activities in which they had been involved. Clients indicated the number of times they had engaged in each of 16 types of crimes. Two summary measures were used in the analyses: the total number of times the client had committed any of the 16 types of crimes and the number of different types of crimes committed.

The Symptom Checklist-90 (SCL-90), Beck Depression Inventory, Manifest Anxiety Scale, and Rosenberg Self-Esteem Scale were used to measure psychological status. All scales were self-administered. The global score from the SCL-90 (Derogatis, 1983) is a measure of symptomatic distress. Overall scores were transformed to t-scores normed separately for females and males from the general population. The Beck Depression Inventory (Beck & Steer, 1981) rates cognitive, affective, somatic, and behavioral and vegetative symptoms of depression. To measure anxiety, a total score from the shortened Manifest Anxiety Scale (Bendig, 1956) was used. The Rosenberg Self-Esteem Scale (Rosenberg, 1965) was used to measure self-esteem. This scale is composed of ten items derived from the Tennessee Self-Concept Scale (Fitts, 1965). An average global score was used.

Portions of the Circumstances/Motivation/Readiness/Suitability (CMRS) scales were included in the baseline battery (De Leon & Jainchill, 1986; De Leon, Melnick, Kressel, & Jainchill, 1994). This is a self-administered instrument designed on the basis of recovery theory to predict retention in treatment among abusers of illicit drugs. Likert-type items are used to rate agreement with each statement. Two of the four available scales were used, including the complete Motivation Scale (that is, to measure internal pressure to change) and the modified Brief Readiness for Treatment Instrument (that is, to measure the perceived need for treatment). Circumstances and Suitability scales were not used because they were not appropriate for nonresidential treatment populations.

Clinic records containing urine toxicological information were obtained for the latter part of the study period. Availability of urine toxicological information was limited to those records released by clinic administration, because urine toxicological data could not be collected as part of the Passages research protocol. The urine toxicological data on drug use measured the presence of four drugs including cocaine and opiates (heroin). In most cases clients were tested weekly although some clients were scheduled to be tested more than once a week and others less often. However, for various practical reasons (for example, illness), clients did not always keep to the schedule. Toxicology merely indicates presence or absence of a drug in urine, not frequency of use; hence the measures of drug use in the present study were defined disjunctively. That is, a client was scored as positive on a drug for a particular time period if the client registered at least one positive result for the drug during that time period. In the absence of any positive results (that is, results available but all negative) the client was scored as negative for that drug. Urine toxicological data also provided a vehicle for validating self-reports of drug use.

A client was defined as a Passages member if he or she completed a short orientation period after voluntarily joining the Passages clinical program. The planned duration of participation in the Passages program included a critical initial period of six months after which some phase-down in daily involvement could occur. Clients were considered still to be active until they failed to attend at least one Passages session for four consecutive weeks. Passages members with a retention potential of six months (that is, clients whose entry date into Passages occurred at least six months prior to the cutoff date for the collection of data used in these analyses) were classified as retained if they remained active for 26 weeks or more; otherwise, they were considered dropouts. Passages members with less than six months retention potential were classified as dropouts if they were known to have left the program. In addition to the dichotomous measure of retention, a continuous measure of retention (that is, number of weeks in active status during the six-month period following the client's entry date) was constructed.

As a proxy variable for actual participation in the Passages clinical program, attendance over the six-month period following program entry was assessed. Scored on a daily basis rather than summarizing involvement during the entire period, attendance is a much more direct estimate of frequency of participation. Moreover, attendance places less emphasis on continuity of participation in treatment and more emphasis on amount (or dosage) of treatment participation. Attendance in Passages (that is, the number of program days a client attended during the six-month period) was operationalized as a continuous measure of program participation.

The present chapter reports data from a nonrandom open clinical trial assessing profile information on clients, retention in the Passages program, and effectiveness of the Passages program. The first two of these inquiries concerned distributions of client characteristics. The third inquiry began by examining effectiveness of membership in the Passages program. It evaluated overall improvement and changes in mean scores from baseline to six-month follow-up on the behavioral and psychological measures. The full set of analyses of change were then repeated to determine the effect of retention in Passages. Analyses were also performed using the continuous measure of retention (that is, number of active weeks in Passages) and then the continuous measure of attendance (that is, number of days attended Passages).

CLIENT PROFILES

Overall Client Profiles

Distributional data were examined for all methadone clients and for comparison groups in the study defined in terms of methadone clinic site and Passages membership. To obtain an overall profile of clients in methadone maintenance therapy, baseline data from the 456 clients were evaluated (Table 10.1). Considerable diversity was revealed for sociodemographic and other background variables. Despite their heterogeneity, clients tended to be under 40 years old, to have had children, to have a limited educational background, and to have had at least one previous admission for drug treatment or some other type of drug-related care. Few MMTP clients were employed either full-time or part-time. Most had an arrest history or had served some time in jail. Many also reported being the victim of either sexual or physical abuse. On the whole, minority ethnic groups were overrepresented, especially Blacks and Hispanics. The average length of stay in MMTP at the time of the baseline interview was just over 15 months. Almost one-third of clients were recent admissions to methadone treatment (that is, within the last month); over one-half had spent 1–19 months as a methadone client; and the remaining one-fifth had been on the clinic roster for 20 months or more.

In general, the methadone sample in this study had poorer scores on all psychological scales than those considered normal for nonpatient populations. Although most mean scores for the SCL-90 were within one standard deviation of the mean reported for normative population data, the methadone sample scored in the high (dysfunctional) end of the normal range. Their average Beck depression score indicated mild to moderate depression.

Site Comparisons

The BP urban site consisted of 105 Passages members and 221 nonPassages clients. By comparison, the NC suburban site had 71 Passages members and 59 nonPassages clients. Baseline profile data obtained from clients at both sites revealed several statistically significant differences (Table 10.1). The overall pattern was for the clients at the urban site to exhibit greater socioeconomic disadvantage, whereas clients at the suburban site were more likely to have made contact with the criminal justice system and more likely to register psychological distress.

Because significant differences in three client background factors emerged between the two Passages sites (namely, level of education, parental status, and race), statistical tests were performed to detect interaction effects between Passages membership and each of these background factors. None of the background factors, however, generated a significant pattern of interaction in predicting change in behavior or psychological functioning over the six-month period. Consequently, data from both sites could be combined to ensure adequate statistical power to detect the effect of Passages over time.

Passages versus NonPassages Clients

Some significant differences emerged between clients who joined the Passages clinical program and those who did not (Table 10.2). In general, Passages clients had been in methadone treatment longer than nonPassages clients and received higher doses of methadone. They also scored higher on both motivation and treatment readiness. Passages members were more likely to be female and to report a history of abuse. They were also less likely to be employed. Passages clients were less likely to be IV drug users at entry into MMTP, registered lower scores on key measures of high-risk behavior (for example, cocaine or heroin injection behavior), and had poorer scores on all of the measures of psychological status. Passages clients were, therefore, more dysfunctional than their nonPassages counterparts. This difference between the methadone clients who opted for Passages and those who declined point to the possibility of self-selection factors contributing to the interpretation of apparent program impact.

Retained Passages Members versus Passages Dropouts

Based on the dichotomous measure of retention, among the 170 Passages members with a retention potential of six months or more, 34 percent were considered retained at six months (that is, 37 percent at BP and 29 percent at NC). On the continuous measure of program retention, there was wide variation in the number of weeks clients remained active following program entry. Fully 29 percent of clients in the Passages clinical program remained active 4 weeks or less, 8 percent remained 5–8 weeks, 10 percent remained 9–12 weeks, 10 percent remained 13–16 weeks, 9 percent remained 17–25 weeks, and 34 percent remained 26 weeks or more. In addition, it is worth noting that, although the continuous measures of attendance (cumulative number of days) and retention (number of consecutive active weeks) were highly correlated (Pearson $r = .72$, $p \leq .01$), they are far from identical. Among clients in the Passages clinical program there was considerable variability in the number of days that they attended: 43 percent attended fewer than one-fourth of the 104 possible days, 18 percent attended at least one-fourth of the days but less than one-half, 22 percent attended at least one-half but less than three-fourths of the time, and 17 percent attended three-fourths or more of the possible 104 days.

Although baseline profile data from retained Passages members and dropouts appeared to be similar (data not shown), one statistically significant difference was evident. More retained Passages members (44 percent) were previously married (for example, divorced, separated, or widowed) than were never married (35 percent) or currently married

TABLE 10.1
Comparison of Clients from Bridge Plaza and Nassau County

	Total (N = 456)	Bridge Plaza (N = 326)	Nassau County (N = 130)	*p*
Profile	%	%	%	
Sex				
Male	60	57	64	N.S.
Female	40	43	36	
Education				
< 12 years	42	46	31	0.01*
12 years	29	29	29	
> 12 years	29	25	40	
Marital status				
Married	34	37	26	N.S.
Unmarried	28	26	31	
Single	38	37	43	
Has at least one child	61	65	52	0.01*
Race				
Black	29	28	31	0.01*
Hispanic	18	24	4	
White	53	47	65	
Other	1	1	0	
Age				
20–29 years	16	18	9	N.S.
30–39 years	53	52	56	
40–49 years	29	28	32	
50+ years	2	2	2	
Employment				
Full-time	11	12	9	N.S.
Part-time	7	7	7	
Unemployed	82	81	84	
Motivation				
Mean	65.66	65.43	66.40	N.S.
Standard deviation	8.43	8.60	7.88	
Readiness				
Mean	29.33	29.40	29.11	N.S.
Standard deviation	4.19	4.03	4.68	
Months in MMTP				
Mean	15.91	11.68	26.66	0.01*
Standard deviation	30.14	25.33	37.87	
Daily methadone dose (mg)				
Mean	54.81	51.81	62.35	0.01*
Standard deviation	22.02	21.39	21.85	
Any previous admission for treatment	94	93	96	N.S.

Profile	Total (N = 456) %	Bridge Plaza (N = 326) %	Nassau County (N = 130) %	p
IVDU at time entering MMPT	55	55	56	N.S.
Shared needles at time entering MMPT	20	23	11	0.01*
HIV/AIDS positive				
(N = 317 clients tested)	23	21	26	N.S.
Homosexual relations in past 6 months	3	4	1	N.S.
Multiple sex partners in past 6 months	20	21	16	N.S.
Ever arrested	87	84	92	0.03**
Ever spent time in jail	66	60	81	0.01*
Youthful offender	23	22	26	N.S.
Involved in criminal justice				
system at baseline	11	9	15	0.05**
Victim of any abuse (sexual or physical)	44	44	43	N.S.
Drug use in the last 30 days:				
Alcohol (any)	51	53	47	N.S.
Alcohol (intoxication)	24	25	18	N.S.
Marijuana	27	25	34	N.S.
Crack	38	36	42	N.S.
Cocaine (snorted)	21	21	22	N.S.
Cocaine (injected)	33	34	29	N.S.
Heroin (snorted)	26	28	22	N.S.
Heroin (injected)	42	45	33	0.03**
Speedball (snorted)	22	22	22	N.S.
Speedball (injected)	29	30	26	N.S.
Cocaine (any form)	52	51	55	N.S.
Heroin (any form)	53	57	40	0.01*
Speedball (any form)	23	24	20	N.S.
Injection (any form)	43	45	37	N.S.
Psychological status				
SCL-90 Global Score				
Mean	61.96	61.25	63.72	0.05**
Standard deviation	11.95	11.89	11.97	
Rosenberg Self-Esteem				
Mean	2.83	2.86	2.77	N.S.
Standard deviation	0.48	0.49	0.44	
Beck Depression Inventory				
Mean	14.56	14.43	14.86	N.S.
Standard deviation	10.45	10.41	10.57	
Manifest Anxiety				
Mean	8.63	8.18	9.38	0.05**
Standard deviation	5.20	4.97	5.50	

Note: Chi-square used to test categorical measures, t-test for continuous measures: $^{*}p \leq .01$, $^{**}p \leq .05$. N.S. = not significant.

TABLE 10.2
Comparison of Passages and NonPassages Clients from Two Sites Combined

	Total (N = 456)	Passages (N = 176)	NonPassages (N = 280)	*p*
	%	%	%	
Sex				
Male	60	51	65	0.03*
Female	40	49	35	
Education				
< 12 years	42	40	43	N.S.
12 years	29	27	30	
> 12 years	29	32	27	
Marital status				
Married	34	29	36	N.S.
Unmarried	28	30	27	
Single	38	41	37	
Has at least one child	61	56	65	N.S.
Race				
Black	29	35	25	N.S.
Hispanic	18	20	17	
White	53	44	57	
Other	1	1	1	
Age				
20–29 years	16	14	17	N.S.
30–39 years	53	52	54	
40–49 years	29	31	27	
50+ years	2	2	2	
Employment				
Full-time	11	5	15	0.01**
Part-time	7	5	8	
Unemployed	82	90	77	
Motivation				
Mean	65.66	67.62	64.47	0.01**
Standard deviation	8.43	8.34	8.28	
Readiness				
Mean	29.33	29.88	28.99	0.05*
Standard deviation	4.19	3.76	4.41	
Months in MMTP				
Mean	15.91	22.01	12.11	0.01*
Standard deviation	30.14	36.93	24.30	
Daily methadone dose (mg)				
Mean	54.81	57.56	53.09	0.04*
Standard deviation	22.02	22.49	21.59	
Any previous admission for treatment	94	94	94	N.S.
IVDU at time entering MMPT	55	49	59	0.05*

	Total (N = 456)	Passages (N = 176)	NonPassages (N = 280)	*p*
	%	%	%	
Shared needles at time entering MMPT	20	17	22	N.S.
HIV/AIDS positive				
(N = 317 clients tested)	23	25	21	N.S.
Homosexual relations in past 6 months	3	3	3	N.S.
Multiple sex partners in past 6 months	20	20	20	N.S.
Ever arrested	87	89	85	N.S.
Ever spent time in jail	66	67	66	N.S.
Youthful offender	23	21	24	N.S.
Involved in criminal justice				
system at baseline	11	9	12	N.S.
Victim of any abuse (sexual or physical)	44	52	39	0.05*
Drug use in the last 30 days:				
Alcohol (any)	51	53	50	N.S.
Alcohol (intoxication)	24	25	23	N.S.
Marijuana	27	32	25	N.S.
Crack	38	34	40	N.S.
Cocaine (snorted)	21	22	21	N.S.
Cocaine (injected)	33	28	36	N.S.
Heroin (snorted)	26	26	26	N.S.
Heroin (injected)	42	34	47	0.02**
Speedball (snorted)	22	19	23	N.S.
Speedball (injected)	29	24	32	N.S.
Cocaine (any form)	52	52	53	N.S.
Heroin (any form)	53	47	56	N.S.
Speedball (any form)	23	17	26	0.04*
Injection (any form)	43	35	47	0.02*
Psychological status				
SCL-90 Global Score				
Mean	61.96	64.74	60.22	0.01**
Standard deviation	11.95	11.89	11.68	
Rosenberg Self-Esteem				
Mean	2.83	2.73	2.90	0.01**
Standard deviation	0.48	0.47	0.47	
Beck Depression Inventory				
Mean	14.56	16.88	13.10	0.01**
Standard deviation	10.45	11.27	9.64	
Manifest Anxiety				
Mean	8.63	10.02	7.45	0.01**
Standard deviation	5.20	5.23	4.99	

Note: Chi-square used to test categorical measures, t-test for continuous measures: $^{*}p \leq .05$, $^{**}p \leq .01$. N.S. = not significant.

(21 percent). In contrast, more Passages dropouts reported never having married (42 percent) than were currently (34 percent) or previously married (24 percent) at baseline.

EFFECT OF PASSAGES AT SIX-MONTH FOLLOW-UP (SELF-REPORT)

Overall Treatment Impact of Passages Membership

To assess the treatment impact of the Passages program, data from clients who completed both baseline and six-month follow-up interviews were used (176 Passages members, 280 nonPassages clients). For each of the major domains of outcomes, measures were entered into a Multivariate Analysis of Covariance (MANCOVA) to detect the overall improvement of Passages members for each relevant domain. The three major domains were HIV-risk related behavior (that is, drug use, needle use, and sexual behavior), criminality, and psychological status. Variables from these three domains combined could not be analyzed using a single MANCOVA because of the reduced sample sizes associated with several of the key variables. Effects because of possible initial differences (that is, time in methadone treatment, methadone dose, employment status, and baseline values of the outcome variables) were controlled statistically by including covariates in the model. In general, Passages clients improved more than nonPassages clients for all domains but not at a statistically significant level.

Retention in the Passages Clinical Program

When Passages members were divided into retained and dropouts, the program's beneficial treatment impact came into sharper focus. Once again, MANCOVAs were run for each of the three domains of outcomes, comparing three groups: retained Passages members, Passages dropouts, and nonPassages clients (the last group being the reference category). In the MANCOVA, improvements for retained Passages members were significant ($p \leq .05$) in two outcome domains (risk behavior and psychological status) and approaching significance ($p \leq .07$) in the third domain (criminality) for which sample size and, thus, statistical power were limited. Dropouts, by comparison, registered no improvement in any domain.

Given the overall differences, comparisons among retained clients, dropouts, and nonPassages clients were examined using data for each outcome measure. The statistical procedure used was ordinary least-squares multiple regressions. The regressions used the six-month follow-up measure of outcome as the dependent variable and Passages retention status plus four control variables as the set of predictors in the equation. Regression coefficients were obtained to indicate the significance of the relationship between Passages retention status and the magnitude (and direction) of change. Based on the multiple regressions for separate outcome measures, retained Passages members (but not the dropouts) showed a significant improvement on several measures of risk (that is, cocaine use, heroin use, and cocaine or heroin injection) and criminal activity (that is, number of different crime types committed).

Based on analyses using Passages members only (N = 170), the continuous measure of retention in Passages was significantly associated with reductions in drug use (that is, cocaine use, heroin use, and injection of cocaine or heroin). Results based on the continuous measure of retention in enhanced treatment are consistent with the findings based on the dichotomous measure, namely, that remaining in Passages had considerably more effect on clients than did simply entering Passages.

Attendance in the Passages Clinical Program

The findings linking attendance and changes in outcomes are somewhat more positive than the parallel findings for the continuous measure of retention. Notwithstanding the limited sample size (Passages members only), attendance in Passages was also associated with reductions in drug use (that is, cocaine use, heroin use, and injection of cocaine or heroin). Results based on the continuous measure of attendance are thus consistent with the retention findings in suggesting a dose-response effect (that is, as participation in the Passages clinical program increases so does degree of client improvement, based on outcome measures in three domains).

EFFECTS OF PASSAGES AT SIX-MONTH FOLLOW-UP (URINE TOXICOLOGY)

Urine toxicological data available from one clinic, BP, confirmed the self-report findings on the impact of retention in Passages on drug use. Even with a limited sample, for whom complete clinic records were released (37 retained Passages members, 35 dropouts, and 167 nonPassages clients), the proportion of clients using cocaine and heroin decreased for the retained Passages groups. At baseline, cocaine use was detected for 51 percent of the retained Passages members, 43 percent of the dropouts, and 48 percent of the nonPassages clients. Six months later, the proportions had decreased to 19 percent of the retained Passages members and 43 percent of the nonPassages clients. No change in cocaine use was detected for the dropout group. A substantially similar pattern emerged for heroin. Roughly 46 percent of retained Passages members, 49 percent of dropouts, and 61 percent of nonPassages clients tested positive for heroin use at baseline. Six months later, all groups showed a reduction in heroin use with only 16 percent of retained Passages members, 29 percent of dropouts, and 49 percent of nonPassages clients testing positive. According to logistic regression analyses, retention in the Passages program for at least six months was significantly associated with reductions in cocaine and heroin use compared to the nonPassages group. By contrast, only a reduction in heroin use emerged when comparing Passages dropouts to nonPassages clients. Therefore, results based on this analysis of urine toxicological data provide support for the self-report findings indicating the beneficial impact of retention in Passages.

CONCORDANCE BETWEEN MEASURES OF DRUG USAGE

To validate self-report measures of heroin and cocaine use directly, a study of concordance between self-report (defined dichotomously as some use versus none) and urine toxicology was performed. However, the individuals for whom both measures were available represent only a subset of clients in the reported study, because access to urine toxicological records was limited to participants who entered during the latter part of the study. Positive urine toxicological reports for cocaine during a specified time period were compared with self-reported usage of crack, cocaine powder, injected cocaine, snorted speedball, or injected speedball during the same period. In the case of heroin, the corresponding comparison was between a positive urine toxicological reading on opiates and self-reported use of snorted heroin, injected heroin, snorted speedball, or injected speedball. When both methods of measurement indicated drug usage, or both indicated absence of use, the two methods exhibited concordance. If self-report indicated usage, but urine tests did not, the resulting discrepancy could not be considered definitive because urine toxicology only measures use during the preceding 48 hours. Hence it is quite possible for a client to self-report usage accurately while registering a negative urine toxicological result. However, if clients registered a positive urine toxicological report but denied usage in their self-reports, the discordance was deemed to result from clients either lying or forgetting about their drug usage. The concordance of self-report and urine toxicological measures of drug use was assessed for both cocaine and heroin use during the 30 days preceding the baseline and separately for the 30 days preceding the six-month follow-up interview.

Despite the limited sample sizes for the weekly urine toxicological records, the data on the concordance of the measures of drug use established a moderate to high level of agreement between self-report and urine toxicology. Agreement between the two methods ranged from 66 percent to 84 percent for measures of usage in the last 30-day period. This level of agreement lent credibility to the general findings based on self-report.

DISCUSSION

Distributional Data on Client Profiles

Compared to normative scores, study participants (Passages and non-Passages methadone clients) exhibited deviant (poor) levels of psychological functioning at baseline measurement (that is, all SCL-90 scores and Beck Depression Inventory). When Passages and nonPassages clients were compared, a pattern emerged. Passages members showed significantly higher levels of psychological dysfunction (that is, all psychological scales evaluated). However, nonPassages clients participated in risk behavior significantly more often than their Passages peers. When juxtaposed, these two findings suggested that a certain level of internal distress (rather than dysfunctional behavior) facilitated client entry into Passages.

Effects of Retention in Passages for at Least Six Months

Supplemented by urine toxicological data, the self-report data point to retention in Passages as having greater positive effect than mere entry into the program. Clients who remained in Passages for at least six months registered substantial overall improvement. Those who separated prior to six months experienced less, or little, change. Significant reductions for retained clients resulted for specific outcome measures in each of the three domains (risk behavior, criminal activity, and psychological functioning). Because the results included reduction in drug use involving injection behavior and, therefore, a decreased risk of contracting or spreading the AIDS virus, these findings are noteworthy. Although both Passages subgroups scored worse than the nonPassages comparison group at baseline on nearly all psychological scales, Passages clients who remained in the program decreased their level of dysfunction to that of the nonPassages clients after six months. These results on retention differences and improvement are consistent with findings in the drug treatment literature documenting a relationship between client outcomes and time spent in programs (Tims & Ludford, 1984). The additional findings linking improvement to continuous measures of retention and, especially, attendance suggest that the degree of exposure to treatment is related to client change. This hypothesis needs to be more thoroughly tested in research utilizing controlled designs and more detailed measures of participation.

Issues of Interpretation

The design limits of this open trial underscore issues of interpretation. In the current open trial design, self-selection factors may have contributed to the significant outcome results associated with the Passages clinical program. The profile data in Table 10.2 exhibit few significant background differences between Passages and nonPassages clients, indicating limited evidence of a selection bias based on static client characteristics. However, other client factors (for example, dynamic factors, such as motivation and readiness for enhanced treatment) point to the possibility of self-selection. Passages clients scored higher on both of these variables than did nonPassages clients. Thus, later studies are planned to assess statistically the interaction effects of client motivation and treatment. A randomized trial offers the most rigorous test of the hypothesis that self-selection alone accounts for the apparent treatment effects. However, randomized field trials pose serious problems of feasibility because clients on methadone would have to be assigned to highly intensive enhanced treatment conditions, such as Passages, which they perceive as very demanding. Randomization may be more feasible at a later stage in the development of the enhanced treatment program. When the enhancement has become an established, valued, and integrated component of the clinic culture, waiting lists of motivated clients may permit random assignment of clients to comparative conditions based upon available slots.

Aside from the issue of self-selection, two related questions that bear upon conclusions concerning effectiveness remain to be addressed. First, although attendance data point to treatment improvement, it is unclear if the improvement in retained Passages members was a specific result of the Passages program or reflects a nonspecific interventional effect of any enhancement (for example, increased counseling, attention, and rewarded activity). Second, there remains the question of identifying the active treatment ingredients that produce the beneficial impact of the Passages program. Studies of the Passages model that include carefully designed process evaluation measures and analyses will help to clarify the specific treatment components most responsible for change.

The above issues of interpretation notwithstanding, the present findings underscore both the feasibility and efficacy of implementing a TC-oriented day treatment model to reduce risk behavior and improve overall clinical status of certain subgroups of clients in methadone treatment. The study provides support for self-help approaches that can be incorporated into methadone maintenance treatment. However, general dissemination of a TC-oriented day treatment model in other methadone clinics will require consideration of the cost-benefit factor. Methadone administrators and policy makers will need to be shown that this type of TC-oriented enhancement, whether integrated into their clinics or incorporated as an adjunct program, produces benefits at costs that do not strain scarce resources or, moreover, may even produce benefits with only a redeployment of resources rather than an additional outlay.

ACKNOWLEDGMENTS

This research was supported by the National Institute on Drug Abuse Grant No. 1 R18 DA06131-05.

REFERENCES

Beck, A., & Steer, R. (1981). *Beck Depression Inventory Manual.* New York: Harcourt Brace Jovanovich.

Bendig, A. W. (1956). The development of a short form of the manifest anxiety scale. *Journal of Consulting Psychology, 43,* 187–190.

Chaisson, R., Bacciati, P., Osmond, D., Brodie, B., Sande, M., & Moss, A. (1989). Cocaine use and HIV infection in intravenous drug users in San Francisco. *Journal of the American Medical Association, 261,* 561–565.

De Leon, G. (1994). Therapeutic communities. In M. Galanter & H. D. Kleber (Eds.), *The American psychiatric press textbook of substance abuse* (pp. 391–414). Chicago: American Psychiatric Press.

De Leon, G. (1986). The therapeutic community for substance abuse: Perspective and approach. In G. De Leon, & J. Ziegenfuss (Eds.), *Therapeutic communities for addictions: Readings in theory, research and practice* (pp. 5–18). Springfield, IL: Charles C. Thomas.

De Leon, G., & Jainchill, N. (1986). Circumstance, motivation, readiness and suitability as correlates of treatment tenure. *Journal of Psychoactive Drugs, 18*(3), 203–208.

De Leon, G., Melnick, G., Kressel, D., & Jainchill, N. (1994). Circumstances, motivation, readiness and suitability (the CMRS scales): Predicting retention in therapeutic community treatment. *American Journal of Drug and Alcohol Abuse, 20,* 495–515.

De Leon, G., Sacks, S., & Hilton, R. (1993). Passages: A modified therapeutic community day treatment model for methadone clients. In J. A. Inciardi, F. M. Tims, & B. Fletcher, (Eds.), *Innovative approaches in the treatment of drug abuse: Program models and strategies* (pp. 125–148). Westport, CT: Greenwood Press.

Derogatis, L. (1983). *SCL-90-R: Administration, scoring and procedures manual — II.* Towson, MD: Clinical Psychometrics Research.

Fitts, W. H. (1965). *Manual for the Tennessee self-concept scale.* Nashville, TN: Counselor Recordings and Tests.

Hubbard, R. L., Marsden, M. E., Rachal, J. V., Harwood, H. J., Cavanaugh, E. R., & Ginzburg, H. M. (1989). *Drug abuse treatment: A national study of effectiveness.* Chapel Hill: University of North Carolina Press.

Kang, S-Y., & De Leon, G. (1993). Correlates of drug injection behaviors among methadone out patients. *American Journal of Drug and Alcohol Abuse, 19,* 107–118.

Lipton, D. S., & Magura, S. (1991). *Methadone maintenance: A policy paper* (Report for the New York State Division of Substance Abuse Services). New York: National Development and Research Institute, Inc.

McLellan, A. T. (1983). Patient characteristics associated with outcome. In J. R. Cooper, & F. Alman (Eds.), *Research on the treatment of narcotic addiction: State of the art* (pp. 500–529). Rockville, MD: National Institute on Drug Abuse.

Rosenbaum, M. (1981). *Women on heroin*. New Brunswick, NJ: Rutgers University Press.

Rosenberg, M. (1965). *Society and the adolescent self-image*. Princeton, NJ: Princeton University Press.

Senay, E. C. (1985). Methadone maintenance treatment. *International Journal of the Addictions, 20,* 803–821.

Tims, F., & Ludford, J. (1984). Drug abuse treatment evaluation: Strategies, progress and prospects. In *Research analysis and utilization system* (Research Monograph Series 51, Publication No. (ADM) (84-1329). Rockville, MD: National Institute on Drug Abuse.

11

Improving Retention and Outcome in the Treatment of Cocaine Addiction

Kimberly C. Kirby, David S. Festinger, Richard J. Lamb, and Jerome J. Platt

Our group has been investigating behavioral interventions in the treatment of cocaine addiction. From our behavior-analytic conceptual framework, cocaine use is an operant behavior controlled by the same or similar factors and principles as other types of operant behavior (Goldberg & Kelleher, 1977; Schuster & Johanson, 1981). Cocaine addiction, like drug addiction in general, has two defining characteristics. First, cocaine reinforces behavior leading to its ingestion. Second, cocaine use produces adverse effects for both the user and society. Cocaine addiction occurs when cocaine ingestion continues despite these adverse consequences. Unfortunately, cocaine is a very effective and easily established reinforcer that can maintain large amounts of behavior (Griffiths, Bradford, & Brady, 1979) and is frequently chosen over other reinforcers (Aigner & Balster, 1978). Thus, cocaine can relatively quickly become a focus for the user, monopolizing much of the individual's time to the exclusion of other activities and rewards. It can be difficult to entice cocaine users to enter treatment, stay in treatment, and effect positive outcomes from treatment.

The basic strategy of behavioral approaches is to identify environmental factors that the clinician can rearrange to increase the likelihood of treatment entry and to improve retention and outcome. This chapter reviews behavioral research that identifies these factors having significant implications for improving treatment entry, retention, and outcomes for cocaine addicted individuals. We have selectively reported studies reviewed in the literature and highlight research results from our own demonstration project addressing these issues.

TREATMENT ENTRY

Successful outreach methods for initiating contact and recruiting substance abusers into treatment have included providing treatment entry vouchers (Iguchi et al., 1994) and training significant others to encourage treatment entry (Sisson & Azrin, 1986). Some data suggest that among out-of-treatment intravenous drug users contacted through street outreach, more are daily cocaine users than are daily heroin users (McCoy, Rivers, & Chitwood, 1993), but little systematic research has addressed outreach specific to cocaine treatment entry. Behavioral outreach and recruitment strategies addressing cocaine users are important, and our research group is in the early stages of initiating investigations regarding these techniques. However, in this project we focused on another important point of treatment entry: initial appointment attendance after treatment need has been identified through scheduling the cocaine user for a treatment intake appointment.

We are not aware of any previously published research addressing first appointment attendance among cocaine dependent individuals, but some studies have examined first appointment attendance with mental health providers. Reports have come from private practice, reporting failed first appointment rates of 20 percent (O'Loughlin, 1990) and community mental health treatment, with failure rates from 29 percent (Turner & Vernon, 1976) to 43 percent (Orne & Boswell, 1991). These rates are high enough not only to disrupt efficiency in health service provision but also to raise important concerns that there may be a substantial proportion of individuals who are identified as needing help but are unable to follow through with treatment entry.

Several studies have searched for possible correlates of failure to attend first appointments, however, many findings are contradictory. Some have found significant relationships between lower socioeconomic status and missed first appointments (Grieves, 1978; Weighill, Hodge, & Peck, 1983), while others have not found socioeconomic status to be a significant predictor (Carpenter, Morrow, DelGaudio, & Ritzler, 1981; Gaines, 1978). Similarly, findings that previous psychological treatment is related to improved first appointment attendance in subsequent psychological treatment (Carpenter, Morrow, DelGaudio, & Ritzler, 1981; Means et al., 1989) is not supported by other studies (for example, Raynes & Warren, 1971). Other studies have examined such factors as impulsiveness (Kirk & Frank, 1976), client gender (Brown & Kosterlitz, 1964; Noonan, 1974; Raynes & Warren, 1971), and race (Raynes & Warren, 1971; Sue, McKinney, & Allen, 1976), with findings again being inconclusive regarding predictors for missed first appointments. The only variable that has consistently predicted failure to attend first scheduled appointment is the delay between initial contact and the first scheduled clinic appointment (Grieves, 1978;

Orne & Boswell, 1991). In these studies, increasing delays were directly correlated with failure to attend the initial appointment. None of the studies we reviewed specifically addressed the cocaine dependent population.

Other studies have evaluated specific interventions aimed at increasing initial attendance. O'Loughlin (1990) found that sending clients a preappointment questionnaire significantly increased initial attendance to clinical psychologist appointments. Similarly, Swenson and Pekarik (1988) found that sending an orientation letter one day before a client's appointment significantly increased his or her attendance at a community mental health treatment. Although these interventions are effective, they depend on getting an accurate and reliable mailing address for a client that can read. Since a significant number of our clients are homeless or are living in transient housing at the time of treatment entry (18 percent), and some have difficulty reading, we were concerned that preappointment mailing would be impossible or ineffective with a significant portion of our clinic population. Only one of the remaining variables examined in the studies we reviewed was an environmental factor under the control of the service provider: the delay between the initial contact and the first scheduled clinic appointment. Thus, our clinic generally attempted to schedule clients' first appointments within 48–72 hours after the initial contact.

We reviewed initial appointment failure rates during the first seven months of our outpatient cocaine treatment program and found 58 percent of the scheduled appointments were not attended despite the general rules we had in place for appointment scheduling (Festinger, Lamb, Kountz, Kirby, & Marlowe, 1995). We began by examining a number of variables as possible predictors of missing intake. During the initial inquiry (which almost always occurred over the telephone) we determined the prospective client's age, distance from treatment, gender, marital status, referral source, primary drug problems, last use of cocaine or other illicit stimulants, and other problem substances. Additional information derived from the inquiries included gender of assigned counselor, gender of operator taking the inquiry, time between phone inquiry and scheduled appointment, and relationship of the individual who made the initial contact to the client who was scheduled for an appointment. Using tabular analysis and backward logistic regression, we found none of the client or demographic variables were significant. However, one environmental factor under our control was a significant predictor of first appointment attendance: the delay between initial contact and the scheduled first appointment. Results indicated that attendance at the first appointment fell from 83 percent for clients scheduled on the same day as the initial contact to 57 percent for clients who were scheduled to come in only one day later. First session attendance continued to decline, although more gradually, with even longer initial appointment delays.

These studies are consistent with earlier reports that greater delays between the initial contact and the first scheduled clinic appointment predict attendance failure for mental health clients (Grieves, 1978; Orne & Boswell, 1991) and they extend the findings to the cocaine treatment population. In addition, our results provide information beyond previous studies focusing primarily on delays of several days or weeks. Our data showed that the greatest decrease in first session attendance occurred in the first 24 hours following the initial contact. This suggests that one variable influencing this aspect of treatment entry is an environmental variable that is largely under the control of the clinic. Although the correlational nature of these data limited statements of causality, the results suggested that cocaine treatment providers may be able to increase treatment entry effectively by making a relatively simple procedural change: scheduling the client's first clinic appointment within 24 hours of the initial contact.

In a subsequent study (Festinger, Lamb, Kirby, & Marlowe, in press) we experimentally examined this scheduling variable. We randomly assigned 78 subjects contacting our outpatient cocaine treatment clinic to either an accelerated intake (where we offered to schedule the first appointment on the same day as the initial contact) or a standard intake (where the first appointment was offered 1–3 days later). Aside from the differences in delays to the first offered appointment, both groups received the same treatment. Client and demographic variables were again examined using chi-square and tabular analysis and none were significant. However, the difference in scheduling the first appointment was significant. Clients who were asked to come in on the initial contact day attended their first appointment at a rate over 40 percent above those asked to come 1–3 days later. Based on the results of this experiment, we concluded that one variable influencing treatment entry is an environmental variable that is largely under the control of the clinic. Cocaine treatment providers may be able to effectively increase treatment entry by offering a clinic appointment within 24 hours of the initial contact.

TREATMENT RETENTION

Once clients have successfully entered treatment, issues of treatment retention and outcome become important. Consistent with the high attrition rates for first clinic appointments, high attrition throughout treatment appears to be a standard in alcohol and substance abuse treatment settings. Previous studies on outpatient alcohol treatment (Baekland & Lundwall, 1975; Roffe, 1981) have indicated that 28 percent to 80 percent of all clients drop out of treatment by their fourth session. Studies of cocaine and crack abusers have found that 47 percent drop out between the initial clinic visit and their first counseling session (Kang et al., 1991) and that 76 percent fail to attend past the fifth session (Kleinman et al., 1992).

A number of studies have focused on client characteristics related to treatment retention. Linn, Shane, Webb, and Pratt (1979) asked whether black and white subjects differed on characteristics measured at intake and whether these characteristics were related to attrition from mental health treatment. Blacks who saw their environment as insightful, spontaneous, autonomous, and practical stayed in treatment longer, while for whites motivation and poorer adjustment increased attrition. Agosti, Nunes, Stewart, and Quitkin (1991) found that completers from outpatient cocaine treatment were more likely to be white and female. However, these findings are contradicted by Sansone (1980), who found much higher drug abuse treatment retention rates among blacks and males, and by Mammo and Weinbaum (1993), who also found better retention among males participating in treatment for alcohol problems.

A comprehensive review by Baekland and Lundwall (1975) focused on attrition in outpatient treatment for a variety of substance abuse and mental health services. Their review indicated a variety of client characteristics, drug use, and treatment variables were related to treatment attrition. Psychopathology, high alcoholic symptomology, and ambivalence toward treatment predicted dropout from alcohol treatment. Dropout from heroin treatment was significantly related to younger age and lack of prior treatment. Means and colleagues (1989), focusing specifically on outpatient cocaine treatment, reported that number of attended sessions was positively related to length of abstinence from cocaine before initiating treatment, number of previous interventions, and secondary substance used. Interestingly, some studies have indicated that both the extent of cocaine use and cocaine-related difficulties are predictors of retention (Carroll, Rounsaville, & Gawin, 1991; Gainey, Wells, Hawkins, & Catalano, 1993). Using multiple substances was actually correlated with longer retention. According to the authors, this may be because long-term cocaine users and multiple drug users may have made more attempts at abstinence and, thus, may be more convinced of the necessity of treatment.

A number of studies have examined social variables predicting treatment attrition. Baekland and Lundwall (1975) found that, for alcohol treatment, social isolation and lower socioeconomic level predicted attrition, although similar social variables (that is, low education, unemployment, and being single) as well as prior arrests predicted dropout from heroin treatment. Means and colleagues (1989) reported that number of attended outpatient cocaine treatment sessions was positively related to educational level and quality of living condition. According to Hawkins and Catalano (1985), involvement in prosocial institutions, such as family, workplace, and other social organizations, increases the opportunity for treatment retention and success. These reinforcing prosocial behaviors may ultimately compete with the cocaine use in both time and level of reinforcement. This is consistent with findings that family involvement in treatment (Higgins, Budney, Bickel, & Badger, 1994; Siddall & Conway, 1988) and degree of social support are related to retention in drug treatment.

To explore possible factors related to retention in our outpatient cocaine treatment, we examined the retention of 92 clients from intake to an initial counseling session 1–3 days later (Lamb, Marlowe, Festinger, & Kirby, 1994). Using a tabular analysis, we identified several client and demographic variables related to treatment retention. Low levels of anxiety, significant depression, previous involvement with Narcotics Anonymous, no current legal involvement, and living in the city where the clinic is located (as opposed to townships within the metropolitan area) all significantly predicted return. The last three variables were also found to interact in a positive manner. Among the clients with previous Narcotics Anonymous experience, lack of current legal involvement and city residence were even greater predictors of retention. Variables not predictive of retention included graduating high school, income, marital status, living arrangements, client gender, client age, frequency of cocaine or alcohol use, previous Alcoholics Anonymous involvement, and number of past treatment attempts. Our results differ from those reported by other researchers because variables that others have reported to predict cocaine and other drug treatment retention (for example, number of past treatment attempts, and client age) were not significant predictors in our study. These differences may partially be because we examined short-term retention from orientation to first counseling session while the other studies examined longer term retention periods.

Unfortunately, few of the variables reported as significant predictors of treatment retention have been environmental factors directly under the control of the clinic. Although environmental factors, such as quality of living condition, involvement in prosocial institutions, and living in the city where the clinic is located, were predictive of retention these factors cannot be directly controlled by the clinic. Clinics can provide access to social work services that may lead to some improvements in clients' living conditions, refer clients to clinics in the area where they live, or encourage clients to include family members in treatment, find work, and become more involved in other prosocial activities. However, few clinical interventions have attempted to take direct action to increase the likelihood that the client complies with these suggestions. Recently, some comprehensive behavioral interventions have developed that focus on assisting the client to improve their own living conditions and become more involved in prosocial activities. Because these interventions have focused on reducing cocaine use in addition to assessing treatment retention, the effects on both dependent variables will be reviewed in the section on treatment outcome.

TREATMENT OUTCOME

The behavioral treatments for cocaine and stimulant abuse that first reported good treatment outcomes tended to focus on behavioral contingency contracting techniques (for example, Anker & Crowley, 1982; Boudin, 1972; Crowley, 1984). Usually these techniques were implemented in the context of more traditional drug counseling approaches, which provided counseling, psychotherapy, and medical care. The behavioral intervention tended to focus only on drug taking and arranged for aversive consequences for drug use (Anker & Crowley, 1982; Crowley, 1984) or positive reinforcement for abstinence (Boudin, 1972). Recently, more comprehensive behavioral approaches have been suggested (for example, Grabowski, Higgins, & Kirby, 1993; Higgins & Budney, 1993; Higgins, Budney, & Bickel, 1994; Lamb, Iguchi, Husband, & Platt, 1993) and the treatment outcomes reported (Grabowski, Higgins, & Kirby, 1993; Higgins & Budney, 1993; Higgins et al., 1994; Kirby, Marlowe, Lamb, Husband, & Platt, 1995). These treatments tend to address both the antecedents and consequences of cocaine use in the context of multiple aspects of the patient's life. In this sense, cocaine use is one among many operant behaviors, each with naturally associated consequences. Problems arise when cocaine comes to maintain a large portion of the patient's behavior, to the exclusion of other reinforcers. The basic strategy is to rearrange the patient's environment so that drug use and abstinence are readily detected, drug abstinence is reinforced, drug use is extinguished or results in loss of reinforcement, and reinforcement from nondrug sources is increased to compete with the reinforcing effects of drugs.

Implementing this basic strategy involves frequent provision of urine samples and immediate screening for benzoylecgonine, a cocaine metabolite. Patients, therapists, and sometimes significant others are immediately informed of urinalysis results. Cocaine-free urines are immediately reinforced by providing the patient with a voucher. These vouchers are, in turn, used to increase reinforcement density from nondrug sources. Voucher exchanges are negotiated with counselors and used to encourage prosocial activities that are in concert with the patient's treatment plan and likely to have naturally reinforcing consequences that will maintain the behavior after cocaine treatment has ended (for example, recreational activities, family outings, and goods that support vocational or educational goals). Other aspects of these programs include helping the patient to identify antecedents of cocaine use and plan to avoid them or to develop skills to respond to those that are unavoidable (Lamb et al., 1993) and contracting with the patient's significant others to participate in treatment (Higgins & Budney, 1993).

The effectiveness of this type of approach relative to traditional 12-step drug abuse counseling approaches was first demonstrated by Higgins, Delaney, Budney, Bickel, Hughes, Foerg, and Fenwick (1991) and Higgins, Budney, Bickel, Hughes, Foerg, and Badger, (1993). Patients given behavioral treatment showed better treatment retention and achieved significantly longer periods of continuous cocaine abstinence than patients given 12-step treatment. Higgins and colleagues (1991, 1994) noted, however, that the generalizability of their results to crack-using minorities living in large inner-city metropolitan areas was unknown because their patient population was comprised of cocaine hydrochloride-using Caucasians living in a small, rural city.

Our research has focused on evaluating components and variations of a comprehensive behavioral approach, but provides some evidence for generalizability of behavioral approaches to crack-using inner-city minorities. Most of our patients are single, black, unemployed males living in Camden, New Jersey, a city near the Philadelphia metropolitan area that has received national attention for its severe social problems (Fedarko, 1992). We conducted a preliminary evaluation of our cognitive-behavioral counseling manual, regressing percent of cocaine-free urines on counseling attendance during treatment for 177 subjects. One-half of these subjects received a voucher incentive system and one-half did not. We found that subjects who attended more counseling sessions provided significantly higher percentages of cocaine-free urine samples ($F[1,175] = 24.94$, $p < .001$), with counseling attendance predicting 13 percent of the variance. These data do not provide experimental confirmation of the efficacy of our behavioral counseling manual because they are correlational in nature. Although positive correlations between treatment tenure and reduced drug use have been found in several investigations of methadone treatment (Hargreaves, 1983; Simpson, 1979; Simpson, Savage, & Loyd, 1979), this relationship did not hold for cocaine use (Hubbard, Marsden, Cavanaugh, Rachal, & Ginzberg, 1988), and a recent study of cocaine abusers did not find a positive relation between treatment retention and outcome (Carroll, Power, Bryant, & Rounsaville, 1993). It seems plausible that treatment retention may correlate positively with improved outcomes only when the treatment is an effective one. If so, the positive relation found in our data would suggest that cognitive-behavioral counseling provides a basis for an effective behavioral intervention for the treatment of crack cocaine addiction. Although our cognitive-behavioral treatment intervention and the behavioral treatment used by Higgins and colleagues (1991, 1994) have several components in common, they also differ in important ways. Therefore, our findings do not confirm the generalizability of that intervention. They do suggest that behavioral approaches to cocaine dependence are hopeful, and that a systematic replication of Higgins and colleagues with inner-city crack-using populations would be promising. Although this preliminary analysis did not systematically differentiate different components of the behavioral approach, additional studies by Higgins' research group and our own have proceeded to examine components and variations of the approach to determine what aspects contribute significantly to positive treatment outcomes.

Vouchers

Higgins and Budney (1993) reported a comparison of their behavioral treatment package (that is, urine testing, informing significant others of urinalysis results, counselors encouraging prosocial activities, and contracting with significant others to participate in treatment) with and without the voucher system. Subjects who received vouchers stayed in treatment longer and achieved better cocaine abstinence. They concluded that the voucher system contributed significantly to the efficacy of their behavioral treatment package, but suggested that other aspects of the package were also important because subjects in both groups showed better treatment retention and longer periods of cocaine abstinence than those in the standard 12-step treatment group of the previous study (Higgins et al., 1991).

We conducted a similar study at our Camden treatment site where one of two randomly assigned groups received the voucher system in addition to the structured behavioral counseling package (Kirby et al., 1995). The purpose of the comparison was to determine if the addition of the contingency management system would have a therapeutic advantage during treatment and if the effects would endure beyond the period that the contingency management program was in effect. In a preliminary analysis of the first 28 subjects to complete intake, a 3-month follow-up that corresponded to the end of the scheduled treatment, and a 12-month follow-up interview, we found trends suggesting a therapeutic advantage of the voucher system that endures beyond the treatment period. Subjects in the group receiving vouchers reported one-half as many days of drug use in the past 30 days at the 3-month follow-up compared to intake and a further reduction was noted at the 12-month follow-up. This trend was not seen for the noncontingent group, where the mean reported drug use was about the same at all three interviews. Unfortunately, between-subject variability in drug use was sufficiently large so that this preliminary analysis did not show significant differences between the groups. We are hopeful that analysis of the completed data set will replicate the results reported by Higgins and Budney (1993).

Other Treatment Factors

In addition to the voucher system, Higgins' research group has reported on two more factors that appear to predict good treatment outcomes. In a study conducted to identify predictors of cocaine abstinence during their outpatient behavioral treatment, Higgins, Budney, Bickel, and Badger (1994) used stepwise logistic regression to examine the influence of demographic, drug use, and other subject characteristics. They found that the single best predictor of cocaine abstinence was whether a significant other participated in a structured form of relationship counseling and behavioral contracting. In this intervention, patients were assisted in choosing significant others who were not drug abusing and appropriate for the role. The patient and significant other develop a contract in which the patient agrees to abstain from cocaine and the significant other agrees to do something reinforcing when the patient successfully does so. Significant others are informed of urinalysis results and engage in the agreed-upon activity with the patient if the result is cocaine-negative. Having a significant other who participated in this structured intervention improved the odds that the patient would achieve a criterion level of cocaine abstinence by a factor of 20. Although others have noted that social support can improve outcome in treatment for cocaine dependence (Havassy, Hall, & Wasserman, 1991; Means et al., 1989), this appears to be the first report specifically examining reciprocal relationship counseling in behavioral treatments for cocaine dependence. While the findings of this retrospective analysis are impressive, Higgins and colleagues (1994) expressed caution in considering their practical utility because attempts to translate social support into an efficacious clinical intervention has been unsuccessful in treatments of smoking cessation (for example, Lichenstein, Glasgo, & Abrams, 1986).

Another factor predicting good treatment outcomes among cocaine-dependent patients with concurrent alcohol abuse or dependence is disulfiram therapy (Higgins, Budney, Bickel, Hughes, & Foerg, 1993). Sixteen patients who met diagnostic criteria for cocaine and alcohol dependence were placed on disulfiram therapy administered under supervision of clinic staff. Both number of days drinking and frequency of cocaine use were suppressed during periods of disulfiram administration. Because patients often determined when disulfiram therapy was terminated, Higgins and colleagues (1993) could not attribute causality for the changes observed, however, disulfiram therapy was clearly associated with significant decreases in cocaine and alcohol use for these patients.

In preliminary analysis of data collected at our research and treatment site, we examined two other factors in relation to treatment outcome. We conducted a preliminary comparison of data from our day-treatment pilot study with that from our outpatient treatment study. We compared treatment retention and drug use outcome measures during the first six weeks of treatment for 97 subjects assigned to the contingency group of the contingent/noncontingent experiment described previously and 12 subjects in a day-treatment pilot study. For both groups, urines were collected three times weekly and tested for a variety of illicit substances. Individual counseling followed the same schedule and the treatment manual for both groups. The day-treatment intervention produced significantly better counseling attendance ($t = 3.54$, $df = 104$, $p = .001$), while improvements in provision of cocaine-free urines approached significance ($t = 1.69$, $df = 104$, $p = .093$). This preliminary comparison suggests that a full day-treatment program may have significant benefits over outpatient treatment. We are currently conducting a controlled study with sufficient power to detect such effects.

We also have conducted a preliminary examination of the differences in treatment outcome and retention between state agency mandated (N = 50) and voluntary participants (N = 175) in our outpatient treatment program (Glass & Marlowe, 1994). We compared subjects on demographic and baseline drug use variables including age, educational level, employment status, race, marital status, drug(s) used, and drug use frequency. The dependent measures were treatment outcome as measured by provision of cocaine-free urine samples and treatment retention as measured by number of counseling sessions attended. Compulsory and noncompulsory subjects did not differ significantly on any of the demographic measures, and they did not show significant differences in counseling attendance or the percent of cocaine-free urines provided during treatment. These data suggest that being mandated to treatment by a state agency does not lead to better or worse treatment attendance or outcome than voluntary participation in treatment. We are currently conducting further data analyses to determine if trends in cocaine use differ between these groups over the course of treatment or if the groups differ in their readiness to change problem behaviors at the point of treatment entry.

SUMMARY AND DISCUSSION

This review identified several environmental factors the clinician can rearrange to improve the likelihood of treatment entry, retention, and outcome for cocaine abusers. To date, the only variable directly shown to influence cocaine treatment entry is an environmental variable that is largely under the clinic control, that is, offering an appointment within 24 hours of the initial contact. However, interventions, such as preappointment contacts, have improved first appointment attendance for other clinical populations, and provision of treatment vouchers and recruitment through significant others have been successfully used in other settings. These factors deserve attention in research on the treatment of cocaine abuse. Besides having potential for increasing treatment entry, vouchers and significant other involvement tend to also improve treatment retention and outcome. Vouchers provided contingent on cocaine abstinence and used to encourage prosocial activities improve both treatment retention and outcome. Involvement of a significant other in a structured reciprocal contract with the cocaine user predicts substantial improvements in outcome. Finally, supervised disulfiram therapy is associated with improved outcomes for cocaine-dependent patients with concurrent alcohol abuse or dependence and preliminary data suggest that providing a structured full-day treatment improves both treatment retention and outcome.

That involvement of significant others and provision of vouchers appear to facilitate compliance with treatment entry and continued treatment attendance and to lead to improved treatment outcomes is noteworthy. Treatment entry involves an agreement to initiate clinic contact, then keep the first appointment. Treatment retention involves compliance in keeping subsequent appointments, while improvements in treatment outcome may be influenced by compliance with counselor suggestions or instructions and with clinic rules regarding drug use. Because of this perspective, vouchers and significant others may be seen as important environmental factors in improving treatment compliance. Research identifying other environmental factors predicting compliance is useful, but identifying predictors of various aspects of treatment compliance is not sufficient to improve our methods for treating cocaine addiction. The factors must also be accessible to the clinic in ways that allow rearrangement of the antecedents and consequences of cocaine use and of competing prosocial behaviors. Both clinic-delivered vouchers and participation of significant others can meet this criterion. It is through the rearrangement of such environmental factors that behavioral interventions can improve treatment compliance and, thus, facilitate treatment entry, treatment retention, and good treatment outcomes.

Treatment entry and retention, while not considered sufficient for effective treatment, are generally considered necessary elements of effective treatment. In other words, a treatment not attended is generally considered to have no effect. Despite the frequent recognition of the difficulty of getting clients needing help to enter and stay in drug abuse treatment, little research has been conducted in this area. However, some general findings are beginning to emerge. These findings can be grouped into two types of interventions: those functioning to improve the reciprocal relationship of the patient and the clinic and those functioning to extend treatment into the natural ecology. An example of the former is making immediate intake appointments. Examples of the latter are significant other participation in treatment and supervised disulfarim administration. Thus, explicating treatment tactics facilitating compliance with the effective treatment strategies already identified by both basic and applied behavioral research is a promising and necessary area of investigation in the development of better substance abuse treatments.

In summary, previous basic and applied research has identified and verified important strategies in the behavioral treatment of drug abuse (compare Higgins & Budney, 1993 and Lamb et al., 1993). These strategies include the explicit reinforcement of abstinence through contingency management systems, the development of natural communities of reinforcement for prosocial activities that serve as alternatives for drug use, and the use of stimulus control and self-control procedures to facilitate the initiation of abstinence and the development of prosocial activities. These strategies are now beginning to be complemented with the development of tactics facilitating compliance and, thus, facilitating treatment entry, retention, and the use of strategies learned during treatment. These tactics generally focus on improving the relationship between the treatment provider and the patient or on extending treatment into the patient's natural ecology. The further development of such tactics will be an important topic of substance abuse treatment research for some time to come. Another area that substance abuse researchers will need to address, but beyond the scope of this chapter, is technology transfer. To date, effective treatment elements have only been slowly adopted by the substance abuse treatment community (compare Holder, Longabaugh, Miller, & Rubonis, 1991). Facilitating this technology transfer should also be an important area of research.

REFERENCES

Agosti, V., Nunes, E., Stewart, J. W., & Quitkin, F. M. (1991). Patient factors related to early attrition from an out-patient cocaine research clinic: A preliminary report. *The International Journal of the Addictions, 26*(3), 327–334.

Aigner, T. G., & Balster, R. L. (1978). Choice behavior in rhesus monkeys: Cocaine versus food. *Science, 201*, 534–535.

Anker, A. A., & Crowley, T. J. (1982). Use of contingency contracts in specialty clinics for cocaine abuse. In L. S. Harris (Ed.), *Problems of drug dependence 1981* (NIDA Research Monograph 41, pp. 452–459). Washington, DC: U.S. Government Printing Office.

Baekland, F., & Lundwall, L. (1975). Dropping out of treatment: A critical review. *Psychological Bulletin, 82*(5), 738–783.

Boudin, H. M. (1972). Contingency contacting as a therapeutic tool in the deceleration of amphetamine use. *Behavior Therapy, 3*, 604–608.

Brown, J. S., & Kosterlitz, N. (1964). Selection and treatment of psychiatric outpatients. *Archives of General Psychiatry, 11*, 425–438.

Carpenter, P. J., Morrow, G. R., DelGaudio, A. C., & Ritzler, B. A. (1981). Who keeps the first appointment? *American Journal of Psychiatry, 138*(1), 102–105.

Carroll, K. M., Power, M. D., Bryant, K., & Rounsaville, B. J. (1993). One-year follow-up status of treatment-seeking cocaine abusers: Psychopathology and dependence severity as predictors of outcome. *Journal of Nervous and Mental Disease, 181*, 71–79.

Carroll, K. M., Rounsaville, B. J., & Gawin, F. H. (1991). A comparative trial of psycho-therapies for ambulatory cocaine abusers: Relapse prevention and interpersonal psychotherapy. *American Journal of Drug and Alcohol Abuse, 17*, 229–247.

Crowley, T. (1984). Contingency contracting treatment of drug-abusing physicians, nurses, and dentists. In J. Grabowski, M. Stitzer, & J. Henningfield (Eds.), *Behavioral interventions in drug abuse treatment* (NIDA Research Monograph 46, pp. 131-146). Washington, DC: U.S. Government Printing Office.

Fedarko, K. (1992, January 20). Who could live here? *Time, 139*(3), 20.

Festinger, D. S., Lamb, R. J., Kirby, K. C., & Marlowe, D. B. (in press). Accelerated intake: A method of reducing initial appointment no-show. *Journal of Applied Behavior Analysis*.

Festinger, D. S., Lamb, R. J., Kountz, M., Kirby, K. C., & Marlowe, D. B. (1995). Pretreatment drop-out as a function of treatment delay and client variables. *Addictive Behaviors, 20*(1), 111–115.

Gaines, T. (1978). Factors influencing failure to show for a family evaluation. *International Journal of Family Counseling, 6*, 57–61.

Gainey, R. R., Wells, E. A., Hawkins, J. D., & Catalano, R. F. (1993). Predicting treatment retention among cocaine users. *International Journal of the Addictions, 28*(6), 487–505.

Glass, D. J., & Marlowe, D. B. (1994, March). Comparing state agency mandated and voluntary outpatients: Treatment outcome and retention in a cocaine addiction program. Paper presented at the biennial meeting of the American Psychology-Law Society, Santa Fe, New Mexico.

Goldberg, S. R., & Kelleher, R. T. (1977). Reinforcement of behavior by cocaine injections. In E. H. Ellinwood, Jr. & M. M. Kilbey (Eds.), *Cocaine and other stimulants* (pp. 523–544). New York: Plenum Press.

Grabowski, J., Higgins, S. T., & Kirby, K. C. (1993). Behavioral treatments of cocaine dependence. In F. M. Tims & C. G. Leukefeld (Eds.), *Cocaine treatment: Research and clinical perspectives* (NIDA Research Monograph 135, pp. 133–149). Washington, DC: U.S. Government Printing Office.

Grieves, R. (1978). An analysis of service delay and client variables as they relate to mental health center pre-therapy drop outs. *Dissertation Abstracts International, 34*, 2126–2135.

Griffiths, R. R., Bradford, L. D., & Brady, J. V. (1979). Progressive ratio and fixed ratio schedules of cocaine-maintained responding in baboons. *Psychopharmacology, 65*, 125–136.

Hargreaves, W. A. (1983). Methadone dosage and duration for maintenance treatment. In J. R. Cooper, F. Alterman, B. S. Brown, & Czechowicz, D. (Eds.), *Research on the treatment of narcotic addiction* (NIDA Treatment Research Monograph, pp. 19-80). Washington, DC: U.S. Government Printing Office.

Havassy, B. E., Hall, S. M., & Wasserman, D. A. (1991). Relapse to cocaine use following treatment: Preliminary findings on the role of social support. In L. S. Harris (Ed.), *Problems of drug dependence 1990* (NIDA Research Monograph

105, pp. 502-504). Washington, DC: U.S. Government Printing Office.

Hawkins, J. D., & Catalano, R. F. (1985). Aftercare in drug abuse treatment. *International Journal of the Addictions, 20*, 917–945.

Higgins, S. T., & Budney, A. J. (1993). Treatment of cocaine dependence via the principles of behavior analysis and behavioral pharmacology. In L. S. Onken, J. D. Blaine, & J. J. Boren, (Eds.), *Behavioral treatments for drug abuse and dependence* (NIDA Monograph Series 137, pp. 97–121). Washington, DC: U.S. Government Printing Office.

Higgins, S. T., Budney, A. J., & Bickel, W. K. (1994). Applying behavioral concepts and principles to the treatment of cocaine dependence. *Drug and Alcohol Dependence, 34*, 87–97.

Higgins, S. T., Budney, A. J., Bickel, W. K., & Badger, G. J. (1994). Participation of significant others in outpatient behavioral treatment predicts greater abstinence. *American Journal of Drug and Alcohol Abuse, 21*(1), 47–56.

Higgins, S. T., Budney, A. J., Bickel, W. K., Foerg, F., Dunham, R., & Badger, G. J. (1994). Incentives improve outcome in outpatient behavioral treatment of cocaine dependence. *Archives of General Psychiatry, 51*, 568–576.

Higgins, S. T., Budney, A. J., Bickel, W. K., Hughes, J. R., Foerg, F., & Badger, G. J. (1993) Achieving cocaine abstinence with a behavioral approach. *American Journal of Psychiatry 150*: 763–769.

Higgins, S. T., Budney, A. J., Bickel, W. K., Hughes, J. R., & Foerg, F. (1993). Disulfiram therapy in patients abusing cocaine and alcohol. *American Journal of Psychiatry, 150*(4), 675–676.

Higgins, S. T., Delaney, D. D., Budney, A. J., Bickel, W. K., Hughes, J. R., Foerg, F., & Fenwick, J. W. (1991). A behavioral approach to achieving initial cocaine abstinence. *American Journal of Psychiatry, 148*, 1218–1224.

Holder, H., Longabaugh, R., Miller, W. R., & Rubonis, A. V. (1991). The cost effectiveness of treatment for alcoholism: A first approximation. *Journal of Studies on Alcohol, 52*(6), 517–540.

Hubbard, R. L., Marsden, M. E., Cavanaugh, E., Rachal, J. V., & Ginzberg, H. M. (1988). Role of drug-abuse treatment in limiting the spread of AIDS. *Review of Infectious Disease, 10*, 377–384.

Iguchi, M. Y., Bux, D. A., Lidz, V., Kushner, H., French, J. F., & Platt, J. J. (1994). Interpreting HIV seroprevalence data from a street-based outreach program. *Journal of Acquired Immune Deficiency Syndromes, 7*, 491–499.

Kang, S., Kleinman, P. H., Woody, G. E., Millman, R. B., Todd, T. C., Kemp, J., & Lipton, D. S. (1991). Outcomes for cocaine abusers after once-a-week psychosocial therapy. *American Journal of Psychiatry, 148*(5), 630–635.

Kirby, K. C., Marlowe, D. B., Lamb, R. J., Husband, S. D., & Platt, J. J. (1995). Cognitive-behavioral cocaine treatment with and without contingency management. In L. S. Harris (Ed.), *Problems of drug dependence 1994* (NIDA Research Monograph 153, p. 346). Washington, DC: U.S. Government Printing Office.

Kirk, B. A., & Frank, A. C. (1976). Zero interviews. *Journal of Counseling Psychology, 23*(3), 286–288.

Kleinman, P. H., Kang, S. Y., Lipton, D. S., Woody, G. E., Kemp, J., & Millman, R. B. (1992). Retention of cocaine abusers in outpatient psychotherapy. *American Journal of Drug and Alcohol Abuse, 18*(1), 29–43.

Lamb, R. J., Iguchi, M. Y., Husband, S. D., & Platt, J. J. (1993). A behavioral model for the treatment of cocaine addiction. In J. A. Inciardi, F. M. Tims, & B. W. Fletcher, (Eds.), *Innovative approaches in the treatment of drug abuse: Program models and strategies*, (pp. 149–160). Westport, CT: Greenwood Press.

Lamb, R. J., Marlowe, D., Festinger, D., & Kirby, K. C. (1994). Predictors of initial treatment retention in cocaine abusers. In L. S. Harris (Ed.), *Problems of drug dependence 1993* (NIDA Research Monograph). Washington, DC: U.S. Government Printing Office.

Lichenstein, E., Glasgo, R. E., & Abrams, D. B. (1986). Social support in smoking cessation: In search of effective interventions. *Behavior Therapy, 17*, 607–619.

Linn, M. W., Shane, R., Webb, N. L., & Pratt, T. C. (1979). Cultural factors and attrition in drug abuse treatment. *International Journal of the Addictions, 14*(2), 259–280.

Mammo, A., & Weinbaum, D. F. (1993). Some factors that influence dropping out from outpatient alcoholism treatment facilities. *Journal of Studies on Alcohol, 54*, 92–101.

McCoy, C. B., Rivers, J. E., & Chitwood, D. D. (1993). Community outreach for injection drug users and the need for cocaine treatment. In F. M. Tims & C. G. Leukefeld (Eds.), *Cocaine treatment: Research and clinical perspectives* (NIDA Research Monograph 135, pp. 190–202). Washington, DC: U.S. Government Printing Office.

Means, L. B., Small, M., Capone, D. M., Capone, T. J., Condren, R., Peterson, M., & Hayward, B. (1989). Client demographics and outcome in outpatient cocaine treatment. *International Journal of the Addictions, 24*, 765–783.

Noonan, J. R. (1974). A follow-up of pretherapy dropouts. *Journal of Counseling Psychology, 1*, 43–44.

O'Loughlin, S. (1990). The effect of a pre-appointment questionnaire clinical psychologist attendance rates. *British Journal of Medical Psychology, 63*, 5–9.

Orne, D. R., & Boswell, D. (1991). The pre-intake drop-out at a community mental health center. *Community Mental Health Journal, 27*, 375–379.

Raynes, A. E., & Warren, G. (1971). Some characteristics of "dropouts" at first contact with a psychiatric clinic. *Community Mental Health Journal, 7*, 144–150.

Roffe, M. (1981). Predictive correlates of treatment program completion in a sample of male alcoholics. *International Journal of the Addictions, 16*, 849–857.

Sansone, J. (1980). Retention patterns in a therapeutic community for the treatment of drug abuse. *International Journal of the Addictions, 15*(5), 711–736.

Schuster, C. R., & Johanson, C. E. (1981). An analysis of drug-seeking behavior in animals. *Neuroscience Biobehavioral Reviews, 5*, 315–323.

Siddall, J. W., & Conway, G. L. (1988). Interactional variables associated with retention and success in residential drug treatment. *International Journal of the Addictions, 23*(12), 1241–1254.

Simpson, D. D. (1979). The relation of time spent in drug abuse treatment to posttreatment outcome. *American Journal of Psychiatry, 136*, 1449–1453.

Simpson, D. D., Savage, L. J., & Loyd, M. R. (1979). Follow-up evaluation of treatment of drug abuse during 1969 to 1972. *Archives of General Psychiatry, 36*, 772–780.

Sisson, R. W., & Azrin, N. H. (1986). Family-member involvement to initiate and promote treatment of problem drinkers. *Journal of Behavior Therapy and*

Experimental Psychiatry, 17(1), 15–21.

Sue, S., McKinney, H. L., & Allen, D. B. (1976). Predictors of the duration of therapy for clients in the community mental health system. *Community Mental Health Journal, 12*(4), 365–375.

Swenson, T. R., & Pekarik, G. (1988). Interventions for reducing missed initial appointments at a community mental health center. *Community Mental Health Journal, 24*(3), 205–218.

Turner, A. J., & Vernon, J. C. (1976). Prompts to increase attendance in a community mental-health center. *Journal of Applied Behavioral Analysis, 9*, 141–145.

Weighill, V. E., Hodge, J. T., & Peck, D. F. (1983). Keeping appointments with clinical psychologists. *British Journal of Clinical Psychology, 22*, 143–144.

12

The DATAR Project: Cognitive and Behavioral Enhancements to Community-based Treatments

D. Dwayne Simpson, Donald F. Dansereau, and George W. Joe

Although there is substantial evidence that community-based treatment for drug addiction is effective for many clients (Anglin & Hser, 1990; De Leon, 1989; Gerstein & Harwood, 1990; Hubbard et al., 1989; Simpson, 1993; Tims & Ludford, 1984), there has been a long-standing recognition of the need to examine treatment implementation and therapeutic process to improve its efficacy (for example, De Leon, 1984; Simpson, 1984). Growing concerns in recent years about AIDS and the spread of HIV through sharing injection equipment prompted the infusion of new research funds that enabled the drug abuse field to initiate several large-scale studies of treatment process and enhancement strategies in naturalistic settings. In particular, it made possible the treatment demonstration research described in this volume in which promising techniques for treatment improvements have been developed, implemented, and evaluated in representative community settings throughout the United States. The findings should help guide programmatic upgrading of services in our public drug abuse treatment system.

Our project, Improving Drug Abuse Treatment for AIDS-Risk Reduction (DATAR), was funded as one of these demonstrations. It began with the premise that treatment services research should have practical objectives and be carried out in real-world settings. That is, experimental interventions should be implemented and evaluated within the constraints intrinsic to the programs they are intended to enhance (for example, Chatham & Simpson, 1994). General goals for the DATAR project have been to improve therapeutic interventions for drug abusers and to understand the treatment dynamics involved. More specifically, we want to find better strategies for engaging clients in treatment, reducing the rates of early dropout, and enhancing the quality of care to reduce drug use relapse rates and related HIV/AIDS risks (Simpson, Chatham, & Joe, 1993).

The rationale for this project follows in part from previous findings based on the Drug Abuse Reporting Program showing evidence for the effectiveness of major treatment modalities (Simpson & Sells, 1982, 1990). Particularly noteworthy were the favorable effects of longer retention on posttreatment outcomes (Simpson, 1979, 1981) and the frequent occurrence of relapses over time (Simpson & Marsh, 1986). In the era of AIDS, implications of these results increase in significance; that is, early dropouts from treatment are more likely to return to drug use and related AIDS-risky behaviors. The DATAR project, therefore, focuses on ways to increase time in treatment, along with engagement and compliance in therapeutic plans, as a means to enhance chances of client recovery.

Our three-part strategy addresses counseling technique, intervention materials, and treatment process. First, we introduced a cognitive approach to drug abuse counseling — "node-link mapping" — as a visual representation technique for improving communication, solution-oriented thinking, and action planning. As we had hoped, this type of graphic conceptualization of problems and their potential solutions has been found to have benefits over simple talking therapy in engaging clients and increasing their therapeutic compliance. It seems to enhance the counselor's repertoire of clinical skills and provides an easy-to-use tool for helping clients to understand and solve their problems.

The second component of our strategy was the development and testing of some new psychoeducational training materials to guide counselors and clients through special treatment issues that we felt had been neglected previously in drug abuse treatment. We reasoned that counselor-friendly manuals that provide better focus and structure for practical educational and skills building training sessions would improve client participation and understanding. These include an HIV/AIDS education module that provides information about the disease and ways to reduce risks of HIV infection, a women's assertiveness training curriculum that addresses specialized health care issues and social skills needed to choose safer sex options, and a transition to aftercare program that helps clients improve their social support networks for maintaining a recovery-oriented lifestyle following release from treatment. Materials are presented in a practical, step-by-step format for use in group counseling sessions, and evaluations have been positive. Two of these manuals are being published by the National Institute on Drug Abuse for national distribution, and the third is under review.

The third part of our strategy focused on behavioral approaches for increasing treatment engagement, including the use of simple and inexpensive reinforcement techniques to improve client participation. Contingency management schedules with inexpensive rewards, for instance, were demonstrated as effective ways to increase session attendance and drug abstinence. In addition, several important studies have been conducted to help identify and understand the formation of therapeutic relationships and how they influence outcomes. They include examination of program and client attributes (such as motivation at intake) in relation to indicators of client commitment to treatment (for example, early dropouts, session attendance levels, and attitudes toward counselors).

Before elaborating on these enhancement strategies and summarizing our research findings, the treatment settings and data collection system in the DATAR project will be described. It should also be noted that the results presented in this chapter are limited to our during-treatment evaluations; one-year posttreatment follow-up studies are in progress.

TREATMENT SETTINGS AND DATA COLLECTION

Between May 1990 and September 1993 a total of 960 opioid addicts were admitted to three methadone treatment clinics participating in the DATAR project. These clinics were located in Corpus Christi, Dallas, and Houston, Texas, and each was part of a larger multimodality agency. Approximately 14 percent of the 960 admissions to DATAR left treatment within 30 days, 25 percent left within 60 days, and 34 percent left within 90 days; 47 percent stayed in the program for 180 days or longer. Methadone dosages averaged between 40 milligrams and 50 milligrams at all three clinics, with daily doses ranging up to 85 milligrams. These medication levels are low by some therapeutic standards, but they are representative. Two-thirds of the methadone clinics surveyed in a recent national study reported average doses of 50 milligrams or less (D'Aunno & Vaughn, 1992).

At the time of admission to treatment, the average age of DATAR clients was 37, and 69 percent were male. In terms of race-ethnic distributions, 21 percent were African-American, 38 percent were Mexican-American, and 37 percent were Caucasian. Forty-two percent were married or living as married, and 55 percent had been employed in the past six months (including 32 percent full-time, 12 percent part-time, and 11 percent at periodic odd jobs). Illegal activities (including prostitution) were reported by 28 percent to be a major source of financial support prior to intake; 95 percent had a history of previous arrests, including 32 percent who had one or more arrests in the past six months. All were daily opioid drug users (usually heroin), and cocaine was the second major drug of choice; 29 percent reported no cocaine use in the last 6 months before treatment admission, 33 percent used cocaine on a daily basis, 16 percent used it weekly, and 22 percent used it less than weekly (crack was used by only 14 percent). Marijuana was used by 54 percent (7 percent used daily), and minor tranquilizers, such as benzodiazepines, were used by 31 percent (3 percent used daily).

Of the 34 counselors involved in the DATAR research project at the three treatment programs, 19 were male and 15 were female; 18 were white, 11 were African-American, 4 were Mexican-American, and 1 was American Indian. Their average age was 35. Twenty had bachelor's degrees, seven had master's degrees, and two had junior college degrees. Of the remaining five counselors, two had completed two years of college, one had attended one year, and two reported finishing high school only. Five were recovering substance abusers.

As part of the treatment admission process, a structured face-to-face intake interview was conducted by a trained intake counselor. It lasted approximately one hour, covering sociodemographic background, family background, peer relations, criminal history, health and psychological status, drug use and treatment history, and behavioral risks for HIV. A self-administered assessment of psychosocial functioning was also completed, addressing psychological problems (including scales for self-esteem, depression, anxiety, and decision-making confidence), social problems (that is, childhood problems, hostility, risk-taking, and social conformity), and treatment motivation (that is, drug use problems, desire for help, and treatment readiness). The conceptual basis and psychometric attributes of these scales are described elsewhere (Joe, Knezek, Watson, & Simpson, 1991; Knight, Holcom, & Simpson, 1994; Simpson & Joe, 1993).

A series of during-treatment assessments occurred at monthly intervals for each of the first three months after admission (and at three-month intervals thereafter). Included were the psychosocial self-rating scales, as well as a brief interview to record changes in behavioral functioning over time (using a core subset of items from the intake form). In addition, clients and counselors each completed monthly rating scales concerning treatment activities, progress, and therapeutic interventions. Finally, counselors documented client attendance and activities after each individual and group session. Research staff at each agency maintained monthly tracking records on client services and contacts including results of urinalyses (see Simpson [1992] for a complete description of the data collection instruments and Chatham and Rowan-Szal [1992] for descriptions of data management systems and procedures).

SUMMARY OF MAJOR FINDINGS

Significant overall improvements occurred during treatment on a variety of drug use, criminal involvement, and psychosocial adjustment measures. In the first three months these specifically included heroin, cocaine, and alcohol use; illegal activity; psychological functioning (self-esteem, depression, and anxiety); and social adjustment (risk-taking and social conformity) (Simpson, Joe, Rowan-Szal, & Greener, 1995). For instance, mean scores for days of illegal activities in the previous month dropped from 11.0 at intake to 1.5 at month three, and average frequency of needle injections was reduced from 108.2 to 9.5 per month (based on 557 clients that completed at least three months of treatment). Persons with one or more days of illegal activity in the past month dropped from 57 percent at intake to 17 percent at month three; those with 15 or more drug injections per month dropped from 98 percent to 12 percent. Self-reported decreases in frequency of use for each of the major drug categories — heroin, cocaine, and speedball — were large. Percentages of users in the month before intake and month three dropped from 94 to 41 for heroin, 46 to 26 for cocaine, and 51 to 24 for speedball; combining reports of cocaine usage into a single indicator (based on cocaine as well as speedball) reflected a drop from 61 percent to 37 percent. These significant decreases in self-reported drug use were validated by urinalysis results. That is, dirty urines for opiates dropped from 86 percent at intake to 38 percent in month three, and from 47 percent to 35 percent for cocaine metabolites. Additional analyses of clients who remained in treatment for six months or longer show that these improvements were sustained over time (Joe, Dansereau, & Simpson, 1994).

Factors that influence these and related measures of during-treatment performance (including engagement and retention) have been examined in a series of studies, discussed below.

Cognitive Enhancements Using Node-link Mapping

Node-link mapping is a visual representation system that can be used in group and individual counseling sessions to illustrate clients' problems, issues, and plans. The nodes contain facts, ideas, actions, or feelings, and the labeled links are used to express their interrelationships. Figure 12.1 shows a sample map developed during a drug abuse counseling session, reproduced from our training manual for counselors (Dansereau, Dees, Chatham, Boatler, & Simpson, 1993). Maps can be developed by counselors and clients or by specialists on particular counseling issues for instructional presentations.

Background and Rationale

Researchers in cognitive psychology have established the importance of representing problems schematically, and the use of visual (diagrammatic) representations are recommended (Larkin & Simon, 1987; Mayer & Gallini, 1990; Winn, Li, & Schill, 1991). Visual representations can cluster

FIGURE 12.1
Sample of Node-link Mapping during a Counseling Session

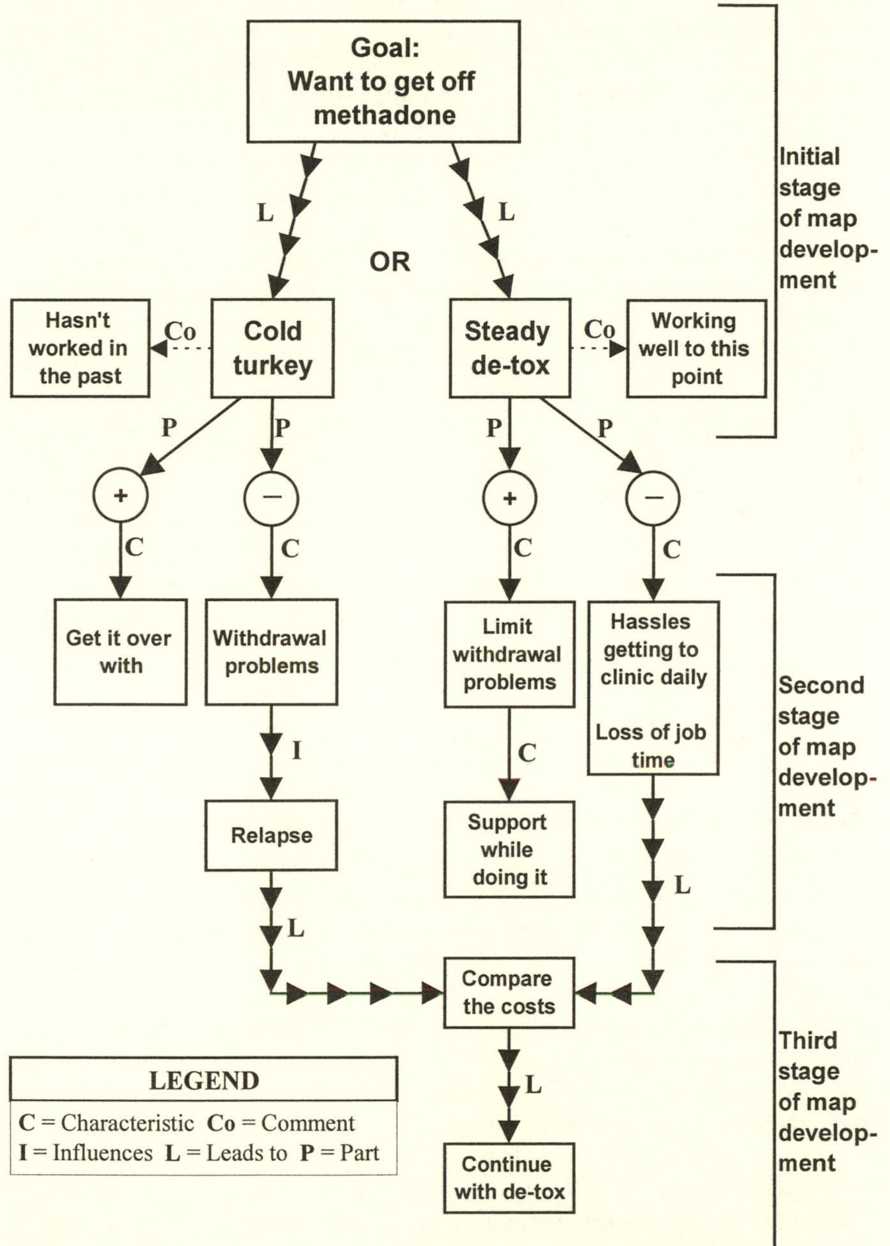

related components together, while natural language (spoken or written) tends to "string them out." Consequently, natural language can be less effective for representing parallel lines of thought, feedback loops, and other elements of complex systems. Because counseling involves working with complex systems of interrelated feelings, thoughts, and actions, it should, therefore, be beneficial to have relevant issues and potential solutions represented visually as much as possible.

In addition to having more potential than natural language for effectively representing complexity, visual representations appear to have other distinct advantages. Because they are visible to both the client and counselor, they help maintain shared cognitive focus on the issue at hand and thereby reduce disruptions caused by attentional lapses. Learning and memory research also indicates that visual displays are often remembered better than natural language (Lambiotte, Dansereau, Cross, & Reynolds, 1989; Patterson, Dansereau, & Newbern, 1992), which is particularly relevant in the light of recent work showing the importance of session recollection in counseling (Cummings, Slemon, & Hallberg, 1993). Finally, the ease of reference associated with well-constructed visual displays makes them potentially valuable in counseling supervision as well as in transferring a client from one counselor to another. Supervisors or counselors can quickly review maps to assess the progression of treatment.

In spite of these advantages, the use of visual representations in counseling has been limited except in some types of family and marital therapy (for example, Cohen & Shlomy, 1986; Parnell & Vanderkloot, 1991). It is likely that one of the reasons is the lack of a widely applicable graphic procedure and its technical adaptation to counseling settings. Therefore, training materials for the node-link mapping system developed at Texas Christian University (see Dansereau & Cross, 1992) were modified in 1989 for use by drug counselors participating in the DATAR project (Dansereau, Dees, Chatham, Boatler, & Simpson, 1993). Counselors were trained to incorporate mapping into their individual and group sessions, with appropriate latitude to tailor it to their own personal counseling styles. The usual scenario involves the counselor producing a map on the basis of comments and discussions with the client(s) during a session. As illustrated in Figure 12.1, words or phrases are used to represent a sequence of actions, observations, and alternatives discussed in the process of analyzing or solving a counseling issue. Clients view the map frequently to help clarify communication, visualize key relationships, and review alternatives for decision making. They sometimes request a copy of the map at the end of the session for later review and planning. Counselors rely on mapping to help structure brief problem-solving discussions and keep clients focused. Mapping is well accepted by both counselors and clients and is especially popular in group settings (Knight, Dansereau, Joe, & Simpson, 1994).

Research Findings

A series of studies has been conducted to assess mapping impact on treatment progress. A randomly selected set of counselors at the three DATAR treatment agencies were given mapping training (Dansereau, Dees, Chatham, Boatler, & Simpson, 1993) as an enhancement to their regular counseling; the other counselors did not receive mapping training and thereby served as a standard counseling comparison group. Clients were randomly assigned to mapping and standard counselors over the course of these studies.

In terms of overall impact, we have found that mapping-enhanced counseling leads to greater client commitment to treatment (as measured by attendance at scheduled counseling sessions), more positive counselor perceptions of the client (for example, communication effectiveness and motivation), and fewer urinalysis results that are positive for opiates and cocaine during the first three months of treatment (Dansereau, Joe, & Simpson, 1993, 1995) as well as during later treatment stages (Czuchry, Dansereau, Dees, & Simpson, 1995; Joe, Dansereau, & Simpson, 1994). Less consistent results have been found with client ratings of the counselor and treatment program where average ratings tend to be high and measurement variance is limited. However, when significant effects have been detected using these variables (for example, Czuchry, Dansereau, Dees, & Simpson, 1995) the results have been in favor of mapping. The observed effect sizes in these studies (involving measures of standardized mean differences where values of 0.2, 0.5, and 0.8 represent small, medium, and large effects, respectively) were typically in the medium range (Cohen, 1988). Given the consistency of results across time and samples — even during the early stages of development and implementation — we are encouraged by the magnitude of these effects.

More recently, our assessments focused on the differential effectiveness of mapping with minority and other identifiable subpopulations of clients. Significant interactions involving ethnicity and counseling condition suggest that mapping is more effective for African-Americans and Mexican-Americans than for Caucasians. It appears that mapping helps reduce cultural, racial, and class communication barriers by providing a visual supplement and a common language that enhances counselor-client interchanges (Dansereau, Joe, Dees, & Simpson, 1996). It also appears to be effective (with respect to the same dependent measures described above) even for difficult clients, such as opioid addicts who use cocaine on a regular basis (weekly or daily) and those with attentional problems (Czuchry, Dansereau, Dees, & Simpson, 1995; Dansereau, Joe, & Simpson, 1995; Joe, Dansereau, & Simpson, 1994). In fact, there is some indication that mapping has a comparatively larger positive impact on these clients than on those with fewer impairments. Our interpretation is that mapping serves to focus and maintain the attention of difficult clients more effectively than standard (verbal) counseling procedures. This increased cognitive engagement of clients in the treatment process then leads to the favorable effects observed.

We are also investigating specific elements of the counseling process that may be influenced by mapping. Using client and counselor ratings of group and individual counseling sessions, Dansereau, Dees, Greener, and Simpson (1995) showed that the use of mapping was related to greater counseling session depth (as measured by the Session Evaluation Questionnaire, Stiles et al., 1994). In this case, a deep session was one that was rated as valuable, full, powerful, and special. It is possible, however, that counselors (and clients) may choose to map when a deeper session is anticipated rather than mapping actually causing it. Further research is needed to settle this issue, but, in either case, there appears to be an important role for mapping during critical stages of a counseling session.

Taken together, the Dansereau, Dees, Greener, and Simpson (1995) study and one conducted by Knight, Dansereau, Joe, and Simpson (1994) indicate that mapping is used by counselors much more frequently in group than individual sessions (that is, in approximately two-thirds versus one-third of the sessions, respectively), and that mapped group sessions are seen as smoother and as leading to greater feelings of positivity than mapped individual sessions. These findings support feedback from counselors indicating that they have more difficulty using mapping regularly during individual sessions. Future efforts are, therefore, planned for facilitating the use of mapping in individual sessions by using simple, prestructured maps designed to focus on specific issues.

Based on the positive findings for mapping from our programmatic series of studies and numerous anecdotal discussions with counselors, we have developed our initial theory-driven expectations into a cognitive framework for counseling that attempts to explain the impact of mapping (Dansereau, Dees, & Simpson, 1994). In brief, we have argued that the graphic portrayal of recovery issues provides the client and counselor with a tool that facilitates the interactive course of a session by enhancing communication, focus, and memory for session content. Mapping provides an easily referenced display that can capture complexities (for example, feedback loops and parallel lines of thought), focus and guide attention during the counseling session, and be easily encoded into memory by both client and counselor.

Psychoeducational Intervention Modules

Besides developing and testing cognitive-behavioral intervention strategies, major attention was devoted in the DATAR project to materials and procedures for client education and skills building. Several substantive training areas were identified that we felt needed greater attention in community-based treatment programs. As priorities, we selected HIV/AIDS education, special needs of women, and ways of improving social support networks for transition to aftercare (including Alcoholics Anonymous, Cocaine Anonymous, and other community self-help groups) to assist clients in sustaining their recovery progress in the community after leaving formal treatment. In our efforts to develop well-organized manuals that provide practical, step-by-step guides to session materials, our presentational designs — along with the clinical appropriateness of the materials — underwent numerous phases of pilot-testing and modification.

HIV/AIDS Education

Our preliminary module was the *AIDS/HIV Risk Reduction Module* (Boatler, 1992). It was developed early in the project for presentation in four group and two individual counseling sessions. It covers general information on HIV transmission and AIDS and emphasizes alternatives and safer strategies regarding drug injection and sexual activities. The module includes more technical information than is usually available in HIV community outreach programs, with a focus on the response of the immune system to drug use, infections, diseases, stress, and nutritional factors as well as the effects of exposure (and reexposure) to HIV through injection and sexual activities. Evaluations of this module have shown that, among clients in treatment less than four months, the intervention increased knowledge about AIDS, reduced AIDS-risky behaviors, and improved attitudes toward achieving and maintaining abstinence from drug use. Thus, our AIDS education and intervention efforts were effective, especially in the early phase of drug abuse treatment (Boatler, Knight, & Simpson, 1994).

The value of using information maps to help improve communication and knowledge has been systematically evaluated in several psychoeducational modules. Our studies of the HIV/AIDS module suggest that clients in a mapping-enhanced version of the program had greater knowledge gains and retention at posttest than those in a standard (nonmapping) version. The use of mapping also increased the knowledge gains of clients in a relapse prevention training module (Knight, Simpson, & Dansereau, 1994). A recent update of the AIDS module, *Approaches to HIV/AIDS Education in Drug Treatment* (Bartholomew & Simpson, 1994), advances our use of information maps and structured "fill-in" maps to help clients plan personal risk-reduction strategies and incorporates new information in the field.

Women's Assertiveness Training

Our intervention module, *Time Out! For Me,* is a sexuality and assertiveness workshop for women (Bartholomew, Chatham, & Simpson, 1994) consisting of six weekly group sessions, each lasting two hours. The development of self-esteem through acceptance of one's personal rights and responsibilities (Lange & Jakubowski, 1978) provides the foundation for assertiveness skills introduced in the module. The importance of using I-Messages (versus You-Messages), listening, negotiating, and overcoming communication roadblocks are discussed and specific skill areas are practiced. In addition, such topics as breast health and breast self-examination, sexual and reproductive anatomy, sexual response, gynecological health, and sexually transmitted disease and HIV/AIDS prevention are introduced. The sessions incorporate a structured format of discussions, exercises, visual aides, handouts, videos, anatomically-correct models, and role-play activities.

The module's primary purpose is to teach basic communication skills, improve health awareness, and enhance self-esteem to help women become more comfortable discussing sexual issues with their partners. This increased comfort level is an important foundation for empowering women to negotiate safer sexual relationships. The module also provides women with an opportunity to dispel sexual mythology and challenge stereotypes that often have a negative impact on women's self-concept and self-esteem. We have found that women who participated frequently in the women's groups (4–6 sessions) showed greater increases in self-esteem and knowledge compared with women who participated infrequently (1–3 sessions). In addition, level of participation was positively associated with length of stay in the treatment program after completing the workshop (Bartholomew, Rowan-Szal, Chatham, & Simpson, 1994).

An evaluation of the module's effectiveness for women in residential treatment also has been conducted to examine its generalizability to other settings (Hiller, Rowan-Szal, Bartholomew, & Simpson, 1996). One-half of the residents were randomly assigned to attend the module while the other one-half served as a control group and participated in regular program activities. Results supported those found in the previous DATAR evaluation; women who attended the module showed significant increases in knowledge and self-esteem, compared with the control group. In addition, they reported significantly more positive attitudes toward being assertive and practicing safer sex. In the second phase of the same study (involving a delayed intervention design), women in the control group later participated in the module. After completion, their knowledge, self-esteem, and attitude ratings were comparable to those of the initial group of module participants. Thus, this special intervention for women appears to be effective in both outpatient and residential settings.

Improving Social Support Networks

A ten-session life skills enhancement module for clients in advanced phases of treatment, *Straight Ahead: Transition Skills for Recovery* (Bartholomew, Simpson, & Chatham, 1993), was the last intervention manual developed as part of the DATAR project. It is designed to help clients improve their social networks and otherwise strengthen their recovery efforts during the treatment-to-aftercare transition period. Training efforts focus on developing recovery maintenance skills and personal relationships, building drug-free social networks, accessing community-based self-help groups, improving communication, managing negative emotions, and solving problems more effectively. The materials are organized for presentation in a weekly series of ten two-hour small-group workshops involving open discussion, interactive exercises, experience sharing, role-playing, and cognitive enhancements, such as structured mapping. The training program is now being evaluated.

Studies of Client Engagement and Treatment Process

To address the process of client engagement and recovery, comprehensive assessments of clients, counselors, and the therapeutic environment are needed. The DATAR data collection system focused specifically on these dimensions, especially during the first few months of treatment. Much of our initial research examined this critical treatment phase. In particular, we have measured client background and program characteristics believed to be related to early dropout as well as to a variety of other indicators of engagement and recovery patterns. These studies include systematic efforts to increase engagement, such as the use of contingency management procedures.

Motivation for Treatment

Our motivation scales reflect three transitional cognitive stages believed to be important conditions for behavior change including self-perceptions of drug-use problem severity, desire for help, and treatment readiness (Simpson & Joe, 1993). Indeed, higher motivation scores at intake, along with social stability (marital status, employment, and fewer prior arrests), previous treatment experience, and the use of higher methadone medication doses, are significant (and independent) predictors of treatment retention of opioid addicts beyond the first 60 days (Simpson & Joe, 1993). Motivational indicators can be transient, however, and are subject to a variety of influences from social relations and legal authorities. More work is needed to identify these sources and how they affect internal and external motivations, as well as their role in maintaining commitment to change.

Client Engagement in Treatment

Previous research has shown that the overall length of time spent in drug abuse treatment is associated with better treatment outcomes (for example, Simpson, 1981), but details about therapeutic engagement are lacking. We, therefore, examined counseling intensity among DATAR clients who remained in treatment for three months or longer (Simpson, Joe, Rowan-Szal, & Greener, 1995). Treatment engagement — operationally defined as the number of sessions attended by 557 clients during their first 90 days after admission — was greater among males and for clients with higher social stability, more previous treatment experience, and lower cocaine use prior to intake. In addition, level of engagement was positively related to favorable behavioral indicators during treatment as well as to positive attributions by both clients and counselors about therapeutic interactions. These predictive relationships were unchanged after making statistical adjustments for the effects of client background and motivational characteristics at intake. Types of therapeutic strategy and content of counseling sessions reported by counselors likewise were related to client engagement. For example, higher engagement was associated with more therapeutic emphasis on improving communication skills, goal setting, personal responsibility, relations with others, and problem solving; the amount of time spent discussing these issues during sessions was directly related to favorability of counselor ratings concerning client motivation and therapeutic rapport.

Treatment Induction

Our initial contingency management study included clients from all phases of treatment and showed that inexpensive rewards for program compliance (for example, using food and gas coupons, token gifts, and so on) increased counseling session attendance and decreased drug use during treatment (Rowan-Szal, Joe, Chatham, & Simpson, 1994). Building on these findings, subsequent work focused more specifically on reinforcing positive behaviors during the first 90 days of treatment (that is, on-time session attendance and drug-free urines). We randomly assigned one-half of all new clients to the contingency management (CM) group, and one-half were assigned to a control group in which no rewards were offered. Comparisons of the two groups showed that CM procedures significantly increased the number of individual sessions attended in the first 90 days of treatment as well as the rate of clean urines (for cocaine use) over the following three months. After six months in treatment, counselors judged the CM group significantly higher than the control group on self-confidence, motivation, and rapport (Rowan-Szal, Joe, Hiller, & Simpson, in press).

Psychological Problems

At the time of admission to treatment, 43 percent of DATAR clients were classified as having psychological problems, based on indicators of depression, anxiety, thought disorders, and suicide attempts (Joe, Brown, & Simpson, 1995). One in five had scores that implied they had significant adjustment problems. Similarly, suicide ideation was reported frequently in this treatment sample — 56 percent for females and 36 percent for males (see Joe, Knight, Dansereau, & Simpson, 1994). Their level of general psychosocial adjustment was related to the quality of their family relations during childhood (Knight, Cross, Giles-Sims, & Simpson, 1995).

Because of the widespread reductions in mental health and other ancillary services at many community-based treatment agencies during the last decade (see Etheridge, Craddock, Dunteman, & Hubbard, 1995), an emerging concern for the field is the degree to which programs can respond adequately to clients who have psychological problems. After classifying DATAR clients on the basis of indicators for psychological problems at intake (for example, anxiety, depression, hallucinations, suicidal ideation, and poor impulse control), however, Joe, Brown, and Simpson (1995) found that the high-problem group was twice as likely to attend the treatment program's recommended minimum number of individual counseling sessions than was the no-problem group. In addition, high-problem clients had significant decreases in drug use and illegal activity in the first three months after admission, and they did not differ significantly from the no-problem group on drug-positive urines or illegal activity at month three.

It was encouraging that these results suggest counselors with limited technical training and expertise in dealing with psychological problems are still able to help clients engage in and benefit from treatment. Records from counseling sessions confirmed that psychological issues were addressed in direct proportion to the level of problems clients reported at intake. Furthermore, clients with higher levels of psychological problems were more likely to attend individual counseling sessions than group meetings. These findings suggest a matching process emerged in which clients (possibly with encouragement from counselors) sought out individualized attention to help resolve personal adjustment problems in therapeutically appropriate one-on-one settings.

Alcohol Problems

A study of the relationship between heavy alcohol use and response to methadone treatment identified the need to distinguish between heavy drinkers who have alcohol dependency symptoms versus those who do not (Chatham, Rowan-Szal, Joe, Brown, & Simpson, 1995). Clients meeting DSM-III-R alcohol dependency criteria were more likely to remain in treatment longer than those who did not. Thus, failure to differentiate between alcohol dependent and nondependent groups of drinkers enrolled in methadone treatment may help account for reported differences in treatment outcome studies. Recognizing these different types of drinkers could help programs plan more effective interventions.

Modeling of Drug Treatment Process and Client Performance

As a way of summarizing and synthesizing findings on client motivation and psychological problems, engagement levels, and counseling procedures, we developed an integrated model to explain during-treatment drug use and time in treatment in terms of the above factors (Joe, Simpson, Rowan-Szal, & Greener, 1994). However, we extended during-treatment measurements across six months in an effort to generalize results beyond the initial three-month period studied earlier. Measures of treatment engagement and therapeutic relationships between clients and counselors during the first three months were incorporated as predictors of subsequent outcomes in a structural equation model. Results were consistent with previous findings based on early treatment relationships, but they provided greater insight into the particular factors influencing during-treatment use of both opiates and cocaine, as well as treatment retention. Specifically, it was shown that enhanced counseling using node-link mapping helped establish stronger therapeutic alliances between counselors and clients, which, in turn, was related to greater client treatment engagement (session attendance). Again, greater engagement was shown to be related to less drug use and increased tenure in treatment. We expanded the model by adding demographic variables, background factors, and methadone dose as predictors but found that the basic relationships still held.

These results show that treatment process variables are more important than most pretreatment variables in determining client outcomes and they support the hypothesis that therapeutic alliance between counselor and client — which is at the crux of counseling — promotes client engagement level and thereby improves during-treatment outcomes. Overall, the analyses support a conceptual and analytical shift from stressing client attributes and treatment structure as outcome predictors to using an expanded measurement system that addresses both counselor and client characteristics and their therapeutic interactions as predictors of client outcomes.

IMPLICATIONS AND FUTURE DIRECTIONS

Our most encouraging finding regarding clinical enhancements in the DATAR project has been that node-link mapping offers counselors an effective new tool in their repertoire of therapeutic skills. This procedure capitalizes on the advantages of graphic representations to promote more effective counseling relationships with clients. Mapping may help counselors identify clients with memory and comprehension difficulties, allowing them to tailor efforts to meet special needs of clients. It seems to be particularly well adapted for use with difficult clients (for example, those with attentional deficits and multiple drug users). Preliminary results also indicate that African-Americans and Mexican-Americans may benefit more from mapping than Caucasians. Having evidence that mapping exerts a positive effect on the therapeutic process and is well suited to virtually all types of patients, work is now proceeding to examine changes in posttreatment outcomes that are associated with mapping.

To facilitate counselor training in the use of this technique, we have written a brief introduction to mapping for practitioners (Dees, Dansereau, & Simpson, 1994) and prepared a detailed manual explaining the use of the mapping system (Dansereau, Dees, Chatham, Boatler, & Simpson, 1993). A two-day workshop with periodic follow-up and trouble-shooting sessions has been sufficient training for the majority of counselors. As with any acquired skill of this type, however, proficiency level for mapping techniques increases with use. In practice, counselors usually draw maps during discussion of a problem situation (working in collaboration with clients), but clients occasionally draw their own maps. Informal feedback from counselors and research on educational applications across a wide range of ages (for example, Lambiotte, Dansereau, Cross, & Reynolds, 1989) suggest that providing clients with mapping training may be helpful. This would offer clients a problem-solving tool that could be used independent of the treatment environment, but more work is needed in this area.

Although mapping therapeutic exchanges has value, there are some instances in which this process may be impeded by a lack of time, knowledge, experience, or energy. In these cases, more systematic use of abbreviated prestructured (fill-in) maps might prove to be beneficial. These can address specific counseling issues that are commonly encountered, such as program rules and compliance problems, causes of drug use lapses or arrests, or social conflicts, and allow straightforward identification of antecedent events and consequences. Preliminary responses of counselors to prototypes of quick, or mini-process, maps have been generally positive and more formal evaluations are planned. Additional development is needed for a more comprehensive set of mapping tools, and studies also are necessary to assess the long-term (posttreatment) effect of mapping and its applications for a wider variety of drug treatment settings.

New materials for structured intervention modules have proven to be beneficial adjuncts to treatment. These are manual-driven interventions that present step-by-step instructions for dealing with special issues and populations in group settings. Materials are easy to use and accommodate the needs of counselors, regardless of experience level. Some incorporate node-link mapping for presenting information, which helps sustain group focus, discussion, and interest. The HIV/AIDS module has been shown to be appropriate for administration during the early stages of treatment, which was important because some counselors originally believed AIDS could not be effectively addressed in the first months after client intake. For personal and public health reasons, therefore, clients should learn how to reduce their risks for HIV early in treatment, especially for the benefit of those who drop out of treatment and return to drug use within a few months after admission. Significant also is the added holding power some of our treatment enhancements offer. Most notable are the findings that women who take an active part in the *Time Out! For Me* program stay in treatment significantly longer than women who do not. This is consistent with anecdotal accounts from counselors who report these women's groups asked to continue meeting after the formal training series was completed. These manuals already have been broadly distributed as a result of requests from workshop presentations as well as module descriptions included in our research newsletter, which is widely circulated to clinical and evaluation research colleagues nationally. Plans by the National Institute on Drug Abuse to publish these manuals will allow much broader dissemination.

Results from CM procedures are consistent with earlier work by Stitzer, Grabowski, and Henningfield (1984) in showing that inexpensive forms of client recognition and reward can increase attendance at sessions and decrease drug use. For example, systematic use of such incentives as coupons to purchase gasoline, bus tokens, or fast foods — items that are often affordable or otherwise accessible to community treatment agencies — fostered positive behavior change. Even simple forms of recognition, such as earning stars on a poster board, have a positive impact on many clients.

Finally, our studies of treatment process help illuminate some of the therapeutic dynamics involved in recovery. Historically, time in treatment has served as one of the most reliable predictors of outcomes (Simpson, 1981), presumably representing a global measure of motivational commitment, treatment engagement, and intensity of services on which retention effects depend. We have found that engagement (that is, session attendance) is positively associated with recovery-oriented perceptions as well as behavioral changes among clients, and the use of a multivariate prediction model helped establish the prominent role of engagement within the larger context of several pretreatment predictors; it made unique contributions beyond the set of client background and baseline characteristics examined. Recovery from addiction, however, represents a complex process involving cognitive readiness for change, perceptions of personal progress in psychological functioning and emotional symptomatology, cognitive awareness and acquisition of better problem-solving skills, therapeutic and social interactions, and behavioral commitment. This dynamic and transitional process is only partially influenced by client interactions within the treatment environment. There are many other contextual and environmental factors that exert direct as well as indirect effects on persons trying to recover from addiction including social influences from peer and family relations (Knight & Simpson, 1996).

Additional research on treatment process is needed to identify significant parameters and formulate more effective analytic frameworks that improve prediction of outcomes during and after treatment. Elaborated models should consider a wider array of therapeutic contacts. It is, likewise, important to test whether increases in session attendance rates lead to improved outcomes for all patients and the extent to which treatment contacts can be tailored to each individual's status in the recovery process. It cannot be assumed that treatment process and other factors that influence client change are constant across clients, time, and settings. These and many other issues with direct and indirect implications for treatment enhancement remain to be explored.

The DATAR studies to date have been encouraging, but, as already noted, they have been based only on data gathered from clients during treatment. Our cognitive and behavioral enhancements have beneficial effects on treatment engagement and performance by clients while in the program, but our one-year posttreatment follow-up data are not yet available.

ACKNOWLEDGMENTS

This work was funded by the National Institute on Drug Abuse (Grant No. DA06162). The interpretations and conclusions, however, do not necessarily represent the position of the National Institute on Drug Abuse or the Department of Health and Human Services. Data were collected in collaboration with treatment programs at the Corpus Christi Drug Abuse Council, DARCO Inc. in Dallas, and adVance Treatment Center in Houston. Special appreciation is expressed to Barry S. Brown and Lois R. Chatham for their editorial advice and comments.

REFERENCES

Anglin, M. D., & Hser, Y. I. (1990). Treatment of drug abuse. In M. Tonry & J. Q. Wilson (Eds.), *Drugs and crime* (pp. 393–460). Chicago, IL: University of Chicago Press.

Bartholomew, N., Chatham, L. R., & Simpson, D. D. (1994). *Time out! for me: An assertiveness/sexuality workshop specially designed for women* (rev. ed.). Bloomington, IL: Lighthouse Institute Publishing.

Bartholomew, N. G., Rowan-Szal, G. A., Chatham, L. R., & Simpson, D. D. (1994). Effectiveness of a specialized intervention for women in a methadone program. *Journal of Psychoactive Drugs, 26*(3), 249–255.

Bartholomew, N., & Simpson, D. D. (1994). *Approaches to HIV/AIDS education in drug treatment*. Bloomington, IL: Lighthouse Institute Publishing.

Bartholomew, N., Simpson, D. D., & Chatham, L. R. (1993). *Straight ahead: Transition skills for recovery*. Bloomington, IL: Lighthouse Institute Publishing.

Boatler, J. F. (1992). *AIDS/HIV risk reduction module*. Fort Worth: Texas Christian University, Institute of Behavioral Research.

Boatler, J. F., Knight, K., & Simpson, D. D. (1994). Assessment of an AIDS intervention program during drug abuse treatment. *Journal of Substance Abuse Treatment, 11*(4), 367–372.

Chatham, L. R., & Rowan-Szal, G. (1992). *Data management system for DATAR project*. Fort Worth: Texas Christian University, Institute of Behavioral Research.

Chatham, L. R., Rowan-Szal, G., Joe, G. W., Brown, B. S., & Simpson, D. D. (1995). Heavy drinking in a population of methadone maintained clients. *Journal of Studies on Alcohol, 56*(4), 417–422.

Chatham, L. R., & Simpson, D. D. (1994). Delivering and evaluating outpatient treatment: Finding a practical balance. In B. W. Fletcher, J. A. Inciardi, & A. M. Horton (Eds.), *Drug abuse treatment: Implementation of innovative approaches* (pp. 181–193). Westport, CT: Greenwood Press.

Cohen, B-Z, & Shlomy, O. (1986, March). The family therapy chronogram: An aid to supervision. *Social Casework: The Journal of Contemporary Social Work, 67*(3), 174–179.

Cohen, J. (1988). *Statistical power analyses for the behavioral sciences*. Hillsdale, NJ: Lawrence Erlbaum.

Cummings, A. L., Slemon, A. G., & Hallberg, E. T. (1993). Session evaluation and recall of important events as a function of counselor experience. *Journal of Counseling Psychology, 40*(2), 156–165.

Czuchry, M., Dansereau, D. F., Dees, S. M., & Simpson, D. D. (1995). The use of node-link mapping in drug abuse counseling: The role of attentional factors. *Journal of Counseling Psychoactive Drugs, 27*(2), 161–166.

Dansereau, D. F., & Cross, D. R. (1992). *Knowledge mapping: Cognitive software for thinking, learning, and communicating*. Fort Worth: Texas Christian University, Department of Psychology.

Dansereau, D. F., Dees, S. M., Chatham, L. R., Boatler, J. F., & Simpson, D. D. (1993). *Mapping new roads to recovery: Cognitive enhancements to counseling*. Bloomington, IL: Lighthouse Institute Publishing.

Dansereau, D. F., Dees, S. M., Greener, J. M., & Simpson, D. D. (1995). Node-linking mapping and the evaluation of drug abuse counseling sessions.

Psychology of Addictive Behaviors, 9(3), 195–203.

Dansereau, D. F., Dees, S. M., & Simpson, D. D. (1994). Cognitive modularity: Implications for counseling and the representation of personal issues. *Journal of Counseling Psychology, 41*(4), 513–523.

Dansereau, D. F., Joe, G. W., Dees, S. M., & Simpson, D. D. (1996). Ethnicity and the effects of mapping-enhanced drug abuse counseling. *Addictive Behaviors, 21*(3), 363–376.

Dansereau, D. F., Joe, G. W., & Simpson, D. D. (1995). Attentional difficulties and the effectiveness of a visual representation strategy for counseling drug-addicted clients. *International Journal of the Addictions, 30*(4), 371–386.

Dansereau, D. F., Joe, G. W., & Simpson, D. D. (1993). Node-link mapping: A visual representation strategy for enhancing drug abuse counseling. *Journal of Counseling Psychology, 40*(4), 385–395.

D'Aunno, T., & Vaughn, T. E. (1992). Variations in methadone treatment in practices: Results from a national study. *Journal of the American Medical Association, 267*(2), 253–258.

Dees, S. M., Dansereau, D. F., & Simpson, D. D. (1994). A visual representation system for drug abuse counselors. *Journal of Substance Abuse Treatment, 11*(6), 517–523.

De Leon, G. (1989). Psychopathology and substance abuse: What is being learned from research in therapeutic communities. *Journal of Psychoactive Drugs, 21*, 177–188.

De Leon, G. (1984). Program-based evaluation research in therapeutic communities. In F. M. Tims & J. P. Ludford (Eds.), *Drug abuse treatment evaluation: Strategies, progress, and prospects* (NIDA Research Monograph Series No. 51, DHHS Publication No. ADM 84-1329). Rockville, MD: National Institute on Drug Abuse.

Etheridge, R. M., Craddock, S. G., Dunteman, G. H., & Hubbard, R. L. (1995). Treatment services in two national studies of community-based drug abuse treatment programs. In R. Moos & J. Finney (Eds.), *Journal of Substance Abuse, 7*, 9–26.

Gerstein, D. R., & Harwood, H. J. (Eds.). (1990). *Treating drug problems.* Vol. 1. *A study of the evolution, effectiveness, and financing of public and private drug treatment systems* (Committee for the Substance Abuse Coverage Study Division of Health Care Services, Institute of Medicine). Washington, DC: National Academy Press.

Hiller, M. L., Rowan-Szal, G. A., Bartholomew, N. G., & Simpson, D. D. (1996). Effectiveness of a specialized women's intervention in a residential treatment program. *Substance Use & Misuse, 31*(6), 771–783.

Hubbard, R. L., Marsden, M. E., Rachal, J. V., Harwood, H. J., Cavanaugh, E. R., & Ginzburg, H. M. (1989). *Drug abuse treatment: A national study of effectiveness.* Chapel Hill: University of North Carolina Press.

Joe, G. W., Brown, B. S., & Simpson, D. D. (1995). Psychological problems and engagement in treatment. *Journal of Nervous and Mental Disease, 183*(11), 704–710.

Joe, G. W., Dansereau, D. F., & Simpson, D. D. (1994). Node-link mapping for counseling cocaine users in methadone treatment. *Journal of Substance Abuse, 6*, 393–406.

Joe, G. W., Knezek, L., Watson, D., & Simpson, D. D. (1991). Depression and decision-making among intravenous drug users. *Psychological Reports, 68,* 339–347.

Joe, G. W., Knight, K., Dansereau, D. F., & Simpson, D. D. (1994). *Suicide ideation in a drug user population: Evidence for a mediational model.* Fort Worth: Texas Christian University, Institute of Behavioral Research.

Joe, G. W., Simpson, D. D., Rowan-Szal, G., & Greener, J. (1994) *Structural equation modeling of drug abuse treatment process and retention.* Fort Worth: Texas Christian University, Institute of Behavioral Research.

Knight, D. K., Cross, D. R., Giles-Sims, J., & Simpson, D. D. (1995). Psychosocial functioning among adult drug users: The role of parental absence, support, and conflict. *International Journal of the Addictions, 30*(10), 1271–1288.

Knight, D. K., Dansereau, D. F., Joe, G. W., & Simpson, D. D. (1994). The role of node-link mapping in individual and group counseling. *American Journal of Drug and Alcohol Abuse, 20*(4), 517–527.

Knight, D. K., & Simpson, D. D. (in press). Influences of family and friends on client progress during drug treatment. *Journal of Substance Abuse.*

Knight, K., Holcom, M., & Simpson, D. D. (1994). *TCU psychosocial functioning and motivation scales: Manual on psychometric properties.* Fort Worth: Texas Christian University, Institute of Behavioral Research.

Knight, K., Simpson, D. D., & Dansereau, D. F. (1994). Knowledge mapping: A psychoeducational tool in drug abuse relapse prevention training. *Journal of Offender Rehabilitation, 20*(3/4), 187–205.

Lambiotte, J. G., Dansereau, D. F., Cross, D. R., & Reynolds, S. B. (1989). Multirelational semantic maps. *Educational Psychology Review, 1*(4), 331–367.

Lange, A., & Jakubowski, P. (1978). *Responsible assertive behavior.* Champaign, IL: Research Press.

Larkin, J. H., & Simon, H. A. (1987). Why a diagram is (sometimes) worth ten thousand words. *Cognitive Science, 11,* 65–99.

Mayer, R. E., & Gallini, J. K. (1990). When is an illustration worth the thousand words? *Journal of Educational Psychology, 82*(4), 715–726.

Parnell, M., & Vanderkloot, J. (1991). Mental health services — 2001: Serving a new America. *Journal of Independent Social Work, 5*(3–4), 183–203.

Patterson, M. E., Dansereau, D. F., & Newbern, D. (1992). The effects of communication aids and strategies on cooperative teaching. *Journal of Educational Psychology, 84*(4), 453–561.

Rowan-Szal, G., Joe, G. W., Chatham, L. R., & Simpson, D. D. (1994). A simple reinforcement system for methadone clients in a community-based treatment program. *Journal of Substance Abuse Treatment, 11*(3), 217–223.

Rowan-Szal, G., Joe, G. W., Hiller, M. L., & Simpson, D. D. (in press). Increasing early engagement in methadone treatment. *Journal of Maintenance in the Addictions.*

Simpson, D. D. (1993). Drug treatment evaluation research in the United States. *Psychology of Addictive Behaviors, 7*(2), 120–128.

Simpson, D. D. (1992). *TCU forms manual: Drug Abuse Treatment for AIDS-Risk Reduction (DATAR).* Fort Worth: Texas Christian University, Institute of Behavioral Research.

Simpson, D. D. (1984). National treatment system evaluation based on the Drug Abuse Reporting Program (DARP) followup research. In F. M. Tims, & J. P. Ludford (Eds.), *Drug abuse treatment evaluation: Strategies, progress, and prospects* (NIDA Research Monograph Series No. 51, DHHS Publication No. ADM 84-1329). Rockville, MD: National Institute on Drug Abuse.

Simpson, D. D. (1981). Treatment for drug abuse: Follow-up outcomes and length of time spent. *Archives of General Psychiatry, 38*, 875–880.

Simpson, D. D. (1979). The relation of time spent in drug abuse treatment to post-treatment outcome. *American Journal of Psychiatry, 136*(11), 1449–1453.

Simpson, D. D., Chatham, L. R., & Joe, G. W. (1993). Cognitive enhancements of treatment in DATAR: Drug Abuse Treatment for AIDS-Risk Reduction. In J. Inciardi, F. Tims, & B. Fletcher (Eds.), *Innovative approaches in the treatment of drug abuse: Program models and strategies* (pp. 161–177). Westport, CT: Greenwood Press.

Simpson, D. D., & Joe, G. W. (1993). Motivation as a predictor of early dropout from drug abuse treatment. *Psychotherapy, 30*(2), 357–368.

Simpson, D. D., Joe, G. W., Rowan-Szal, G., & Greener, J. (1995). Client engagement and change during drug abuse treatment. *Journal of Substance Abuse, 7*(1), 117–134.

Simpson, D. D., & Marsh, K. L. (1986). Relapse and recovery among opioid addicts 12 years after treatment. In F. M. Tims & C. G. Leukefeld (Eds.), *Relapse and recovery in drug abuse* (NIDA Research Monograph 72, DHHS Publication No. ADM 86-1473). Rockville, MD: National Institute on Drug Abuse.

Simpson, D. D., & Sells, S. B. (1982). Effectiveness of treatment for drug abuse: An overview of the DARP research program. *Advances in Alcohol and Substance Abuse, 2*(1), 7–29.

Simpson, D. D., & Sells, S. B. (Eds.). (1990). *Opioid addiction and treatment: A 12-year follow-up*. Malabar, FL: Krieger.

Stiles, W. B., Reynolds, S., Hardy, G. E., Rees, A., Barkham, M., & Shapiro, D. A. (1994). Evaluation and description of psychotherapy sessions by client using the Session Evaluation Questionnaire and the Session Impacts Scale. *Journal of Counseling Psychology, 41*(2), 175–185.

Stitzer, M., Grabowski, J., & Henningfield, J. (1984). Behavioral intervention techniques in drug abuse treatment: Summary of discussion. In J. Grabowski, M. Stitzer, & J. Henningfield (Eds.), *Behavioral intervention techniques in drug abuse treatment* (National Institute on Drug Abuse Monograph 46, DHHS Publication No. ADM 89-1578). Washington, DC: U.S. Government Printing Office.

Tims, F. M., & Ludford, J. P. (Eds.). (1984). *Drug abuse treatment evaluation: Strategies, progress, and prospects* (NIDA Research Monograph No. 51, DHHS Publication No. 84-1329). Washington, DC: U.S. Government Printing Office.

Winn, W., Li, T-Z., & Schill, D. (1991). Diagrams as aids to problem solving: Their role in facilitating search and computation. *Educational Technology Research and Development, 39*(1), 17–29.

13

The Effectiveness of a Day Treatment Therapeutic Community

Joseph Guydish, Monica Chan, David Werdegar, Barbara Tajima, and Alfonso Acampora

The day treatment modality, although well accepted in the areas of mental health and geriatric care, is not well accepted in the area of drug abuse treatment. In recent years, pressure to develop alternative models of care has prompted drug treatment providers to experiment with this modality. Although available literature is sparse, there is growing interest in implementing, describing, and evaluating drug abuse day treatment programs. This chapter describes one such program, developed using the principles and practices of the residential therapeutic community (TC), and preliminary findings about program effectiveness. It concludes that day treatment for drug users is feasible, can serve clients who have a wide range of demographic and drug use characteristics, and can contribute to positive treatment outcomes. Last, implications of findings and future directions for research are discussed.

Day treatment describes an intermediate level of care, more intensive than traditional outpatient care, and less intensive than 24-hour inpatient or residential care. Day treatment programs, referred to in different fields as day hospital, partial hospitalization, and adult day care, fill a particular niche in the continuum of care. They target patients who require more service, structure, and support than that customarily available on an outpatient basis, but who can be adequately treated without the resources and expense of inpatient care. Day treatment is an accepted model of service in the areas of mental health (Creed, Black, & Anthony, 1989; Schinnar, Kamis-Gould, Delucia, & Rothbard, 1990), geriatric care (Eagle, Guyatt, Patterson, & Turpie, 1987; Weissert et al., 1990) and, to a lesser extent, alcoholism treatment (Bensinger & Pilkington, 1983; McLachlan & Stein, 1982).

In the area of drug abuse, the treatment modalities most widely researched and reported are methadone maintenance and residential treatment (Institute of Medicine, 1990). Outpatient programs in general are not well researched, and until 1990 there were few reports specifically concerning day treatment (Feigelman, 1987; Feigelman, Hyman, & Amann, 1988; Feigelman, Hyman, Amann, & Feigelman, 1990). The search for alternative and potentially less costly models of care has prompted renewed interest in drug abuse day treatment (for example, Alterman & McLellan, 1993; Alterman, O'Brien, & Droba, 1993; De Leon, Sacks, & Hilton, 1993). As day treatment begins to develop in the drug abuse treatment field, there is a need for research that both describes and evaluates such programs.

This chapter reports on the development and evaluation of a drug abuse day treatment program. The program was developed by Walden House, Inc., an agency with a history of providing residential TC services, and was designed to incorporate TC philosophy and clinical tools. Researchers at the University of California, San Francisco, in collaboration with Walden House and with support from the National Institute on Drug Abuse, are evaluating the effectiveness of the day treatment program. This chapter first describes the day treatment program, then summarizes the evaluation design and methods. Major research findings to date are reviewed, along with a few general observations concerning the day treatment modality. In the final section we consider some of the important research questions now emerging, as the day treatment modality is increasingly applied in the field of drug abuse treatment.

PROGRAM DESCRIPTION

The day treatment facility operates seven days a week including holidays. Hours of operation are 8 a.m. to 8 p.m., Monday through Friday, with abbreviated schedules on weekends. Therapeutic groups and activities are scheduled throughout each day and, to further promote a sense of community, meals are served on site. The level of participation varies for each client, depending on the phase of treatment and specific treatment plan.

The philosophy of the day treatment program is adapted from that of the residential TC, which operates on the family concept of a mutually supportive environment. This functional Walden House family tries to reparent the client, abolish old behaviors related to drug use, and develop self-esteem, self-awareness, discipline, and self-reliance. In essence, the TC views substance abuse as a result of learned behaviors that must be identified and corrected. The structure of the program is based on the phase system, a series of treatment steps designed to move the client from addictive behavior to sobriety and self-sufficiency.

The phase system, which describes the treatment process in terms of four stages, was borrowed from the residential program and adapted to fit the needs of day treatment clients. Each successive phase allows the clients more responsibility in dealing with the outside world, and completion of each phase is marked by ritual and celebration to symbolize the client's achievement. Unlike the residential TC, where clients may be sheltered from the outside world for a period of weeks, dealing with the outside community and "testing one's strength" begins early on. Day treatment clients return to their own home every night, often walking through heavy drug use neighborhoods, and begin to address problems in relationships with spouses and family members.

The orientation phase is an introduction to TC rules, principles, and philosophy. Within the first 30 to 45 days, initial assessment and treatment planning are completed, and daily attendance and participation in groups and functions is expected. Clients are assigned a big brother or sister who initiates them into the rituals and rules of the TC. During the orientation period, clients detoxify, and begin to take care of unfinished legal and medical matters. This begins the forging of bonds between clients and treatment staff, the learning of tools, and the teaching of responsibility for actions and behaviors.

After successful completion of the orientation phase, as determined by staff and peers, clients begin the treatment phase. In this phase, which may last four to six months, clients continue establishing bonds and friendships with peers. Specific therapeutic issues are identified and addressed, and clients are assigned to specific groups and caseloads. Clients also earn privileges (special outings, core groups, and specific duties) and start attending Narcotics Anonymous or Alcoholics Anonymous meetings. At some point during the treatment phase, again depending upon each individual, the treatment plan is re-evaluated and modified as needed.

The third phase, pre-reentry, lasts an average of two to three months. In this phase, clients deal with resocialization and start assessing future long- and short-term goals. Such topics as transferred addictions, relationships, and socializing are addressed. Clients also take part in vocational rehabilitation, educational avenues, job training, resume writing, and money management. In addition, clients begin to fulfill required community-service hours. During this phase, privileges are extended, and clients' schedules are modified to accommodate classes and other activities.

In the last phase, reentry, clients continue the reentry process. Volunteer work, education or vocational training, and employment are maintained as each client establishes a support system and reevaluates goals and treatment plans. Often, reentry clients attend evening rather than day groups to participate in more outside activities. Clients also prepare for graduation by completing 40 hours of community work and fulfilling the following requirements: strong support and recovery system, stable legal commitments, consistency with job and school, and secured housing. The philosophy, structure, and tools of the day treatment program are also discussed in Guydish and colleagues (1993).

SUMMARY OF RESEARCH METHODS

Conducting a rigorous evaluation of the new day treatment program, in a community setting and in partnership with a community-based agency, offered many challenges (Guydish, Werdegar, Chan, Nebelkopf, & Acampora, 1994). Chief among these were the needs to develop and refine the day treatment program, to gain acceptance for the program among staff and clients alike, and to pilot test a series of evaluation instruments and procedures. To accomodate these needs, the evaluation was designed to include two phases: a descriptive phase and a clinical trial phase.

The descriptive phase, completed in the first two years of study (1990–92), was intended to develop the main features of a day treatment program, and to recruit and follow a sample of clients entering the program. The research objectives were to describe the nature of the program, study treatment retention and transfer rates, test the evaluation protocol, and assess treatment outcomes over time. At the same time, although the day treatment program was developing and changing, it had not yet gained acceptance among Walden House staff as a freestanding treatment program. Many clients entering day treatment during this early period were transferred to residential treatment in a period of weeks or months, reflecting that some staff regarded day treatment more as a preresidential orientation program than as a distinct treatment modality. In summary, the descriptive evaluation phase was a pilot study, conducted at a time when the day treatment program was rapidly evolving. It was vital in preparing treatment staff, research staff, and clients for the next evaluation phase, the clinical trial.

The clinical trial phase, in progress at the time of this writing, is intended to assess the effectiveness of day treatment in comparison with residential treatment. The evaluation plan for this phase uses a randomized design in which all clients entering the Walden House system, unless excluded for specific reasons, were randomly assigned to either the day treatment program or a residential treatment program. Clients were excluded from the study if they were homeless, referred by a court agency specifically to residential treatment, or when extenuating conditions precluded them from entering one or the other treatment setting. The last category consisted of individuals who, for example, had daily family or childcare responsibilities and could not participate in residential treatment.

Except for procedures associated with sample selection and random assignment described above, data collection methods were the same in the descriptive phase and clinical trial phase of study. Only clients who remained in treatment for approximately two weeks were asked to participate. This was to ensure that research participants had some uniform minimum level of exposure to the treatment being studied. The baseline interview included the Addiction Severity Index (ASI) (McLellan, Luborsky, O'Brien, & Woody, 1980), Beck Depression Inventory (BDI) (Beck, 1972), Symptom Checklist-90 (SCL-90) (Derogatis, 1983), and a measure of social support (Chan, Razban, & Guydish, 1994; Havassy, Hall, & Tschann, 1987). Participants were followed and reinterviewed at 6, 12, and 18 months after baseline.

MAJOR RESEARCH FINDINGS

Findings from the Descriptive Phase

A convenience sample of clients entering day treatment (N = 66), and remaining in day treatment for a period of two weeks, were recruited into the descriptive cohort. The sample had a mean age of about 33 years, and most (73 percent) had completed high school or a general equivalency diploma. Ethnicity for the sample was diverse, with 53 percent African-American, 35 percent Caucasian, 6 percent Hispanic and 6 percent Asian. Most (82 percent) were male, and cocaine was the most frequently reported drug of choice (54 percent).

As in many drug treatment programs, the length of time clients remained in treatment varied widely. The median length of time participants remained in day treatment was about 1 month, and the range for individual participants was from 2 weeks to 11 months. As noted earlier, many clients (64 percent) entering day treatment at this early stage of program development were later transferred to a residential treatment program. The median length of time participants remained continuously in treatment (day treatment plus later residential treatment) was about 4 months, and the range for individual participants was from 2 weeks to 15 months.

At the time of six-month follow-up, 58 percent of the sample were located and reinterviewed. To assess bias associated with loss to follow-up, those successfully followed (N = 38) were compared with those not followed (N = 28) on selected demographic and outcome variables at baseline. The two groups did not differ significantly in terms of age, gender, education, or ethnicity, and did not differ significantly on mean values for nine key outcome variables measured at baseline.

To assess change over time, or treatment effects, mean scores for key outcome measures at baseline and six months were compared using paired t-tests. The outcome variables used in this analysis included six ASI composite scores (medical, employment, legal, alcohol, drug, and social), total scores on the BDI and social support measures, and the SCL-90. ASI composite scores represent a measure of problem severity in each area (McGahan, Griffith, & McLellan, 1986). Those participants completing the six-month follow-up (N = 38) showed significant improvement in four ASI problem areas (legal, alcohol, drug, and social), significant decreases in psychiatric symptoms as measured by the BDI and SCL-90, and significant increases in social support.

In summary, findings from the descriptive phase of the evaluation indicate that the development of drug abuse day treatment is feasible and that such programs can attract and retain clients having a broad range of demographic and drug use characteristics. In the descriptive phase, day treatment was not used for most clients as a single treatment modality but, rather, was used in combination with (and often as a precursor to) residential treatment. Consequently, while significant treatment gains were observed at six-month follow-up, these gains cannot be attributed to either day treatment or residential treatment alone. Nevertheless, clients participating in this combination of treatments showed significant improvement in drug and alcohol use, social problems and social support, legal status, and psychiatric symptomatology.

Findings from the Clinical Trial Phase

Recruitment for the randomized clinical trial took place over a two-year period (1992–94). During that time, 1944 individuals were admitted to treatment. Of those, 1410 were excluded because of homelessness (N = 495), court mandates (N = 693), or for clinical reasons determined by treatment staff (N = 222). The remaining 534 clients were randomly assigned to either residential or day treatment, and 283 were enrolled in the clinical trial two weeks after admission. It was necessary to assign approximately 200 percent of the desired total because of high dropout during the first two weeks of treatment.

Of the 534 clients who were randomly assigned, 266 were assigned to day treatment, and 268 to residential treatment. Two-week retention for randomly assigned clients was 53 percent overall, however, a difference in retention rates was observed between those assigned to day treatment and those assigned to residential treatment. Of those assigned to day treatment, 47 percent stayed in treatment the requisite two weeks prior to enrollment in the clinical trial. Of those assigned to residential treatment, 59 percent remained in treatment for the first two weeks. This statistically significant difference in early retention suggests that residential treatment may be more effective in limiting client dropout during the first few days of treatment.

Once aware of the differential two-week retention rates however, day treatment staff developed strategies to improve retention in their program, including a more structured orientation phase similar to that used in the residential program. After implementation of these retention strategies, two-week retention rates for the two programs were again compared. For the last four months of recruitment, a period in which about one-fourth of the sample was recruited, two-week retention rates were 51 percent in day treatment and 55 percent in residential treatment. The difference between these early retention rates, no longer statistically significant, indicate the success of the retention strategies introduced at day treatment.

Observations of significant differential retention rates also prompted the recording of client preferences at time of assignment to treatment to determine if those who received their preferred treatment were more likely to remain in treatment. Records were maintained for the last 12 months of recruitment, and initial treatment preferences of 324 clients were recorded. In this client sample, approximately 15 percent had no treatment preference, 25 percent initially preferred day treatment, and the remaining clients (60 percent) initially preferred residential treatment. About one-half of the clients in this sample (52 percent) received their preferred treatment. Two-week retention among those who received their preferred treatment was significantly higher (63 percent) than two-week retention among those who did not receive their preferred treatment (49 percent). This finding suggests that client retention in treatment may be improved by allowing clients to enroll in their preferred treatment program.

In preliminary analyses of available baseline data (N = 108), key outcome measures were compared to assess potential differences between randomly assigned groups. Mean scores for depression (BDI), psychiatric symptoms (SCL-90), and social support showed no significant differences between the two groups. Similarly, a comparison of ASI composite scores, which measure problem severity in seven areas, indicated no significant differences between day treatment clients and residential treatment clients at baseline. These preliminary analyses suggest that clients assigned to either group were generally comparable at baseline and that differences observed on follow-up will be attributable to treatment assignment.

In summary, findings from the randomized clinical trial showed that there was a high dropout rate early in treatment for both the day and residential treatment programs. Initially, clients assigned to day treatment were significantly more likely to drop out in the first two weeks after admission. However, after day treatment staff improved orientation procedures early retention rates were similar for both programs. Two-week retention was also significantly higher for those who received their preferred treatment assignment, indicating the possibility of improving retention in treatment by allowing clients to choose their treatment assignment. Preliminary analyses comparing the two treatment groups indicate that they were similar at baseline in terms of addiction severity, psychiatric symptoms, and social support. Consequently, differences observed through follow-up will reflect the type of treatment received by the client and will provide information on the comparative effectiveness of each treatment modality.

OBSERVATIONS ABOUT DAY TREATMENT

In addition to the specific findings reported above, the project team developed a few general impressions concerning the day treatment modality. These relate to the adaptation of residential TC tools and principles to the day treatment setting, acceptance of this day treatment program by clients and staff, and specific strengths of day treatment.

Adaptation of Residential Therapeutic Community Tools

There are at least two strategies for developing a drug abuse day treatment program. One is to build from an outpatient clinic visit model by increasing therapeutic and support services provided, while another is to modify a residential program into an intensive outpatient program. In developing its day treatment program, Walden House chose the latter strategy, which required transfer of existing residential TC technology into a day treatment setting. This was accomplished by eliminating the residential component of treatment but applying in day treatment many of the activities of the residential program.

Some tools of residential treatment fitted easily into the nonresidential setting. For example, many of the specific groups (morning meetings, HIV prevention groups, and relapse prevention groups) and services (legal, educational and vocational, and tutoring for the general equivalency diploma) could be provided equally well in day treatment and residential settings. Many specific clinical tools such as "the chair," where a client sits to reflect about their commitment to treatment, or "contracts," which specify corrective behaviors in the wake of an infraction, were readily put to use in the day treatment program. Some adaptations were necessary. For example, in the orientation phase of traditional residential treatment clients are often required to have little or no contact with family and friends for some specified number of days. However, clients in the orientation phase of day treatment cannot be separated from contacts in the larger community because they leave the program and return home each day. To help clients bond with the program and develop a sense of community early in the course of treatment, the day treatment program assigned an orientation counselor who met with new clients each day and organized social reinforcements for clients who returned to treatment each day.

Over a period of months, by applying residential TC tools in the day treatment setting and modifying these tools when necessary, Walden House developed a specific kind of day treatment program that preserved the community qualities of the traditional residential TC. Consequently, this program may be described as a modified TC (De Leon, Sacks, & Hilton, 1993) or as a nonresidential TC (Bucardo, Guydish, Acampora, & Werdegar, in press).

Acceptance of Day Treatment by Clients and Staff

One of the most difficult aspects of implementing the day treatment program was overcoming resistance by clinical staff, most of whom had backgrounds or experience in residential treatment. These staff members believed that the protected environment of a residential facility was necessary to keep clients drug-free, and there would be too many risks inherent in a day treatment environment. The new program challenged their beliefs that residential TC was the most appropriate treatment for every client. Some staff were also concerned about job security and the possibility that the new day treatment program, if successful, would diminish the need for residential services. In addition to earning acceptance by treatment staff, the day treatment program needed the acceptance of clients. Walden House had long been known for its residential TC, but day treatment was unknown to incoming clients who expected to receive residential treatment.

Changes in clinicians' attitudes began when a core group of staff recognized day treatment's potential. They worked to develop the program and articulate to their peers the idea that day treatment could expand rather than replace existing Walden House services. At the same time, clients were progressing successfully in day treatment. Although success in day treatment was often met with skepticism initially, the growing number of successful graduates could not long be ignored. Moreover, day treatment graduates eventually entered the staff ranks in both counseling and administrative positions. Continued exposure to successful day treatment clients gradually earned the program acceptance among most clinical staff, who now see day treatment as an integral part of the Walden House treatment services.

Client acceptance grew as individuals began to bond with one another, their counselors, and the social structure of the day treatment program. The realization that they could do well and remain drug-free even without being in the residential facility increased clients' self-confidence and their belief in day treatment. As clients became more invested in the program, they helped develop the new TC, with rituals unique to day treatment. These successes increased client identification with day treatment and their sense of being a unique and important part of the Walden House family.

Specific Strengths of Day Treatment

In comparing day treatment with residential treatment, where both programs shared the philosophy of intensive treatment within a nurturing community, two particular strengths of day treatment emerged. First, day treatment was preferable to residential treatment for many clients who had family or job responsibilities, and, second, some clients commented that leaving the day treatment program each day was a kind of "daily reentry."

In the traditional residential TC, clients entering treatment withdraw from family and other responsibilities to participate fully in treatment. Parents transfer childcare responsibilities to others, clients holding jobs end their employment, those caring for sick or disabled family members stop being caretakers. Such separation from external ties and responsibilities is thought to be necessary so that clients can focus on their own drug problem and drug treatment and bond effectively with their new TC family. After clients have bonded with the TC and can benefit from its guidance and emotional support, they gradually resume their roles and responsibilities in the larger social community. In working with the day treatment program over a period of years, the project team observed that many clients could bond with the nonresidential TC and still maintain family or employment responsibilities. The day treatment modality enables some clients to participate in intensive treatment and do so without giving up their responsibilities in the larger social community. Although day treatment cannot replace residential treatment, it is an important innovation in the continuum of care for clients experiencing drug problems.

The second specific strength of day treatment concerns reentry. In the traditional residential TC, reentry describes the gradual return to the larger social community. Clients in reentry have fully participated in the life of the TC, have completed the main phases of treatment, and are preparing to leave the TC. Reentry, which may extend to six months, involves participation in vocational and educational activities, job-seeking and employment, accrual of savings necessary to begin independent living, and finding a suitable living situation. Reentry is often a formidable task because each client's ability to remain drug-free has relied, in part, on the protection afforded by the living environment. In reentry, the client is challenged to maintain sobriety while moving to a less controlled living environment. In day treatment, clients have the guidance and emotional support of the nonresidential TC family, but they do not have the benefit of a controlled and drug-free living environment. Their withdrawal from the larger social community is, at most, eight hours each day. Although they participate in intensive treatment, they also go home each day to face conflicts and problems of living and the ready availability of drugs and alcohol. When day treatment clients begin reentry, they face educational, vocational, and employment challenges. They do not face the challenge of maintaining sobriety while moving out of a protected living environment. The daily reentry associated with day treatment is not suitable for all clients entering drug treatment. For those who are able to participate effectively in day treatment, the burdens of reentry, and, possibly, the dangers of relapse associated with reentry are confronted by the client in smaller doses over a longer period of time.

IMPLICATIONS AND FUTURE DIRECTIONS

Our research project, over the past four years, has been exploring the utility of intensive day treatment and its potential contribution to the continuum of services available for the treatment of drug abuse. The experience gained thus far is encouraging. The early, descriptive phase of the project demonstrated that day treatment is a feasible approach and that it can attract and retain clients of diverse backgrounds, ethnicity, and patterns of drug abuse with severe degrees of addiction. It has been possible to create, in the day treatment model, many of the fundamental elements of the TC approach that are familiar in residential drug treatment. Follow-up studies of the day treatment clients gave clear evidence of improvement in the areas of drug and alcohol use, social support, and psychological symptoms. However, in this early phase of the project, day treatment was often combined to some extent with residential treatment, and the follow-up results could not be ascribed to day treatment exclusively. The findings of the second phase of the research project — the randomized clinical trial still in progress — will provide more definitive data.

Although the randomized clinical trial is not yet complete, we have already derived valuable information. From a methodological viewpoint it was gratifying to find that it was possible to conduct a randomized clinical trial in the setting of a community-based drug treatment program. Random assignment was shown to be successful by the close similarity between day treatment and residential treatment clients in demographic and clinical characteristics. Many investigators in the drug abuse treatment field commented on the need for randomized clinical studies on outcomes of care but often despaired of its difficulties, especially in the setting of community-based treatment programs. Our experience was a process of mutual education and development of shared goals between research and treatment teams, enabling successful implementation of the randomized clinical trial. The demonstrated ability to conduct outcome studies using randomized clinical trials has significant implications for advancing understanding of community drug abuse treatment programs.

The randomized trial initially suggested that retention of clients, at least in early weeks of treatment, was better in residential treatment. This would be understandable, considering the contained and structured environment of residential TCs. However, it proved possible to enhance early retention in day treatment by providing prompt attention to orientation, counselor assignment, and client involvement in structured activities so that the retention rate in the two settings became more similar.

The clinical trial has also provided insights into the applicability of the TC approach in an alternative, nonresidential environment. It is possible to develop and sustain a valid TC program in an outpatient setting, borrowing and adapting from the long experience and clinical wisdom of residential TCs. In the process of developing the day treatment program, one gains empirical clues to those elements of the TC that are essential and other aspects that may not be critical and can be modified or even discarded. Certainly the mutually supportive family structure is the foundation on which the process of developing the desired skills, knowledge, attitudes, and behaviors is built.

The project has provided empirical clues to suggest that certain clients may especially benefit from the availability of the day treatment alternative. They would likely include those unable or unwilling to forego parenting and family responsibilities (this was particularly true for many women with children); those with stable job situations; and those who avoided residential treatment, feeling it was too confining. It was of great interest that a significant proportion of the clients in the randomized trial (25 percent) actually had a preference for day treatment and that, generally speaking, retention in treatment was significantly better when clients were assigned to the treatment modality they preferred.

Another clinical insight of the day treatment experiment was the observation, by a number of clients, that the daily reentry was a process in which social coping skills and self-confidence were continuously strengthened.

Follow-up studies on the outcomes of the randomized clinical trial should provide definitive data to compare the effectiveness of the day treatment TC against the standard of residential treatment. These data are currently being analyzed and, although early impressions are encouraging, we cannot anticipate what the data will disclose.

If follow-up studies were to document favorable outcomes for day treatment, it would represent valuable information and encourage further development of this modality as part of the spectrum of drug abuse treatment services. However, many related questions would arise. What client characteristics best guide, at intake, the selection of day treatment or residential treatment? How can clients be optimally matched to treatment modality? Should there be more fluid interaction between the treatment modalities, allowing clients to move more freely from one to the other? What are the optimal lengths of treatment? What are the relative costs and benefits?

Information about day treatment for drug abuse is essential to clinicians who seek to provide effective treatment. As health care delivery systems move increasingly in the direction of managed care, and reimbursements increasingly toward capitated payments, demands for information about drug treatment programs will increase. The emphasis on cost containment will require more precise information about the relative costs, benefits, and optimal lengths of stay in different treatment programs. Hopefully, there will be equal interest in access to drug abuse treatment and in measures of quality, as attested by outcome research. In this context, the data provided by clinical trials, such as that being conducted by the University of California/Walden House research project, may prove especially useful.

ACKNOWLEDGMENTS

The authors gratefully acknowledge the many members of the project team who developed the day treatment program and implemented the research protocol. In particular, Dolores Alvarez led the treatment team and collaborated generously in the research effort. Larry Nelson and Steve Maddox delivered exceptional effort to ensure the completion of random assignment. Last, Marilyn Price, Claudia Ponath, and Roland Dumontet carefully executed complex research demands in the treatment setting. This work was supported by NIDA Grant No. R18-DA06979.

REFERENCES

Alterman, A. I., & McLellan, A. T. (1993). Inpatient and day hospital treatment services for cocaine and alcohol dependence. *Journal of Substance Abuse Treatment, 10,* 269–275.

Alterman, A. I., O'Brien, C. P., & Droba, M. (1993). Day hospital vs. inpatient rehabilitation of cocaine abusers: An interim report. In F. M. Tims & C. G. Leukenfeld (Eds.), *Cocaine Treatment: Research and Clinical Perspectives* (NIDA Research Monograph 135, NIH Publication No. 93-3639, pp. 150–162). Rockville, MD: National Institute on Drug Abuse.

Beck, A. T. (1972). *Depression: Causes and treatment.* Philadelphia: University of Pennsylvania Press.

Bensinger, A., & Pilkington, C. F. (1983). An alternative method in the treatment of alcoholism: The United Technologies Corporation day treatment program. *Journal of Occupational Medicine, 25,* 300–303.

Bucardo, J., Guydish, J., Acampora, A., & Werdegar, D. (in press). The therapeutic community model applied to day treatment of substance abuse. In G. De Leon (Ed.), *Community as method: Modified therapeutic communities for special populations and special settings.* Westport, CT: Greenwood Press.

Chan, M., Razban, A., & Guydish, J. (1994, March). *Data collection instruments* (Day Treatment Evaluation Project Research Report No. 6). San Francisco: University of California, Institute for Health Policy Studies.

Creed, F., Black, D., & Anthony, P. (1989). Day-hospital and community treatment for acute psychiatric illness: A critical appraisal. *British Journal of Psychiatry, 154,* 300–310.

De Leon, G., Sacks, S., & Hilton, R. (1993). Passages: A modified therapeutic community day treatment model for methadone clients. In J. A. Inciardi, F. M. Tims, & B. Fletcher (Eds.), *Innovative approaches in the treatment of drug abuse: Program models and strategies* (pp. 125–148). Westport, CT: Greenwood Press.

Derogatis, L. R. (1983). *The SCL-90-R: Administration, scoring & procedures manual-II.* Towson, MD: Clinical Psychometric Research.

Eagle, D. J., Guyatt, G., Patterson, C., & Turpie, I. (1987). Day hospitals' cost and effectiveness: A summary. *The Gerontologist, 27,* 735–740.

Feigelman, W. (1987). Day-care treatment for multiple drug abusing adolescents: Social factors linked with completing treatment. *Journal of Psychoactive Drugs, 19,* 335–344.

Feigelman, W., Hyman, M. M., & Amann, K. (1988). Day-care treatment for youth multiple drug abuse: A six-year follow-up study. *Journal of Psychoactive Drugs, 20,* 385–395.

Feigelman, W., Hyman, M. M., A mann, K., & Feigelman, B. (1990). Correlates of persisting drug use among former youth multiple drug abuse patients, *Journal of Psychoactive Drugs, 22,* 63–75.

Guydish, J., Bucardo, J., Chan, M., Nebelkopf, E., Acampora, A., & Werdegar, D. (1993). Drug abuse day treatment using the therapeutic community model. In J. A. Inciardi, F. M. Tims, & B. Fletcher (Eds.), *Innovative approaches in the treatment of drug abuse: Program models and strategies* (pp. 171–190). Westport, CT: Greenwood Press.

Guydish, J., Werdegar, D., Chan, M., Nebelkopf, E., & Acampora, A. (1994). Challenges in developing a drug abuse day treatment program. In B. Fletcher, J. Inciardi, & A. Horton (Eds.), *Drug abuse treatment: The implementation of innovative approaches* (pp. 195–207). Westport, CT: Greenwood Press.

Havassy, B. E., Hall, S. M., & Tschann, J. M. (1987). Social support and relapse to tobacco, alcohol and opiates: Preliminary findings. In L. S. Harris (Ed.), *Problems of drug dependence, 1986: Proceedings of the Committee on Problems of Drug Dependence* (DHHS Publication No. (ADM) 87-1508, pp. 207–214). Washington, DC: U.S. Government Printing Office.

Institute of Medicine (1990). *Treating drug problems.* Washington, DC: National Academy Press.

McGahan, P., Griffith, J., & McLellan, A. T. (1986). *Composite scores for the Addiction Severity Index: Manual and computer software.* Philadelphia, PA: Veterans Administration Press.

McLachlan, J.F.C., & Stein, R. L. (1982). Evaluation of a day clinic for alcoholics. *Journal of Studies on Alcohol, 43,* 261–272.

McLellan, A. T., Luborsky, L., O'Brien, C. P., & Woody, G. E. (1980). An improved evaluation instrument for substance abuse patients: The Addiction Severity Index. *Journal of Nervous and Mental Disease, 168,* 26–33.

Schinnar, A. P., Kamis-Gould, E., Delucia, N., & Rothbard, A. B. (1990). Organizational determinants of efficacy and effectiveness in mental health partial care programs. *Health Services Research, 22,* 387–420.

Weissert, W., Elston, J., Bolda, E., Zelman, W., Mutran, E., & Mangum, A. (1990). *Adult day care: Findings from a national survey.* Baltimore, MD: Johns Hopkins University Press.

14

The Comprehensive Vocational Enhancement Program: Results of a Five-year Research/Demonstration Project

Paula H. Kleinman, Robert B. Millman, Martin L. Lesser, Holly Robinson, Paul Engelhart, Ching Hsu, and Irving Finkelstein

The Comprehensive Vocational Enhancement Program (CVEP), a five-year National Institute on Drug Abuse-funded research/demonstration project, was designed to implement and evaluate the effect of a vocational enhancement program for recovering substance abusers. The project was put into effect in a well-run, New York City-based, outpatient methadone treatment program, the Greenwich House Methadone Treatment Program, and has been completed at the time of this writing. This chapter briefly addresses the development of the project, describes the CVEP intervention, presents the main findings of the project, and discusses the implications of the results.

Heroin addicts entering methadone maintenance treatment present staff with a multitude of problems that reach far beyond the immediate effects of their heroin addiction. Paid employment is an effective way for the recovering substance abuser to integrate (or reintegrate) into the community. For the former addict, employment is a critical alternative to drug use. Employment offers a direct path out of the drug subculture by providing a stable, predictable source of income that does not depend on crime or prostitution. Work also makes a significant contribution to one's positive self-concept and identity.

Even though role models of productively employed persons were absent in the lives of many methadone patients, individuals in methadone treatment themselves seem to recognize the importance of work in their own rehabilitation. In a nationwide survey, persons in methadone treatment identified vocational services as one of their most important needs that were unmet by drug treatment programs (Craddock, Hubbard, Bray, Cavanaugh, & Rachal, 1982).

Unfortunately, in light of its salience to many addicts, systematic attempts to implement and study vocational rehabilitation in methadone treatment programs are rare. A review of the literature identified relatively few relevant studies. A 12-hour job seeker's workshop was offered to methadone clients on a pilot basis, and it was found that participants were more likely than nonparticipants to be employed three months later (Hall, Loeb, Norton, & Yang, 1977). The pilot study was later replicated in an experimental design, and employment three months later was again found to be higher among the participants (Hall, Loeb, Coyne, & Cooper, 1981).

An interpersonal problem-solving approach focused specifically on employment issues was developed by Platt and Metzger (1987). This was a ten-week intervention, delivered in group sessions, that focused on barriers to job participation and utilization of a variety of resources to overcome them. Unemployed clients were randomly assigned to intervention and control groups. Treated clients were significantly more likely than controls to be employed at the 6-month follow-up but were similar in terms of employment at the 12-month follow-up period. These investigators are currently evaluating the efficacy of further training directed toward job maintenance (J. Platt, personal communication, May 1994).

The effects of the placement in a methadone clinic of a full-time vocational integrator were investigated in another study. The task of the integrator was to train staff in vocational rehabilitation but not to work directly with clients. It was found that vocational activities increased as a result of the presence of the integrator, but there was no effect on client vocational status (Arella, Deren, Randell, & Brewington, 1990a).

In a study of supported work, former drug abusers were assigned to a standard group (or to an experimental group with small supportive work crews), an in-house training program, and vocational counselors. Subjects in the experimental group were more likely to work, to work more hours, and to have higher earnings than subjects in the control group (Friedman, 1978).

In another supported work study, former addicts were randomly assigned to either a standard group or a group earning more than the minimum wage. Supported work was found to reduce arrests and jail time significantly, and to increase both level of employment and income (Hollister, Kemper, & Maynard, 1984).

Additional work in the employment area is currently in process at Yale (Schottenfeld, Pascale, & Sokolowski, 1992) and at the Research Triangle Institute (Dennis, French, & Karuntzos, 1992).

RESEARCH DESIGN

The study was designed as a quasi-experiment. The project was implemented in the Greenwich House Methadone Treatment Program, which has two clinics located a few miles from each other in Manhattan. The CVEP was introduced into only one of the clinics (the experimental clinic), while the other was the comparison clinic. Preliminary data indicated that sociodemographic characteristics of patients, staffing, and program policies in the two clinics were similar. It was, therefore, planned that outcomes of project participants in the experimental and control clinics would be compared, based on an intention to treat model.

Subjects of the data analyses to be reported here are the 446 subjects, 289 in the experimental clinic, and 157 at the comparison clinic, or subsets of this entire group as indicated. Subjects of the study are persons retained in treatment at the experimental or comparison clinic for 30 days or more, who agreed to participate in the vocational enhancement program (experimental clinic only) and in an extensive and ongoing data collection process (both clinics). Before being admitted to the study, subjects read and signed an informed consent document that had been approved by the Committee on Human Subjects of Cornell University Medical College. Data shown here were collected between January 1990 and November 1993.

Subjects were interviewed at entry into the study, and, where possible, at two follow-up time periods. The intention was to interview all subjects at 6 and 18 months after entry, regardless of whether they had been retained in treatment, but it was not possible to locate many of those who had dropped out. Eighty-two percent of the original sample was interviewed at the 6-month follow-up, and 58 percent at the 18-month follow-up.

The baseline interview was a detailed, semi-structured interview, that covered employment, legal, medical, drug use, psychological, and social functioning issues. Embedded in this interview were several instruments in standard use, including the Addiction Severity Index (ASI) (McLellan et al., 1985; McLellan, Luborsky, O'Brien, & Woody, 1980), the Symptom Checklist-90 (SCL-90) (Derogatis, 1983), and the Psychopathy Checklist (Hare, Cox, & Hart, 1989). In addition, there was a brief psychiatric interview, administered by a psychiatrist or research psychologist that resulted in a DSM-III-R diagnosis based on clinical criteria. The follow-up interviews were abridged versions of the baseline interview. In addition, for subjects in the experimental clinic who attended one or more vocational sessions, the vocational counselors maintained notes on each session attended.

COMPREHENSIVE VOCATIONAL ENHANCEMENT PROGRAM INTERVENTION

In developing the CVEP, it was important to consider the many obstacles that men and women in treatment must face as they move toward the goal of employment. These obstacles include early age of drug use, history of incarceration, failure to graduate from high school, poor or no work history, and minority group membership, often a source of job discrimination. Quantitative data on these variables are provided in the review of the subjects' sociodemographic characteristics at the beginning of the following section.

To address these multiple and enmeshed needs realistically as well as clients' anxieties and fears about entering or returning to work the vocational rehabilitation intervention was designed as a comprehensive, long-term program that allowed for gradual progress and even temporary setbacks. The CVEP is a nine-level program that was designed to empower clients to move from unemployment or under-employment (part-time, temporary, or off-the-books jobs) to competitive employment. It was designed to help clients develop a sense of their interests and abilities and to address deficits that limit their ability to work, by providing needed support, guidance, and resources.

The realistic needs of both higher functioning and lower functioning clients were taken into account. The program goal for higher functioning clients was to move from unemployment or under-employment to skills training and competitive employment. For lower functioning clients, the immediate goals were to solve some of the pressing prevocational issues that interfere with employment-relevant activities and to encourage them to address psychological issues that may present obstacles to employment.

A client's progress through the nine sequenced levels of activities (see Figure 14.1) was facilitated through individual counseling sessions with one of the two vocational rehabilitation counselors hired for this project. Clients had 24 months to participate in the program. Although there were guidelines for an individual's time in a specific level, these were flexible. Clients could stay in each level for as long or as short a time as necessary to develop the skills needed to proceed to the next level.

Activities for the clients included vocational interest and aptitude testing, addressing prevocational and psychological issues where necessary, educational remediation (adult basic education and high school equivalency preparation), occupational skills training, job readiness training, and vocational counseling.

The Adkins Life Skills Program designed by Columbia University's Institute for Life Coping Skills provided many of the materials used in the job preparation activities. The materials were used in conjunction with

FIGURE 14.1
Summary of Comprehensive Vocational Enhancement Program Levels

Level 1	Orientation (2 months) Assessment of math and reading levels Completion of Self-directed Search (SDS) and Career Assessment inventory (CAI)
Level 2	Remediation (2 months) Attendance at necessary remediation services
Level 3	Aptitude Assessment (1 month) Continuation in necessary remediation services Diagnostic vocational evaluation or appropriate vocation aptitude battery (agency selection)
Level 4	Introduction to the World of Work (2 months) Continuation in necessary remediation services
Level 5	Work Adjustment (2 months) Participation in part-time volunteer experience
Level 6	Training (6 months) Attendance requirement at specific training program
Level 7	Job Hunting and Placement Ongoing
Level 8	Employment Establishment (varied time frame) Vocational counseling sessions
Level 9	Completion — Graduation (1 month) Individual exit counseling sessions

role-playing exercises and videotaped mock interviews designed by the two vocational rehabilitation counselors. Where appropriate, clients were referred to outside agencies for education, occupational skills training, mental health services, and other special services that could not be provided at the methadone program. Outside resources were carefully selected to match clients' specific needs as closely as possible.

All of these activities were coordinated with the clients' primary therapists, who were responsible for overall case management. The vocational activities and behaviors served as additional sources of information upon which the primary therapists could evaluate clients' overall clinical progress. As a general rule, clients moved to a higher level of CVEP based upon their completion of more fundamental tasks in the preceding lower level. For example, as a general practice, a client would not be referred for skills training until he or she had completed the occupational interest and aptitude testing that helped to identify a realistic employment goal. In addition, clients were not referred for employment or for outside vocational training unless they were abstinent from all illicit drugs. The inability to provide a pattern of clean urines, according to the clinic's general policy of random urine testing, indicated that the client might be inappropriately managing stress, and suggested that additional intervention on the part of the primary or vocational counselor was probably necessary before the client was ready to proceed to the next CVEP level.

The vocational rehabilitation counselors also researched and identified specialized resources appropriate to the wide variety of client needs. Examples of community linkages include agencies providing temporary shelter, clothing, food, social services advocacy, AIDS support groups, psychiatric services, long-term educational remediation, and occupational training for specific jobs.

FINDINGS

In this chapter, we present findings focused on treatment outcomes. A number of other issues have been investigated, based on data collected from Greenwich House clients as part of the CVEP project. Among these topics are predictors of lifetime needle sharing (Kleinman et al., 1994), gender and ethnic differences in psychopathology (Millman et al., 1992), factors influencing condom use (Kleinman et al., 1992), predictors of employment at entry into the enhanced program (Feigelman et al., 1993), dual addiction to drugs and gambling (Feigelman et al., 1994), and an exploration of the antisocial personality diagnosis (Kail et al., 1994).

Characteristics of Study Subjects

Almost three-fourths (71 percent) of the study subjects were male, and nearly one-half (47 percent) were 35 years old or older. Over one-half of the sample were Latinos (31 percent) and African-Americans (22 percent), while the remainder were Caucasian. Almost one-half (47 percent) had never graduated from high school or received a general equivalency diploma. More than three-fifths (63 percent) had not been employed in the 30 days before the baseline interview, and one-half (49 percent) had been unemployed or in jail for most of the last three years. Three-fifths (61 percent) had been incarcerated at some time in their lives, and one-third (34 percent) had spent more than 12 months in jail. Two-fifths (41 percent) had first used drugs intravenously before the age of 18.

Participation in Vocational Counseling Sessions

Consistent with the expressed desire of many methadone patients for vocational assistance noted in the introduction, the CVEP project was extremely successful in recruiting clients to the vocational intervention. Fully 75 percent of all 289 subjects in the experimental clinic who indicated interest in the project, or 216 persons, actually attended at least one vocational counseling session. These clients were offered no inducement for attendance other than the content of the intervention itself. Of the 216 who attended one session, 125 (58 percent) returned repeatedly to attend 11 or more sessions. (These 125 individuals represent 43 percent of all 289 subjects who initially indicated interest in participating in the program.)

Differences between Experimental and Control Programs

Based on the baseline data, it was found that more subjects in the experimental than in the comparison clinic had been employed in the pretreatment period. Subjects in the experimental clinic had higher scores on the ASI employment index, higher scores on an index of social integration, higher scores on the ASI drug use index, lower scores on an index of physical health status, and were less likely to be rated as having antisocial personality characteristics (based on the Hare Psychopathy Checklist — Clinical Version). In the outcome analyses that focused on comparisons between subjects in the two clinics, we controlled for these differences by entering them as covariates in multiple regression analyses.

Outcomes

Outcomes were analyzed in two ways. The first approach was according to the quasi-experimental design, in which outcomes for clients in the experimental clinic were compared with outcomes for clients in the comparison clinic. A second approach was to restrict comparison to clients at the experimental clinic and to examine outcomes according to level of participation in the vocational enhancement program.

The Quasi-experimental Design

Retention in treatment of all subjects admitted to the study in the experimental and control clinics was compared. Cox regression methods were used, with covariates entered to control for variables on which the two clinics differed at the outset of the study. This comparison was done 18 months after the last subject was admitted to the study, and retention was measured by subtracting date of dropout from date of admission to study. Similar to findings from a number of previous studies of methadone populations (Allison & Hubbard, 1985; Collins & Allison, 1983; Kleinman & Lukoff, 1980; McLellan, 1983; Simpson & Joe, 1993), it was found that subjects with the highest levels of previous drug and criminal justice involvement were the most likely to be early dropouts from treatment. However, there was not a significant difference in retention between the experimental and comparison clinics, although in the 16–20-month period there was a somewhat greater level of retention in the experimental than in the comparison clinic (see Hsu, Lesser, & Kleinman [1994] for more detail on these findings).

In addition to retention in treatment, outcome analyses focused on employment and drug use. These analyses were restricted to subjects whom research staff were able to interview at the 18-month follow-up period. Using regression analysis, pretreatment differences between the two clinics were controlled in these analyses. No significant differences between the clinics with respect to drug use or employment were found.

Outcome by Level of Program Participation

A second set of outcome analyses was restricted to subjects in the experimental clinic only. In these analyses, the effect of level of participation in CVEP (number of sessions attended) on employment and drug use was examined. No association between employment and level of participation was found.

However, using urinalysis data as the basis for drug use analyses, it was found that attendance at vocational enhancement sessions was significantly associated with cocaine abstinence. Attendance at CVEP sessions was also associated with reduced use of heroin, the only drug in addition to cocaine that was in widespread use among these subjects, but this relationship was not signficant. This was established based on a series of analyses.

First, the relationship between 18-month cocaine use and an ordered categorization of sessions attended was examined. There was a clear dose-response relationship, with only 37 percent of those who attended 3 or fewer sessions being abstinent from cocaine, while 65 percent of those who attended 22 or more sessions were abstinent; this association was found to be significant at the 0.007 level. Second, the simple correlation coefficient between number of sessions and 18-month cocaine score was calculated ($r = -0.22$, $p < 0.019$). Then, a logistic regression analysis was performed with dichotomous posttreatment cocaine use being the dependent variable and number of sessions as the only predictor. It showed that the likelihood of using cocaine was inversely related to the number of sessions attended at better than the 0.01 level of significance.

We wondered whether this association was a spurious one; perhaps persons who used less cocaine at baseline were both more likely than others to attend a large number of CVEP sessions and less likely to use cocaine at 18 months. If this were so, then the association between 18-month cocaine use and number of sessions might be explained by the low levels of cocaine use of the same individuals at both baseline and follow-up.

To investigate this possibility, the relationship between baseline cocaine use and cocaine use at 18 months was examined. As expected, it was found that those who did not use at baseline were significantly less likely to use cocaine at follow-up than others ($p = 0.008$). In a more sophisticated logistic regression analysis, the effect of number of sessions on posttreatment cocaine use with baseline cocaine use controlled was examined. In this analysis baseline cocaine use remained a significant predictor of posttreatment cocaine use. However, most importantly, a significant relationship between posttreatment cocaine use and number of sessions was still found, even with baseline cocaine use controlled.

Possible confounding effects of two personality variables, symptomatic psychological distress and self-esteem, were also examined. There was found to be no significant relationship between baseline distress, as measured by both the nine subscales of the SCL-90 and the SCL-90 total score, and number of sessions completed. There was also no significant relationship between cocaine use at the 18-month follow-up and baseline distress. Thus, psychological distress was determined not to be a confounding factor in the relationship between number of CVEP sessions and cocaine use at follow-up.

A significant positive correlation ($r = 0.30$; $p < 0.01$) between baseline self-esteem score and number of sessions completed was found. However, there was no relationship between baseline self-esteem and cocaine score at follow-up ($r = 0.01$; $p = 0.89$). Thus, it was determined that self-esteem did not account for the relationship between number of CVEP sessions completed and cocaine use at follow-up.

SUMMARY AND DISCUSSION

Comparisons between Clinics

No differences with respect to retention, employment 18 months posttreatment, or drug use 18 months posttreatment were found between clients at the experimental and comparison clinics. This failure to find any differences in outcomes between clinics may be related to the fact that a fairly large proportion of clients at the experimental clinic received too few sessions to benefit from the intervention. Although 43 percent of all experimental subjects attended 11 or more sessions, there was a substantial minority who received little benefit from the program: One-fourth (25 percent) agreed to participate in the study, but attended no CVEP sessions. An additional 13 percent attended only one or two sessions. Thus, in total, 38 percent received fewer than three CVEP sessions. It is unlikely that the program could have an impact on persons who attended fewer than three sessions.

Effects of Participation in CVEP in the Experimental Clinic

Employment

There was no association found between number of CVEP sessions attended and posttreatment employment. This is particularly puzzling in light of the fact that the CVEP sessions were targeted specifically toward improving job related skills.

The CVEP project worked predominantly with clients who were unemployed; those clients who already had jobs rarely needed to avail themselves of the vocational services. In the experimental clinic, 37 percent were already employed at entry into the project. Therefore, the vocational services were addressed to that 63 percent of the clinic population who were least likely to be employable. There was an extremely high degree of severity of handicaps to employment in this group. The nature of these handicaps is suggested by the high percentages of subjects in this study who not only had convictions but also had spent time in jail (63 percent), who had been unemployed or in jail for most of the past three years (47 percent), who had failed to graduate from high school or receive a general equivalency diploma (47 percent), or who were HIV-positive (an estimated 40 percent).

Probably the most important reason for the lack of an employment impact lies in the rising unemployment rate in New York City between 1990 and 1994, the years during which the CVEP was active. In December 1990, the unemployment rate in New York City was 6.3 percent; in December 1991, it had gone up slightly to 6.9 percent. By November 1992, when entry into the study ended and more than one-half of the clients had participated in it for over six months, the unemployment rate in the city had risen to 10.5 percent. By November 1993, it was virtually unchanged at 10.2 percent, and by July 1994, it was still higher than it had been in 1991, at 8.8 percent (*New York Times*, 1991, 1992, 1993, 1994). Consistent with these rates, data collected by the New York State Office of Alcoholism and Substance Abuse Services indicate that, in March 1990, 31 percent of clients in New York City methadone programs were employed full- or part-time, while by 1994 that percentage had dropped to 24 percent (J. Randell, personal communication, May 1994). These data were collected from the Treatment Program Monthly Census and Vocational Activities Report submitted to the New York State Office of Alcoholism and Substance Abuse Services by all publicly funded treatment programs. They were compiled at the request of Joan Randell, Assistant Deputy Director for Vocational Services.

Especially in light of the forbidding job market, clients who had weak or nonexistent job histories were probably extremely fearful of taking a job. Taking a job would mean giving up their Medicaid coverage; and then, if at a later point the job were no longer available for any reason, the process of renewing Medicaid eligibility would be lengthy, perhaps leaving them and any children living with them without coverage for a substantial period of time. (The importance of disincentives for employment was also noted by Arella, Deren, Randell, & Brewington, 1990b). If some form of universal medical coverage were instituted, it would probably eliminate this obstacle to employment, and, thereby, result in some increment in the proportion employed among methadone clients.

Drug Use

Among clients in the experimental clinic, a clear dose-response relationship between number of sessions completed and cocaine abstinence was found. Although those with lower cocaine use at baseline were more likely to complete a large number of sessions, the relationship between number of sessions completed and cocaine use at follow-up was maintained even with control on level of cocaine use at baseline. It was further found that neither baseline self-esteem nor baseline level of symptomatic distress accounted for the relationship between number of sessions completed and cocaine use at follow-up.

How should this finding be interpreted? It might be that the result is entirely an artifact of the presumed high level of motivation of those who completed a large number of sessions. According to this interpretation, individuals with a high level of motivation to change would have become abstinent from cocaine even in the absence of the vocational enhancement. An alternative explanation is that the association is caused by CVEP; that in the absence of the vocational enhancement program, especially because drug abstinence was required before referral to a job or any outside vocational resources, there would have been no decline in cocaine use.

Both interpretations may represent an aspect of the truth. Probably individuals who attended a large number of sessions tended to be more highly motivated to change than others. However, they may not have been able to change, in spite of their high level of motivation, without the support and assistance of the vocational counselors. The synergistic effect of motivation in combination with counseling assistance provides the most plausible explanation of the cocaine abstinence of those who completed a large number of CVEP sessions.

Why should a vocational enhancement program have an effect on cocaine abstinence? There are a number of possible explanations. Involvement with the vocational counseling program is likely to lead to instillation of hope, a necessary ingredient for any change effort. The vocational counselors offered emotional support over and above that offered by the primary counselor. At the least, the availability of another person who is interested in the client means that the client has two opportunities instead of just one to form a therapeutic alliance with a caring person. In addition, in spite of his or her best efforts, the primary counselor is often seen in a somewhat punitive light because of the charge to confront the client with dirty urines. It may be easier for the client to see the vocational counselor, who is free from that obligation, as an unambiguous source of support.

The vocational sessions may also counteract the anhedonia associated with cocaine cessation. Although many abusers find it relatively easy to stop using cocaine, they do not find it easy to deal with the dysphoria that occurs after continued nonuse (Gawin & Kleber, 1986). Attendance at the vocational counseling sessions offsets the dysphoria by offering social support and the opportunity for mastery of new information and skills.

These new skills may also increase the client's feelings of self-efficacy, which, in turn, is likely to buttress his or her ability to remain abstinent from cocaine. A person who feels capable in one area, for example, mastery of vocational skills, is likely also to feel capable in another, for example, remaining drug-free.

In conclusion, the data presented in this chapter strongly suggest that the addition to a methadone treatment program of psychosocial support services can be effective in reducing cocaine use. At least one other study supports this conclusion. Introduction into a methadone program of a treatment enhancement based on the neurobehavioral model has also been found to result in decreased cocaine use (Magura et al., 1994). Even though there was no effect on employment status, largely because of the extremely high unemployment rates during the period of the study, the probable benefits of the program in terms of reduced human misery related to cocaine use are important. Although these services are not inexpensive, they are probably cost-effective if they prevent even a few individuals from becoming HIV-positive. The implementation of new research/demonstration programs designed to explore the efficacy of vocational rehabilitation programs and other well-conceived psychosocial interventions is indicated.

REFERENCES

Allison, M., & Hubbard, R. L. (1985). Drug abuse treatment process: A review of the literature. *International Journal of the Addictions, 20*, 1321–1345.

Arella, L. R., Deren, S., Randell, J., & Brewington, V. (1990a). Increasing utilization of vocational services in methadone maintenance treatment programs: Results of a one-year intervention. *Journal of Applied Rehabilitation Counseling, 21*(2), 45–57.

Arella, L. R., Deren, S., Randell, J., & Brewington, V. (1990b). Structural factors that affect provision of vocational/educational services in methadone maintnenance treatment programs. *Journal of Applied Rehabilitation Counselin,. 21* (2), 19–26.

Collins, J. J., & Allison, M. (1983). Legal coercion and retention in drug abuse treatment. *Hospital and Community Psychiatry, 34,* 1145–1149.

Craddock, S. G., Hubbard, R., Bray, R., Cavanaugh, E., & Rachal, J.V. (1982). *Client characteristics, behaviors, and in-treatment outcomes: 1980 TOPS admission cohort* (Report No. 6895, Contract No. 271793511). Rockville, MD: National Institute on Drug Abuse.

Data on Region's Economy Improve. (1992, December 5) *New York Times,* A, 47:1.

Dennis, M. L., French, M. T., & Karuntzos, G. T. (1992, November). *Training and Employment Program (TEP) trials: Draft research plan.* Research Triangle Park, NC: Research Triangle Institute.

Derogatis, L. (1983). *SCL-90-R: Administration, scoring and procedures Manual-II.* Towson, MD: Clinical Psychometrics Research.

Feigelman, W., Kleinman, P. H., Millman, R. B., Robinson, H., Lesser, M. L., Hsu, C., Engelhart, P., & Finkelstein, I. (1994, June). Problem gambling among former opiate addicts. Poster presented at the 56th annual meeting of the College on Problems of Drug Dependence, Palm Beach, Florida.

Feigelman, W., Kleinman, P. H., Millman, R. B., Robinson, H., Lesser, M. L., Hsu, C., Engelhart, P., & Finkelstein, I. (1993). *Correlates of employment among former opiate addicts.* Poster presented at the 55th annual meeting of the Committee on Problems of Drug Dependence, Toronto, Canada.

Friedman, L. (1978). *The wildcat experiment: An early test of supported work.* New York: Vera Institute of Justice.

Gawin, F. H., & Kleber, H. D. (1986). Abstinence symptomatology and psychiatric diagnosis in cocaine abusers. *Archives of General Psychiatry, 43,* 107–113.

Hall, S. M., Loeb, P., Coyne, K., & Cooper, J. (1981). Increasing employment in ex-heroin addicts II: Methadone maintenance sample. *Behavior Therapy, 12,* 443–460.

Hall, S. M., Loeb, P., Norton, J. W., & Yang, R. (1977). Improving vocational placement in drug treatment clients: A pilot study. *Addictive Behaviors, 15,* 438–439.

Hare, R. D., Cox, D. N., & Hart, S. D. (1989). *The psychopathy checklist: Clinical version.* Vancouver: University of British Columbia.

Hollister, R. G., Jr., Kemper, P., & Maynard, R. A. (Eds.). (1984). *The national supported work demonstration.* Madison: University of Wisconsin Press.

Hsu, C., Lesser, M., & Kleinman, P. H. (1994, August). *Retention time in drug rehabilitation programs: Application of survival analysis.* Poster presented at the Joint Statistical Meeting, Toronto, Canada.

Jobless Picture Brightens in New York & New Jersey. (1993, December 4). *New York Times,* A, 48:33.

Job Losses in New York Region Erode 80's Growth. (1991, December 20). *New York Times,* A, 1:3.

Kail, B. L., Kleinman, P. H., Millman, R. B., Robinson, H., Engelhart, P., Lesser, M. L., Hsu, C., & Finkelstein, I. (1994, June). *Are all persons with ASP true psychopaths?* Paper presented at the 56th annual meeting of the College on Problems of Drug Dependence, Palm Beach, Florida.

Kleinman, P. H., & Lukoff, I. F. (1980). *Life cycle of treated heroin addicts.* Report to the National Institute on Drug Abuse. Unpublished manuscript.

Kleinman, P. H., Millman, R. B., Robinson, H., Engelhart, P., Lesser, M.L., Hsu, C., & Finkelstein, I. (1992, June). *Condom use in a methadone population.* Poster presented at the 54th annual meeting of the Committee on Problems of Drug Dependence, Keystone, Colorado.

Kleinman, P. H., Millman, R. B., Robinson, H., Lesser, M. L., Hsu, C., Engelhart, P., & Finkelstein, I. (1994). Lifetime needle-sharing: A predictive analysis. *Journal of Substance Abuse Treatment, 11*(5), 449–455.

Magura, S., Rosenblum, A., Palij, M., Lovejoy, M., Foote, J., Handelsman, L., & Stimmel, B. (1994, June). *Treatment intensity predicts abstinence and reduction in drug use for cocaine-dependent methadone patients.* Paper presented at the 56th annual meeting of the College on Problems of Drug Dependence, Palm Beach, Florida.

McLellan, A. T. (1983). Patient characteristics associated with outcome. In J. R. Cooper, F. Altman, B. S. Brown, & D. Czechowicz (Eds.), *Research on the treatment of narcotic addiction: State of the art* (Treatment Research Monograph Series, pp. 500–529). Rockville, MD: National Institute on Drug Abuse.

McLellan, A. T., Luborsky, L., Cacciola, J., Griffith, J., Evans, F., Barr, H. L., O'Brien, C. P. (1985). New data from the Addiction Severity Index: Reliability and validity in three centers. *Journal of Nervous and Mental Disease, 173,* 312–328.

McLellan, A. T., Luborsky, L., O'Brien, C. P., & Woody, G. E. (1980). An improved diagnostic evaluation instrument for substance abuse patients: The Addiction Severity Index. *Journal of Nervous and Mental Disease, 168,* 26–36.

Millman, R. B., Kleinman, P. H., Robinson, H., Engelhart, P., Lesser, M., Hsu, C., & Finkelstein, I. (1992, June). *Gender and ethnic differences in psychopathology in a methadone population.* Paper presented at the 54th annual meeting of the Committee on Problems of Drug Dependence, Keystone, Colorado.

New Jersey's Jobless Rate Fell in July. (1994, August 6). *New York Times,* A, 44:1.

New York City Jobless Rate Dips. (1991, January 5). *New York Times,* A, 39:1.

Platt, J. J., & Metzger, D. S. (1987). Cognitive interpersonal problem-solving skills and the maintenance of treatment success in heroin addicts. *Psychology of Addictive Behaviors, 1*(1), 5–13.

Schottenfeld, R. S., Pascale, R., & Sokolowski, S. (1992). Matching services to needs: Vocational services for substance abusers. *Journal of Substance Abuse Treatment, 9*(1), 3–8.

Simpson, D., & Joe, G. W. (1993). Motivation as a predictor of early dropout from drug abuse treatment. *Psychotherapy, 30*(2), 357–368.

15

The Effect of Treatment on High Risk Sexual Behaviors and Substance Use: St. Louis' Effort to Reduce the Spread of AIDS among Injection Drug Users

Linda B. Cottler, Renee M. Cunningham, and Wilson M. Compton, III

In 1989, investigators at Washington University School of Medicine were awarded a National Institute on Drug Abuse (NIDA) demonstration project entitled St. Louis' Effort to Reduce the Spread of AIDS among IDUs (ERSA). The primary objectives of the ERSA study were to attract injection drug users (IDUs) and other drug users into substance use treatment, to improve drug-free and methadone maintenance treatment at two city programs, and to educate persons about how to change high-risk behaviors. One unique aspect of this project was the comparison group, that is, those users who did not wish to enter treatment.

The ERSA study was jointly carried out by investigators from Washington University School of Medicine, a drug-free and methadone treatment program, and the St. Louis City Public Health Department under the guidance of the health commissioner. This study was the first area-wide collaborative effort of such a multidisciplinary team. Its goals were to accommodate more drug users and to expand HIV prevention efforts and street outreach efforts targeted at an underserved population. All of these efforts were designed to identify individual characteristics that predict changes in outcomes among individuals, regardless of treatment status. The analyses presented in this chapter examine changes in substance use and high-risk sexual behaviors from baseline to the terminal 18-month interview among persons assigned to the treatment group compared with those who did not wish treatment at the time of their enrollment in the study. Our analyses address several issues: whether the treated and untreated populations differ on sociodemographic variables, patterns of drug use, sexually transmitted diseases (STDs), prior treatment history and incarceration; whether the groups are differentiated by sexual behavior risk; and whether, over 18 months, persons undergoing treatment were more likely to change their behavior than persons who were not assigned to treatment.

METHODS

Sample

The ERSA project recruited its 479 subjects through street-based outreach efforts conducted by the St. Louis Public Health Department's program called the Community Outreach for Risk Reduction (CORR). CORR was just getting underway as the city's first and only street outreach program to educate high-risk populations about their risk for HIV infection and how they could practice safer sex. The ERSA study, through funding from NIDA, proposed to expand and enhance CORR rather than create a new and competing outreach program. HealthStreet, two storefront offices strategically placed in at risk areas in St. Louis city, served as home bases for this project. Once the HealthStreet operations were underway, community health outreach workers were hired and trained for the effort. Outreach workers engaged people on the street in conversation about HIV, drug use, and treatment and invited potential participants in the project to HealthStreet for more information. Upon arriving at HealthStreet, persons were seen by an information specialist who recorded the reason for the visit, the source of referral, problems experienced recently, sociodemographic information, medical history, and history of illicit drug use in the preceding 12 months. Regular drug users were eligible for the study; once eligible, they were given the option of at least 12 months of free drug treatment at one of two places, depending on their drug of abuse — either the drug-free or methadone program. Eligible users who did not want treatment were recruited for the comparison sample. In this study, randomization was not conducted.

In addition to street-based recruitment through the HealthStreet offices, the participating drug-free and methadone programs referred persons interested in their specific treatment but not yet admitted (that is, on the waiting list) to our study. The programs were chosen for our study for their distinct client characteristics and because the directors of the programs were eager to enhance their treatment protocols. Because of the potential for differences in drug use patterns between the methadone and drug-free treatments to effect behavior change, the analyses in this chapter are restricted to the 203 persons in the drug-free treatment group and an equal number of persons in the comparison group. When 18-month data are presented, the sample size is reduced from 406 to 385; this excludes persons who did not complete the 18-month wave of data collection (95 percent completion of baseline and 18-month follow-up interviews).

The drug-free treatment program selected for the study is a culturally-specific program, developed to make counseling, treatment, and aftercare more relevant to and effective for African-Americans. At the time of the ERSA study, admission to that program was allowed only after the client was drug-free for at least ten days. The program includes a 12-Step approach, and each week has 1 hour of individual and 5 hours of group counseling and a 90-minute substance abuse educational lecture. One unique aspect of this program is the aftercare. Clients who successfully complete their outpatient treatment of approximately 150 days (21 weeks) graduate to a 14-week aftercare program that includes attendance at a weekly 3-hour counselor-facilitated group session and, as needed, individual counseling sessions. Treatment graduates meet individually with their counselor to assess sobriety three months and six months after graduation. The ERSA project made possible several important enhancements to the program including the expansion of services and space, the implementation of urine and HIV antibody testing, and a child activity center with babysitting arranged during counseling sessions.

Eligible subjects referred to treatment through HealthStreet were considered part of the treatment group if they entered the methadone or the drug-free program within 30 days and stayed at least 7 days. Desisters, those who do not enter treatment within 30 days of their HealthStreet debut or persons who entered treatment but stayed less than 7 days, were placed in the comparison group, along with the persons who declined treatment at study enrollment.

Protocol

Although drug treatment was conducted by the staff of each program, and the outreach component was conducted by the CORR staff, the ERSA evaluation component — consisting of sampling, data collection, urine and blood collection, testing, and data analysis — was carried out by the Washington University investigators and staff. These persons had extensive experience on the proper administration of the interviews and the proper completion of administrative, locating, and tracking forms. Each interviewer was supervised in their administration of one or two taped interviews on pilot subjects. Thereafter, 10 percent of the interviews were audiotaped and reviewed for quality control. Ongoing editing and cleaning of data was completed with computer data entry programs after manual editing. In addition to a baseline assessment, subjects were interviewed at 3, 6, 9, 12, and 18 months to determine changes in behaviors. Among the Washington University staff were several interviewers who had extensive experience in tracking and locating subjects as well as converting refusals to agreements; the 18-month completion rate was 95 percent among those included in this chapter.

Respondents were paid $10 for each completed research assessment. Because cash payments might be considered to be coercive or might be used to purchase drugs, ERSA subjects were compensated with gift certificates for food, which could be redeemed at a major supermarket chain in St. Louis. Treatment subjects who completed their course of treatment of 150 days (21 weeks) were eligible to receive an additional $15 in certificates as a bonus. All subjects received a bonus of $15 in certificates for participating in the 18-month follow-up.

Assessment of Behavior Change

Structured, standardized assessments were included in our protocol. Data from the following assessments were used in these analyses:

WHO/NIH Composite International Diagnostic Interview — Substance Abuse Module and Treatment Modules

Written in collaboration with researchers at the World Health Organization (WHO), the National Institute on Drug Abuse (NIDA), and NIAAA, the Substance Abuse Module (SAM) is a structured diagnostic assessment tool for use in epidemiological and clinical studies (Cottler & Compton, 1993; Cottler, Robins, & Helzer, 1989; Robins, Cottler, & Babor, 1990). It covers the use of alcohol, tobacco, sedatives, opioids, cocaine, other stimulants, PCP, hallucinogens, cannabis, and inhalants. For each substance used, a detailed history of treatment and attitudes toward treatment, and DSM-III, DSM-III-R, ICD-10, and DSM-IV criteria are covered. In addition, the SAM obtains information on the course of substance use, age of onset and recency of each positive symptom, duration of use, recency of use, route of administration, and information on quantity and frequency.

National Institute on Drug Abuse AIDS Risk Behavior Assessment

These questions, developed by NIDA's Community Research Branch in 1988, include high-risk sexual behaviors (number of partners, and use of condoms) and needle use behavior (frequency of injection, cleaning habits, and number of needle-sharing partners). It also includes questions concerning attitudes toward the AIDS epidemic and knowledge of HIV infection. To this assessment, we added questions on STDs and health services related to those illnesses.

Sociodemographic Factors

Each of the instruments described above contain sociodemographic information, such as age, race, gender, marital history, number of children, occupation, health care utilization, education, income, and geographic mobility.

Operationalizaton of Risk Behaviors

The determination of sexual behavior change was based on three high-risk behaviors experienced in the six months prior to interview: the number of partners with whom the subject had sexual contact (SEXMATES), whether the subject had a partner who injected drugs (IDUMATES), and the types of sexual activities that were experienced (SEXTYPE). In defining the SEXTYPE score, each behavior was given a score based on its perceived risk for contracting HIV infection (Table 15.1). The scores ranged from 1 to 4, with 1 indicating the lowest risk for HIV infection (for example, oral-vaginal sex or oral-anal sex) and 4 indicating the highest risk (for example, receptive anal sex). Scores for sexual behavior types reported in the six-month period were added; the sum became the SEXTYPE score.

TABLE 15.1
SEXTYPE Scores for the Last Six Months

Oral vaginal sex	+ 1
Oral anal sex	+ 1
Vaginal sex	+ 2
Vaginal sex during menstruation	+ 2
Oral sex during menstruation	+ 2
Active anal sex	+ 3
Receptive anal sex	+ 4

Shown in Table 15.2 is the actual operationalization of individual risk levels attributed to each behavior and the proportion of persons in each category. Because of the skewed distributions for each behavior, the median was the best measure of central tendency to use in subsetting the data into risk levels. For example, although the upper range of partners was 96, the median number of sex partners in this sample was 1. Thus, persons who reported having more than one sexual partner in the last six months were considered to be at higher risk than those who reported having only one partner. Similarly, all those with a sexual activity type score above 3, that is, those who either had receptive anal sex or

TABLE 15.2
Determination of Risk Level

(ERSA Baseline; N = 406)

Variable	Mean	Median	Range	Definition	Percent	Risk Level
SEXMATES	2.76	1	0–96	0–1 partners	57	Single partner
				2+ partners	43	Multiple partners
SEXTYPE	2.85	3	0–14	0–3 partners	51	Low
				4+ partners	49	High
IDUMATES	0.11	1	0–9	0 partner	93	None
				1+ partners	7	1+ partners

those engaging in a number of behaviors to warrant a score above 3, were considered at higher risk than those with scores of 3 or lower.

How these risks were combined into one of four composite scores is shown in Table 15.3. Subjects who had either no sexual partners or only one sexual partner, engaged in only low-risk sexual behavior, and did not have an injection drug using partner were labeled low-risk. Persons reporting multiple partners and injecting drug using partners, irrespective of the type of sexual activity they engaged in, were considered at the highest risk for HIV infection. All other combinations of behaviors were labeled either medium or moderately high-risk.

TABLE 15.3
Composite Sex Risk Score
(ERSA Sample)

SEXMATES	SEXTYPE	IDUMATES	Composite Sex Risk Score
Single partner	Low risk	None	Low
Single partner	Low risk	1+ partners	Medium
Single partner	High risk	None	Medium
Single partner	High risk	1+ partners	Moderately high
Multiple partner	Low risk	None	Medium
Multiple partner	Low risk	1+ partners	High
Multiple partner	High risk	None	Moderately high
Multiple partner	High risk	1+ partners	High

RESULTS

Demographics

Table 15.4 summarizes the differences in baseline characteristics between the treatment and comparison groups on selected demographic variables. A significant proportion of the sample was African-American (94 percent) and male (73 percent). The subjects ranged in age from 18 to 57, with an average age of 31 years. More than half of the sample graduated from high school (52 percent) with an average of 11.6 years of education. The only statistically significant difference between the treatment and the comparison groups was in employment status in the year prior to the interview. The comparison group was significantly more likely to be unemployed than the treatment group (71 percent versus 52 percent; $p < .0001$).

TABLE 15.4
Demographics of ERSA Treatment and Comparison Groups

Characteristic	Treatment Group	Comparison Group	Total
Sample size	N = 203	N = 203	N = 406
Race			
Black	97%	92%	94%
Other	3%	8%	6%
Gender			
Male	72%	75%	73%
Female	28%	25%	27%
Mean Age			
Male (SD)	31(6.65)	32(7.00)	32(6.84)
Female (SD)	32(5.50)	31(4.90)	31(5.22)
Graduation from high school			
No	43%	52%	48%
Yes	57%	48%	52%
Mean years of education (SD)	11.9(1.81)	11.5(1.82)	11.6(1.91)
Employment in past year*			
No	52%	71%	62%
Yes	48%	29%	38%

*$p < .0001$

Selected Characteristics

Table 15.5 summarizes the lifetime rates of using cocaine and opiates more than five times, DSM-III-R dependence on those drugs, lifetime and past six months injection drug use, STDs, incarceration history, and drug treatment history. Overall, 93 percent reported using cocaine and 40 percent reported using opioids; there were no differences in lifetime use of cocaine and opioids between the groups. Although not shown, 91 percent of those dependent on cocaine and 100 percent of those dependent on opioids were dependent in the six months prior to the interview. The groups did not differ in their lifetime use and past six months use, but they did differ in reported consequences of use. Interestingly, the comparison sample, those who declined treatment, were more likely than the treatment sample to have met DSM-III-R criteria for cocaine and opioid dependence.

The groups also differed in reports of injection drug use; the comparison subjects were nearly twice as likely as treated subjects to have ever injected drugs and more than three times as likely to have injected in the

TABLE 15.5
Selected Characteristics among ERSA Treatment and Comparison Groups

Characteristic	Treatment Group	Comparison Group	Total
Sample size	N = 203	N = 203	N = 406
Cocaine use†	91%	94%	93%
Percent DSM-III-R dependent†*	22%	33%	28%
Opiate use†	37%	43%	40%
Percent DSM-III-R dependent†*	5%	17%	12%
Injection drug use†**	18%	31%	24%
In last six months**	16%	58%	42%
Sexually transmitted diseases (excluding HIV)†	50%	43%	47%
Ever incarcerated			
No	28%	27%	27%
Yes	72%	73%	73%
Drug treatment (prior to ERSA)***	92%	63%	77%

†Lifetime
* $p < .05$
** $p < .01$
*** $p < .001$

past six months (lifetime: 31 percent versus 18 percent; past six months: 58 percent versus 16 percent).

Two additional characteristics, STDs and incarceration, were examined for their relationship with treatment status because of their association with high-risk sexual and drug behavior. Although reports of contracting an STD (other than HIV), such as syphilis, gonorrhea, trichomonas, and herpes, were no more likely among the comparison than the treated group, they were common among both groups. Almost half of the subjects self-reported contracting an STD at some point in their lives. Although there were no differences in incarceration history between the groups, a significant proportion of ERSA subjects reported a lifetime history of being in jail or prison (73 percent).

When respondents were asked about their treatment experience prior to ERSA, overall 77 percent reported having received some drug treatment before becoming involved in the ERSA study. Treatment experience was defined as ever having seen a doctor, other professional, receiving methadone, or attending a clinic for a drug-related problem. Those in the treatment group were significantly more likely than the comparison group to have had a prior drug abuse treatment episode of any length (92 percent versus 63 percent).

18-Month Treatment History

Over the 18 months of the ERSA study, the 406 respondents reported being in treatment an average of 30.7 weeks (Table 15.6). Among those subjects assigned to treatment at the time of study enrollment, 56 percent completed at least 21 weeks of treatment — the number of weeks required for graduation from the program — and were labeled completers. Of note was the fact that they reported an average of 54.6 consecutive weeks in treatment, which was twice that required for graduation. The noncompleters — those assigned to the treatment group who did not complete the program — received less than 10 weeks of treatment on average.

TABLE 15.6
18-month Treatment History of ERSA Subjects

Site	Status	N	Mean Weeks in Treatment (SD)	
Treatment group	Noncompleters	90	9.8	(6.2)
(N = 203)	Completers	113	54.6	(19.0)
Comparison group	No treatment	103	0.4	(0.3)
(N = 203)	Tried treatment later	100	22.2	(23.7)
Total		406	30.7	(26.7)

Among the subjects assigned to the comparison group upon enrollment, 49 percent reported seeking treatment at some time in the 18 months. On average, comparison subjects who reported any treatment were in that treatment half as long as completers (22.2 weeks). Notably, their time in treatment was twice as long as the noncompleters. As shown in Table 15.6, on average the 103 comparison subjects tried treatment for less than one week.

Distribution of Composite Sex Risk Score by Treatment Status

Our findings suggest that the distribution of composite sex risk scores did not differ by treatment status. The majority of our subjects, regardless of treatment status, engaged in behaviors that placed them at the lower end of the risk score. As shown in Table 15.7, 67 percent of both the treatment and comparison groups fell into either the low or medium sex risk level. Only 14 persons overall engaged in behaviors that placed them into the highest risk category.

TABLE 15.7
Distribution of Composite Sex Risk Score by Treatment Status (ERSA Baseline; N = 406)

Composite Sex Risk Score	Treatment Group			Comparison Group		
	Noncompleters	Completers	Total	No Treatment	Tried Treatment Later	Total
Sample size	N = 90	N = 113	N = 203	N = 103	N = 100	N = 203
Low	33%	39%	36%	43%	39%	41%
Medium	33%	28%	31%	25%	27%	26%
Moderately high	32%	29%	31%	29%	27%	28%
High	1%	4%	2%	3%	7%	5%

Condom Use and Risk Behaviors

Condoms were not included as a component of the risk behavior index because, when used consistently, they become a positive behavior that protects from the negative effects of the high-risk behaviors. Not including condom use in the composite risk score allowed us to examine their use among persons with different composite sex risk levels.

Table 15.8 shows the rate of condom use in the six months prior to interview among treatment and comparison subjects stratified by composite sex risk score. Of the 371 subjects who reported having sex, 11 percent reported always using a condom. No significant differences in reports of always using a condom were found between the treatment and comparison groups when stratified by their composite sex risk score.

TABLE 15.8
Consistent Use of Condoms in the Past Six Months by Composite Sex Risk Score and Treatment Status
(ERSA Baseline; N = 371)*

Composite Sex Risk Score	Treatment Status	N	Percent Always Used
Low	Treatment	58	7
Medium	Treatment	62	8
Moderately high	Treatment	61	20
High	Treatment	5	40
Low	Comparison	67	12
Medium	Comparison	53	9
Moderately high	Comparison	56	13
High	Comparison	9	11

*Excludes persons who reported no sex in the past six months.

Individual Changes in High-risk Behavior

As shown in Table 15.9, average baseline scores were compared with the score tallied at the terminal 18-month interview. If subjects changed for the better, these changes were denoted by a plus (+) sign; changes for the worse were denoted by a minus (–) sign. Statistically significant changes were denoted with an asterisk (*).

Composite Sex Risk Score

When average baseline composite sex risk scores for the treatment and comparison groups were compared, statistically significant changes were noted for individuals in the treatment group if they completed their

TABLE 15.9

Average Change in Behavior for Individuals from Baseline to the 18-month Interview by Treatment Status (ERSA Sample; N = 387)

Behaviors in the Six Months Prior to Interview	Treatment Group			Comparison Group		
	Noncompleters	Completers	Total	No Treatment	Tried Treatment Later	Total
Sample size	N = 82	N = 112	N = 194	N = 96	N = 97	N = 193
Composite score	+	+*	+*	+	–	–
SEXMATES	+	+*	+*	+	+	+
SEXTYPE	+	+	+*	+*	+	+*
IDUMATES	–	+	+	+	–	–
Drug use						
Cocaine	+*	+*	+*	+*	+*	+*
Opiates	+	+*	+*	+*	+*	+*
Injection drug use	+*	+*	+*	+*	+*	+*

*Statistically significant change from baseline to 18-month interview ($p < .05$)

Plus (+) = Change for the better

Minus (–) = Change for the worse

treatment. The changes were primarily because of a reduction in the number of sexual partners. Overall, the treatment group significantly reduced their SEXTYPE scores. Noncompleters did worse at 18 months than they did at baseline in terms of the number of injection drug using partners; although the change is not statistically significant, it may be clinically meaningful.

Comparison subjects, in contrast, had an increase in their overall composite sex risk score. Although this change was not statistically significant, it may be clinically meaningful, because the negative change was seen among those who attempted some treatment. A negative change was also seen in the number of drug injecting sexual partners reported for individuals in the comparison group who tried treatment later.

Cocaine and Opiate Use

Both the treatment and comparison groups were found to have made statistically significant improvements in reported drug use in the six months prior to interview regardless of treatment status or completion status.

Injection Drug Use

All of the subjects made positive changes in their injection drug use by the end of the study when response in the six months prior to baseline was compared to response in the six months prior to the 18-month interview.

Comparison of Sex Behaviors and Drug Use between Treatment and Comparison Groups

In contrast to the findings presented in Table 15.9, those shown in Table 15.10 compare the average change score for the treatment and comparison groups. Shown are the actual scores for baseline and 18 months. The change in those scores, for the two groups, were compared. Surprising to us, the only statistically significant changes in scores were found for composite sex risk score — persons in treatment did better over 18 months in reducing their high-risk behaviors than persons who declined treatment at the baseline (the comparison group). Although by looking at the scores in Table 15.10 one can see that the comparison group had higher scores on almost all indices, their changes in drug use from the baseline to the 18-month interview were not any different from the changes made by persons in treatment. Upon further examination, we did not find differences by completion status.

TABLE 15.10
Comparison of Sex Behaviors and Drug Use from Baseline to the 18-month Interviews for ERSA Treatment and Comparison Groups

	Treatment Group		Comparison Group	
Behaviors in the Six Months Prior to Interview	**Baseline**	**18-month**	**Baseline**	**18-month**
Sample size	N = 406	N = 387	N = 406	N = 387
Composite score*	.99	.78	.97	.99
SEXMATES	2.23	1.57	3.29	2.11
SEXTYPE	2.81	2.45	2.90	2.48
IDUMATES	0.5	.03	.18	.15
Drug use				
Cocaine	.69	.27	.83	.39
Opiates	.14	.06	.18	.08
Injection drug use	.33	.02	.43	.11

***Treatment and comparison group changes from baseline to 18-month, statistically significant difference ($t = 2.0832$; $p = .0379$).**

SUMMARY

In response to St. Louis' HIV epidemic, the Washington University School of Medicine investigators proposed the ERSA treatment demonstration project. This area-wide project sought to reduce the spread of HIV among drug abusing populations and the wider heterosexual populations by increasing and improving drug treatment in the most vulnerable inner-city area.

The ERSA project has allowed a multidisciplinary team to collaborate on ways to improve drug treatment, increase treatment availability to susceptible populations, and initiate outreach efforts. These collaborative endeavors have been among the most worthwhile for all team members. The ERSA project has significantly enhanced HIV prevention efforts in St. Louis. Treatment availability has been improved, treatment programs have been enhanced, and outreach has become an integral part of the city's public health strategy to help its most underserved population. Efforts to ensure the continuation of this area-wide collaboration began with a second project, upon completion of the ERSA project.

What has the ERSA effort demonstrated? In these analyses, the investigators have been able to show that HIV prevention efforts do, in fact, work for IDUs, non-IDUs, treatment completers, and noncompleters. However, when individuals in the treatment group are compared with individuals in the comparison group, little difference is found overall, except for composite sex risk scores where the comparison group was found to do worse. This demonstrates that the ERSA treatment providers gave clear messages about reducing all high-risk behaviors including sexual behaviors. This is a message that out-of-treatment subjects apparently did not hear.

Additionally, the fact that we did not find more significant differences in drug use does not mean that treatment does not work. On the contrary, we may have seen a Hawthorne Effect in our data — meaning that the improvement seen in the treatment group is wearing off in the comparison group and that all community subjects are deriving some benefit from this demonstration project. Perhaps in our future work, we may see a difference in groups if we combine the treatment failures with those persons from the comparison group who had at least 21 weeks of treatment — the amount needed to graduate from the program. In this way, we may see differences attributed to actual treatment rather than merely to assignment to treatment.

The analyses presented in this chapter highlight the additional types of analyses that can be done to determine effects of treatment-related variables on later change in behavior. From this work, we become more aware of the nature of the effect of treatment on behavioral changes. Further, we realize how much work is still needed in this field to continue to make this a priority in HIV prevention at a time when education is the only sure prevention tool.

ACKNOWLEDGMENTS

The authors acknowledge the respondents who participated in this research, the staff of the drug-free program, the outreach workers and staff at the St. Louis Public Health Department, the ERSA interviewers, and the technical assistance of Donna Fonseca, Greg Asmus, and Arbi-Ben Abdallah.

REFERENCES

Cottler, L. B., & Compton, W. M. (1993). Advantages of the CIDI family of instruments in epidemiological research of substance use disorders. *International Journal of Methods in Psychiatric Research, 3*, 109–119.

Cottler, L. B., Robins, L. N., & Helzer, J.E. (1989). The reliability of the Composite International Diagnostic Interview Substance Abuse Module (CIDI-SAM) — A comprehensive substance abuse interview. *British Journal of Addiction, 84*, 801–814.

Robins, L. N., Cottler, L. B., & Babor, T. (1990). *WHO/ADAMHA Composite International Diagnostic Interview-Substance Abuse Module (CiDI-SAM)*. St. Louis, MO: Washington University School of Medicine, Department of Psychiatry.

Index

About the Contributors

ALFONSO ACAMPORA is Chief Executive Officer of Walden House, Inc., the largest publicly funded substance abuse program in San Francisco. He is government liaison for California Therapeutic Communities. Acampora is on the executive board of Therapeutic Communities of America and the executive council and international organizing committee of the World Federation of Therapeutic Communities.

M. DOUGLAS ANGLIN is Director of the UCLA Drug Abuse Research Center (Neuropsychiatric Institute) and Director of the California Drug Abuse Information and Monitoring Project. He is author or coauthor of nearly 80 articles for scientific books and journals.

JEFFREY J. ANNON is Research Associate at the UCLA Drug Abuse Research Center. His research interests include the emotional and cognitive processes involved in drug use and abuse.

KARST J. BESTEMAN is Director of the Substance Abuse Center of the Institutes for Behavior Resources and is active in national policy debate and health service research with a special emphasis on the evaluation of treatment effectiveness in addiction.

PETER J. BOKOS has served as President and Chief Executive Officer of Interventions since the corporation's inception in 1974. He has published in more than 30 professional publications.

JOSEPH V. BRADY is Professor of Behavioral Biology and Professor of Neuroscience at the Johns Hopkins University School of Medicine. He is also President and Chairman of the Board of Trustees of the Institutes for Behavior Resources, a nonprofit human service, educational, and scientific organization with research and service programs in the District of Columbia and Baltimore. He is presently a member of the National Academy of Sciences Committee on Toxicology and Chairman of the NIDA Clinical and Behavioral Initial Review Committee (Study Section).

RONALD BRADY is Medical Director of Bridge Plaza Treatment and Rehabilitation Services, P.C., a multimodal methadone maintenance and detoxification program in New York City, and Assistant Professor of Clinical Psychiatry at Columbia University. He is an advisor and research scientist with the Institute for Behavioral Resources in Washington, DC.

MONICA CHAN is Research Analyst for the Drug Abuse Day Treatment Evaluation Project. Her current interests in substance abuse treatment are in the areas of relapse prevention and family and social relationships.

PHYLLIS A. COLE is the Program Manager for the Weekend Intervention Program at Wright State University School of Medicine.

WILSON M. COMPTON, III, is Assistant Professor of Psychiatry at Washington University School of Medicine and was Coinvestigator of St. Louis' Effort to Reduce the Spread of AIDS among IDUs program. Compton's research interest has been the cultural and sociodemographic correlates of psychiatric disorders, including substance use disorders. Recently he has focused on the comorbidity of psychiatric disorders with HIV risk behaviors.

LINDA B. COTTLER is an Associate Professor of Epidemiology in Psychiatry at Washington University School of Medicine and is Director of a National Institute of Mental Health postdoctoral program in epidemiology and biostatistics. Her interests are in the areas of assessing substance abuse and dependence disorders, HIV risk behaviors and antisocial personality disorder, and child and adolescent psychiatric disorders and mental health services.

RENEE M. CUNNINGHAM is a National Institute of Mental Health postdoctoral fellow in the Department of Psychiatry at Washington University School of Medicine. Her interests include child and adolescent mental disorders, drug abuse, sexual risk taking and impulsive behaviors, and adolescence-adult transition.

DONALD F. DANSEREAU is a Professor of Psychology at Texas Christian University. His research focuses on cognitive approaches for improving education, technical training, and drug abuse prevention and counseling. He has also developed theoretical models of how individuals acquire and represent complex information. He has published more than 100 articles in professional journals and books.

GEORGE DE LEON is Director of the Center for Therapeutic Community Research, Deputy Director for Clinical Research at National Development and Research Institutes, Inc., a member of the Extra Mural Scientific Advisory Board of the National Institute on Drug Abuse, and Research Associate Professor of Psychiatry at New York University School of Medicine. He has published extensively in the field of substance abuse and psychology.

PAUL ENGELHART is Director of Education for the National Association on Drug Abuse Problems and on the faculty of Mollow College's Alcoholism and Drug Addiction Counselor Education Program.

DAVID S. FESTINGER is a graduate student in Clinical Psychology at Hahnemann University School of Medicine and a Research Assistant at Addiction Research and Treatment–Camden, a clinical research facility that is investigating new treatments for cocaine abuse. He is particularly interested in variables influencing treatment entry and retention.

IRVING FINKELSTEIN is the Director of the Greenwich House Methadone Treatment Programs. He is currently a board member and is past Chairman of the New York State Committee of Methadone Program Administrators.

JAMES H. FISHER is an Assistant Professor in the Department of Community Health at Wright State University and Research Director of the Enhanced Treatment Through Induction and Case Management Project. His research interests include cultural and behavioral aspects of health and habitat.

BENNETT W. FLETCHER develops large-scale longitudinal drug treatment evaluation research for the National Institute on Drug Abuse. This includes the Drug Abuse Treatment Outcome Study (DATOS), begun in 1989 to evaluate treatment outcomes for clients in five treatment modalities, and parallel studies designed around the DATOS core, such as the Drug Abuse Treatment Outcome Study of Adolescents (DATOS-A) begun in 1990.

RAY FROST is a Consultant for Marathon, Inc. of Rhode Island.

FRANCES B. GARFIELD is a Research Associate at Spectrum Addiction Services, Inc., where she is a Project Director onsite for NIDA study No. RO1DA06151, AIDS Prevention, Four Residential Treatment Models.

LAWRENCE GREENFIELD is a Behavioral Psychologist with the Institutes for Behavior Resources, Inc.

CHRISTINE E. GRELLA is an Assistant Research Psychologist at the UCLA Drug Abuse Research Center. Her research interests include evaluation of alcohol, drug, and mental health treatment and prevention programs, with a focus on special populations, such as women, adolescents, the homeless, and the dually-diagnosed.

BENJAMIN GROSS is the Director of Development at Nidus Corporation.

JOSEPH GUYDISH is Project Director for the Drug Abuse Day Treatment Evaluation Project and Assistant Adjunct Professor of Medicine at the University of California, San Francisco. His clinical specialty is in behavioral medicine, and current areas of research include substance abuse treatment, evaluation of community-based service organizations, HIV related risk behavior among injection drug users, and the effectiveness of needle exchange.

ROBERT HILTON is Clinical Director for the Therapeutic Community Methods in Methadone Maintenance (Passages) study. He is responsible for the clinical design, staff training and supervision, and technical assistance. He is a cofounding and board member of Community Studies Institute in New York City.

ARTHUR McNEILL HORTON, JR., is a Research Psychologist and Project Officer in the Treatment Research Branch of the Division of Clinical Research of the National Institute on Drug Abuse. Horton is the author or editor of four books.

CHING HSU is Research Statistician, Division of Biostatistics at North Shore University Hospital. His research interests are in the areas of mathematical statistics and clinical trials.

JAMES A. INCIARDI is Director of the Center for Drug and Alcohol Studies at the University of Delaware; Professor in the Department of Sociology and Criminal Justice at the University of Delaware; and Adjunct Professor in the Department of Epidemiology and Public Health at the

University of Miami School of Medicine. He has published 34 books and more than 175 articles and chapters in the areas of substance abuse, criminology, criminal justice, history, folklore, social policy, AIDS, medicine, and law.

GEORGE W. JOE is a Research Scientist in the Institute of Behavioral Research at Texas Christian University. His research has focused on the etiology of drug abuse, components of the treatment process, the use of toxicant inhalants, statistical methodology, and psychometric theory. He has published approximately 70 articles in books and professional journals.

KIMBERLY C. KIRBY is an Assistant Professor of Mental Health Sciences at Hahnemann University School of Medicine where she is a member of the Division of Addiction Research and Treatment. She is also the Research Director at Addiction Research and Treatment–Camden, a clinical research facility that is currently investigating new treatments for cocaine abuse. She conducts research in drug abuse treatment evaluation and human behavioral pharmacology.

PAULA H. KLEINMAN is Assistant Professor of Sociology, Department of Public Health, Cornell University Medical College, and the Research Director of the CVEP project. She has published widely in sociological and substance abuse journals.

RICHARD J. LAMB is an Associate Professor of Mental Health Sciences at Hahnemann University School of Medicine where he is a member of the Division of Addiction Research and Treatment. He conducts behavioral pharmacological research into both the basis and treatment of drug addiction.

MARTIN L. LESSER is Director of the Division of Biostatistics at North Shore University Hospital and Associate Professor of Biostatistics at the Department of Public Health, Cornell University Medical College. His areas of statistical applications are in clinical trials, clinical epidemiology, epidemiology, and diagnosis and screening. Lesser has coauthored two book chapters and over 85 papers in medical and statistical literature.

BENJAMIN F. LEWIS is a Senior Research Fellow in the School of Public Health at the University of Massachusetts/Amherst, Associate Director of the AIDS Research Unit at the University of Massachusetts/Amherst, and principal investigator on NIDA research studies No. R01DA5615, Comprehensive Surveillance of HIV Among IVDUs — Greater Worcester,

Massachustts, and No. R01DA6151, AIDS Prevention, Four Residential Models.

BRUCE G. LINK is a Research Scientist at the Epidemiology of Mental Disorders Research Unit, New York State Psychiatric Institute, and an Associate Professor of Public Health at Columbia University. He has researched and published extensively on aspects of labeling theory, help-seeking, service delivery, and the homeless.

DOROTHY LOCKWOOD is an independent contractor conducting program evaluations for drug treatment and social service agencies, courts, corrections, and prevention programs. She serves as a consultant to state and county governments and provides training for professionals in the corrections and treatment fields. Her research interests include juvenile delinquency, women and drug use, drug abuse treatment, and corrections.

JAMES F. MADDUX is a Professor in the Department of Psychiatry, the University of Texas Health Science Center at San Antonio. He is the principal investigator of the NIDA-supported project to improve retention on methadone and author of 1 book and 56 articles and chapters.

STEVEN S. MARTIN is an Associate Scientist with the Center for Drug and Alcohol Studies in the Department of Sociology and Criminal Justice at the University of Delaware. He has coauthored a number of articles on the epidemiology, etiology, prevention, and treatment of substance abuse.

E. MICHAEL MASLAR is the Case Manager Supervisor and a Case Manager for Interventions and has been with the project since its inception. He is currently enrolled in a doctoral program at the Chicago School of Professional Psychology.

JANE McCUSKER is Professor of Epidemiology and Director of the AIDS Research Unit in the School of Public Health, University of Massachusetts/Amherst. She is principal investigator of the evaluation team for Project IMPACT and is involved in other AIDS prevention research in Massachusetts.

KAREN McKENDRICK is the Research Associate for the Therapeutic Community Methods in Methadone Maintenance (Passages) study.

CHERYL L. MEJTA is a Research Consultant with Interventions, Project Director of the Illinois Addiction Training Center, and a Professor of

Addictions Studies at Governors State University. She has published in numerous professional publications.

RONALD MELCHIONDA is a Certified Social Worker and Director of Drug Treatment Services for the Nassau County Department of Drug and Alcohol Addiction. He is also the Director of Nassau County's Substance Alternative Clinic, a comprehensive methadone treatment program serving over 575 substance abusers and their families.

JUDITH H. MICKENBERG has served as the Interventions Case Management Study Supervisor for three years.

ROBERT B. MILLMAN, the Saul P. Steinberg Distinguished Professor of Psychiatry and Public Health at Cornell University Medical College and acting Chair of the Department of Public Health at Cornell University Medical College, is the principal investigator of the CVEP project. He is also the Director of Alcohol and Substance Abuse Services at the Payne Whitney Psychiatric Clinic–New York Hospital, the Project Director of the Adolescent Development Program, the Medical Director of the Employee Development Center, and the Director of the Midtown Center for Treatment and Research, all at the Cornell University Medical Center, New York Hospital. Millman serves as consultant to numerous governmental and foundation advisory groups on substance abuse affairs and has written over 100 scientific articles, chapters, and reviews.

DAISY NG-MAK is the statistician of the MICA Research Demonstration Project and a doctoral candidate in biostatistics at Columbia University School of Public Health.

AMIE L. NIELSEN is currently doing doctoral work in sociology at the University of Delaware. Her research entails examining rape law reforms and racial and ethnic differences in substance use. She has published in the area of drug treatment programs.

LARRY NUTTBROCK is a Sociologist with postdoctoral training in psychiatric epidemiology. His research interests include sociological aspects of depression, violence among the mentally ill and the evaluation of substance abuse treatment programs.

BERT PEPPER is the Executive Director of the Information Exchange on Young Adult Chronic Patients, Inc.; Clinical Professor of Psychiatry at New York University; and Director of the Consultation Service of the American Psychiatric Association. He has been conducting staff training at Harbor House and serves as its psychiatric consultant and trainer.

THERESA E. PERLIS is Assistant Project Director for the Therapeutic Community Methods in Methadone Maintenance (Passages) study.

JEROME J. PLATT is Professor of Mental Health Sciences at Hahnemann University School of Medicine, where he is Director of the Division of Addiction Research and Treatment. He conducts research into the social and psychological bases of addiction; one of his main areas of focus has been interpersonal cognitive problem-solving skills in the assessment and treatment of substance abusers.

MICHAEL RAHAV is the principal investigator of the MICA Research Demonstration Project.

RICHARD C. RAPP is Project Director of the Enhanced Treatment Through Induction and Case Management Project at Wright State University, School of Medicine, and an Instructor in the School of Medicine and Adjunct in the Department of Social Work.

JAMES J. RIVERA's interests are in planning and evaluating service delivery for the persistently mentally ill.

HOLLY ROBINSON is the Project Manager for the CVEP project.

STANLEY SACKS is the Deputy Director of the Center for Therapeutic Community Research at National Development and Research Institutes, Inc. He is the coprincipal investigator on Modified Therapeutic Community for MICA Clients, funded by the National Institute on Drug Abuse, and principal investigator of Documentation of a Modified Therapeutic Community for Homeless MICA Clients, funded jointly by the Center for Mental Health Services and the Center for Substance Abuse Treatment.

FRANK R. SCARPITTI is a Professor in the Department of Sociology and Criminal Justice at the University of Delaware. His research interests and publications have been in the areas of community mental health, juvenile delinquency, female criminality, therapeutic communities, organized crime, and substance abuse. He currently is involved in the process analysis of two large drug treatment programs in Delaware.

EDWARD C. SENAY is a Professor of Psychiatry at the University of Chicago. He has published more than 100 articles and books on substance abuse treatment and research.

HARVEY A. SIEGAL is a Professor in the Department of Community Health and the Department of Sociology and Director of Substance Abuse

Intervention Programs at Wright State University, School of Medicine. He is also principal investigator of the Enhanced Treatment Through Induction and Case Management Project.

D. DWAYNE SIMPSON is Director of the Institute of Behavioral Research and the S. B. Sells Professor of Psychology at Texas Christian University. He has published more than 150 articles in books and professional journals.

GRAHAM L. STAINES is Senior Project Director of the Therapeutic Community Methods in Methadone Maintenance (Passages) study. His current research evaluates the use of modified therapeutic communities for methadone maintenance clinics.

ELMER L. STRUENING is the Director of the Epidemiology of Mental Disorders Research Unit and the Community Support System Evaluation Program at the New York State Psychiatric Institute. He has published extensively in the field of evaluation research.

ELIZABETH L. STURZ is Founder, President, and Chief Executive Officer of Argus Community, Inc. She has developed a number of innovative programs for substance abusers and high-risk populations, and has published three books on related subjects.

HILARY L. SURRATT is a Research Associate in the Comprehensive Drug Research Center at the University of Miami School of Medicine and Project Director of a NIDA-funded AIDS seroprevalence and prevention study in Rio de Janeiro, Brazil. She has published in the areas of AIDS, substance abuse, and drug policy.

BARBARA TAJIMA is a Research Associate at the University of California, San Francisco, where she leads the data collection team for the Day Treatment Evaluation Project.

FRANK M. TIMS is Deputy Chief, Treatment Research Branch, National Institute on Drug Abuse. Among his recent research monographs are *Relapse and Recovery in Drug Abuse*, *Drug Abuse Treatment in Prisons and Jails*, and *Compulsory Treatment of Drug Abuse*, each in collaboration with Carl Leukefeld.

JOSEPH H. WAGNER is an Instructor in the Department of Community Health at Wright State University and a Research Associate in the Enhanced Treatment Through Induction and Case Management Project.

DAVID WERDEGAR is Professor of Family and Community Medicine at the University of California, San Francisco, and principal investigator for the Drug Abuse Day Treatment Evaluation Project. His research interests include innovative approaches to substance abuse treatment, AIDS prevention education, the relationship of health services to community needs, the organization of health services, and health team approaches to primary care and prevention.

STUART E. WUGALTER is a Staff Research Associate with the UCLA Drug Abuse Research Center. His expertise is in measurement and analytic methods for categorical data. His most recent publication will appear as a chapter in *Analysis of Categorical Variables in Development Research.*

ISBN 0-313-30065-8
90000>
EAN
9 780313 300653
HARDCOVER BAR CODE